BUDDHISM—A NON-THEISTIC RELIGION

BUDDHISM-
A NON-THEISTIC
RELIGION

With a selection from Buddhist Scriptures,
edited by Heinz Bechert

by

HELMUTH VON GLASENAPP

Translated from the German by
IRMGARD SCHLOEGL

London
GEORGE ALLEN AND UNWIN LTD
RUSKIN HOUSE · MUSEUM STREET

First published as *Buddhismus und Gottesidee. Die
Buddhistischen Lehren von den überweltlichen Wesen
und Mächten und ihre religionsgeschichtlichen Paral-
lelen,* in *Abhandlungen der geistes- und sozialwissen-
schaftlichen Klasse der Akademie der Wissenschaften
und der Literatur in Mainz,* 1954, Nr. 8.

© Copyright 1966 by Szczesny Verlag KG, Munich

For the present publication Prof. Heinz Bechert,
Göttingen, has selected the most important quotations from the Buddhist Scriptures referred to by
the author, and appended them in translation.

This translation © George Allen & Unwin Ltd, 1970

SBN 04 294062 1

PRINTED IN GREAT BRITAIN
in 11 on 12 point Old Style
BY UNWIN BROTHERS LIMITED
WOKING AND LONDON

TRANSLATOR'S FOREWORD

The author introduces an aspect of Buddhism which is perhaps foreign to our way of thinking yet crucial for an understanding of the subject—the religiosity of a non-theistic religion. This made it imperative that the translation avoid as much as possible terms that have strong Christian connotations.

Buddhism has always accommodated the local gods in its framework, and never denied 'the holy' in Rudolf Otto's definition as an aspect of man's perceptive faculty. However, the Buddha is said to be the teacher of both men and gods. Buddhism as a religion seems to aim at the apperception of 'the holy' rather than denying it *a priori*. It is indeed owing to this misunderstanding that the question of whether Buddhism is a religion arose.

IRMGARD SCHLOEGL

REFERENCES

An asterisk * in the text refers to a footnote.

A superior figure ¹ refers to a note at the end of the book (usually indicating source material).

A figure in square brackets [1] refers to the numbered selections from the Buddhist Scriptures, which the reader will find at the end of the book.

THE PRONUNCIATION OF INDIAN WORDS:
Vowels are pronounced as in Italian: *ā, ī, ū, e, o, ai, au* are always long.

The consonants are pronounced as usual; *ñ* as in Spanish. *c* = *ch* in *church*. *H* in the Indian combinations *bh, ch, dh, gh, jh, kh, ph, th* is always sounded (*Buddha* = *Budd-ha*).

The stress, as in Latin, depends on the vowel in the last syllable but one. If this is short, the preceding syllable is stressed (*dévatā*); if long—either because the vowel itself is long, or by its position (a syllable ending in a double consonant, for example *nd, tt*)—it carries the stress (*Vasubándhu*).

CONTENTS

PREFACE

This admirable translation by Dr Irmgard Schloegl of a work which first appeared in 1954 as *Buddhismus und Gottesidee* puts before English-speaking students of Buddhism its suggested place in the field of religion. Professor von Glasenapp, a scholar of international standing, having analysed his very mixed material, concludes that whether or not Buddhism is a religion depends on the definition of religion. Much turns, in such analysis, on the Buddhist school under review, and the author assumes that the Pāli Canon is nearest to the Buddha's message to mankind. It is with this school that he is mostly concerned, and the same applies to the admirable 'Brief Note on Buddhist Scriptures' by M. O'C. Walshe and the 'Selections from Buddhist Scriptures', edited by Heinz Bechert, which together form the second half of the volume.

The paradox contained in the English title is highly topical. Western thought is rapidly abandoning God, in the sense of an Absolute Creator who is yet a personal saviour of mankind, and for the many it is becoming true to say that 'God is dead'. But his disappearance from the field of higher thought, and from the needs of the heart, is becoming increasingly felt. In the absence of any substitute-concept of the Beyond of purely material existence the younger generation is left in a spiritual and moral chaos, without a purpose in life beyond pleasure or a guide/exemplar on a more worthy way.

Considering this vacuum, what can Buddhism offer the West which will satisfy both heart and mind, and also that faculty of intuition by which the developed mind contacts the beyond of feeling-thought?

The writer considers, the gods of Buddhism and then seeks for its concept of God. In a single chapter he clears away the former, for they too, from the highest *deva* to the lowest nature-spirit, are bound upon the Wheel. Turning to the God-concept, Professor von Glasenapp examines the God of Christianity and cognates ideas in other religions; but he makes it clear, with a wealth of quotation, that such a thought is anathema in the Pāli Canon. His examination of anything even superficially comparable in Buddhism shows the profound distinction between a hypostatic principle, such as the Dharmakaya or Alayavijnana or mind-only, and creator of the universe; for if someone created the universe, who created him?

True, as the author admits, there are figures in the Buddhist pantheon which approach in the religious sense the status of God. Amitabha, for example, is worshipped in every sense of the term in the Pure Land schools of China and Japan, and the same applies to some extent to Vairocana in the Shingon school. But this devotion is still to a virtue, as of wisdom or compassion, and knowingly so, and never to a creator.

What then can replace the God-concept in the Western mind for those who seek an acceptable alternative? The writer corroborates the view of a handful of Western Buddhists who, forty years ago, suggested the twin doctrines of *karma*/rebirth. Buddha was not concerned with ultimates, such as a first cause, but he clearly maintained the existence of 'a moral world order' under the reign of law for which he used the term *dharma*. This provides the cosmic ground of unity and harmony upon which field the individual treads the middle way to enlightenment. Here is the static aspect of the Godhead, a reflection in manifestation of the 'unborn'. The dynamic, all-embracing, infinitely adjustable law of karma, and its inevitable corollary rebirth provides, and with greater dignity, that which in theistic faiths calls for the personal attention of a Creator-God.

The author dilates upon the relative merits of the two concepts, and makes it clear why the Buddhist can politely say to his Christian brother that in Buddhism there is just no place or need for a theistic God. Nor is *karma* itself a god, still less God. Here is law, impersonal, utterly just which the individual may use precisely as he will. Nor is the heart left out. The twin concepts of *prajna*/*karuna*, wisdom and compassion are, as Dr Suzuki pointed out, the twin pillars on which the Mahayana rests, and neither can exist without the other.

Was not Buddha himself raised from man to superman and thence to the rank of God? Undoubtedly he reached very near it; but when to concepts such as *sunyata* and *tathata* and the like are added the Buddha-mind, is this not a reflection of the 'unborn, unoriginated, unformed' of which the Buddha spoke, and into awareness of which he entered by that enlightenment which earned him the title of Buddha? Such is the goal of Buddhism and of every Buddhist, and whether or not the word religion applies the purpose of endeavour is the same. Such personal awareness, such direct, immediate experience of the living fact that Nirvana is to be found within *samsāra*, that the Buddha-light already shines within, that the Absolute, however named and the relative, however known are one and the same and utterly indivisible—such experience is surely in the field of religious enterprise, whether or not religion is the right term to apply to the means by which this supernal end was attained?

Professor von Glasenapp deserves congratulation by fellow scholars in the field of comparative religion. His name should equally be remembered by the growing body of seekers who weary of an outworn form of God, but are looking for satisfaction for the heart and mind in that mighty field of thought and spiritual attainment known as Buddhism.

CHRISTMAS HUMPHREYS

INTRODUCTION

The word 'god' is used in various connotations.

In its most general sense it means each and every of the many supernatural beings that are prayed to, or made images of by man. The etymology of the word indicates the Old-Indian *hū*, to call (upon), or the Greek *khéein*, to cast, i.e. cast an image, hence idol.

Under Judaeo-Christian influence it became the name of the *one* eternal, supernatural, personal being who created the world, and who rules it.

In philosophy, it takes on the meaning of the Absolute, the impersonal *Ens realissimum* which is the ground of being irrespective of whether it coincides with the world, surrounds the world, or is active within the world.

To the ideology of gods, god, and the divine there belong further the image of a divine order of things, of a moral world order (in Fichte's sense), and finally the belief in 'men who became gods', who have become superhuman as incarnation (*avatāra*) of a higher power or by self-power, and who are worthy of veneration.

To the extent that this whole complex of religious ideas has found expression in Buddhism, it will be treated in detail. Such examination is also of special interest for the study of comparative religion because within this subject Buddhism differs from most of the other religions. Buddhism believes in the existence of a great number of impermanent gods (*devas*) and of men who became gods (*buddhas*). It believes in a moral world order (*dharma*), but emphatically denies the existence of an eternal creator and ruler of the world.*

This Buddhist 'atheism' excited the interest of the first Europeans who came in contact with it during the seventeenth

* This is especially stressed by modern Buddhist scholars. In his 1926 lectures on 'Main Buddhist Tenets'[3] to Prince Takamatsu, Junjiro Takakusu said: 'The first of the fundamental Buddhist principles is atheism. . . . However many stages and realms of intelligent beings there are above the human, we acknowledge them all; but we firmly deny recognition of a creator god who is ruler of all creatures.' And again:[4] 'Buddhism is atheist beyond all doubt.'

century.[1] Kant represents this opinion in the chapter on Siam of his *Lectures on Physical Geography*. 'They repudiate divine providence but teach that by fatal necessity vices are punished and virtues rewarded.'[2] Kant mentions the Buddhist teaching only shortly and without further comment; Schopenhauer, however, was profoundly impressed by it. In numerous quotations from the then existing literature he illustrates that Buddhism 'is *ex professo* according to our expression atheist'.[5] He specially stresses that the equation of atheism with materialism, irreligiosity or absence of morals is erroneous. Above all he insists that it is 'scandalous that German scholars to date and without exception consider religion and theism as identical and synonymous; yet religion relates to theism as does genus to one single species'.[6]

Since then, over a hundred years have passed. Some scholars of comparative religion still refuse to call Buddhism an atheistic religion, for it seems to be a *contradictio in adjecto* to those who have grown up within habitual Christian thought. However, the words 'atheist' and 'theist' express but the opinion of a man about the idea of a personal god; from it nothing else can be deduced as to his further religious or irreligious views. Moreover, the concept has another meaning as well; ancient writers called the Christians 'atheists' because they did not believe in the gods of the state.[7] In India it is usual to classify the *Sāmkhya*, Buddhism and Jainism as *Nirīshvara-vāda* (a teaching that denies a personal ruler of the world), and yet nobody doubts that they, too, are religious systems that teach the existence of impermanent gods, of a moral world order, and of liberation.

Wilhelm Schmidt in his textbook on comparative religion *Origin and Growth of Religion*[8] defines the concept of religion as 'the knowledge and feeling of dependence on supramundane personal powers with whom one enters into a mutual relationship'; he continues: 'here the words "personal powers" need an explanation. Though one can feel oneself dependent on impersonal powers, yet it is impossible to enter into a mutual relationship with them, for they cannot respond. This applies irrespective of whether it is a material power, for example the whole material universe; or whether it is the inexorable law of the universe. Both remain rigid and silent with regard to the human individual. Therefore basic Buddhism with its denial of personal gods cannot be considered a religion but only a philosophy. But wherever later Buddhism grew into a popular religion, it permitted innumerable personal gods to re-enter its wide system by a thousand back doors.'

This definition of religion by Schmidt is insufficient. It excludes many religious forms, especially those which, objectively considered, are veritable peaks of religious thinking. To the latter belong the various forms of 'all-one' mysticism. Moreover, creeds which are expressed by action, and which Schmidt himself counts as religions, could by his own definition not be called religions, i.e. creeds expressed by sacrifices, austerities, observation of ethical or moral codes, etc.

And finally, Schmidt's definition does not consider the fact that the Romans, who coined the word *religio*, did not understand by it 'the mutual relationship with supramundane personal powers'[9] alone.

With regard to Buddhism, Schmidt's statements are based on an erroneous assumption. Buddhism has never denied the existence of personal gods (*deva*), and only negated the existence of an eternal creator and ruler of the world. Even according to Schmidt's own definition, then, Buddhism is a religion.

The work of this great scholar, however, illustrates how very important it is to study the changing history of Buddhism, and to present its relationship with the image of the divine in detail.[10] It is obvious that an exhaustive treatment cannot be expected in so vast a field. I have therefore limited my researches mainly to Indian Buddhism. Linguistically, too, I am only qualified for this.

The presentation of such a study would be incomplete without the endeavour to integrate its results into the wider framework of the history of religions. I have therefore tried to find parallels from other religions analogous to specific points of Buddhist doctrine, as I wished to show that the Buddhist representation of gods, god, and the divine, is by no means exceptional, and has parallels in various other forms of religion.

Tübingen, summer 1954.

HELMUTH VON GLASENAPP

I. THE IMPERMANENT GODS

I THE BUDDHIST REPRESENTATION OF DEVAS

In Candalakappa, the young Brahmin Sangārava asked Buddha: 'Are there gods?' The Buddha answered: 'There are. The world is loud in agreement that there are gods' [26]. The existence of gods is also indirectly affirmed when king Pasenadi asks the same question [24], and in the *Milinda-Pañha* by the existence of the *Yakshas* [30].

These texts confirm unmistakably and authoritatively that since the oldest times Buddhists believed in the existence of gods (*deva*). The importance of the gods is shown also by the fact that *devatānusmriti* (Pāli: *devatānussati*), i.e. the proper consideration of the gods, belongs to the six *Anusmritis*; the others are: Buddha, teacher, community, discipline, and generosity in giving.[1] The meaning of this contemplation is that the meditator calls to mind the gods in their power and glory, and ponders by what virtues they have become heavenly beings. By keeping these virtues in mind, the heart of the mediator becomes free of delusions and passions [3].[2] The importance of popular belief in gods is confirmed by the edicts of the emperor Ashoka.[3] In the fourth rock-edict the 'Lord Beloved of the Gods' says that he showed his subjects images of gods and columns of flame (perhaps images of the fires of hell) together with processions of elephants, and that this resulted in a considerable uplift of general morals. In another edict Ashoka claims that, due to his religious fervour, gods who had no connection with man (*amissā*, literally, 'were not mixed'), are now again united with man.[4] And so it must be concluded that since their beginnings both the Buddhists and their founder have believed in a multiplicity of gods. The supposition that 'polytheism' only arose later is untenable.

If we want to get a clear picture of which specific ideas the early Buddhists connected with the Devas, we can most usefully start with the definition of the word *deva* by the commentators. Three different etymologies are given.

The first connects the word *deva* with the root *div*, i.e. to shine: 'the gods shine in their beauty' (*siriyā jotanti*).

A second etymology takes up the connotation 'to play, to sport' of the same root: *dibbantī ti devā, pañcahi kāmagunehi kīlanti*, i.e. 'they enjoy the five sense pleasures'.

If we connect these two meanings, we get: The gods are beings with a shining, supernatural body and spend their existence in sensual pleasures.

In a third etymology we learn of the function of the gods. It connects the related word *devatā* (divine being) with the word *deti* (he gives): *devatā yesam deti*, 'divine beings are beings to whom one brings gifts'. There are five types of such divine beings: (1) ascetics; (2) domestic animals like elephants, horses, cows, cocks, crows; (3) forces of nature and of the elements, such as fire and stones; (4) the lower gods like snakes, birds, *Yakshas, Asuras, Gandharvas*; (5) the higher gods who live in the specific world of the gods, like sun, moon, Indra, Brahmā.

This last connotation of a god as 'a being to whom one has to present something in order to receive his benevolence or to continue in it', seems to connect with still another classification.[5] It lists three kinds of gods:

Gods by consensus (*sammutti-deva*), i.e. humans who are referred to politely as *devas*, such as kings, princes, etc. (in Ancient Indian drama, '*deva*' is the usual form of address for royalty). Then, gods by purification (*visuddhi-deva*), i.e. humans who have cleansed their being to the extent that they have become free of the passions and possess higher insight and power, such as Arahats, Buddhas, etc. And finally reincarnated gods (*upapat ti-deva*), i.e. beings who are reborn in a supernatural world.

The Pāli Canon repeatedly mentions all kinds of sacrifices made to supernatural beings. The (113th) *Jātaka of the Jackal* tells us that fish, pieces of meat, and cups filled with wine were placed at crossroads by the local farmers. This religious observance is called *Yakkha-bali-kamma*.[6] Apparently pre-Buddhist in origin is the veneration of the holy trees (*rukkha-cetiya*) near Vesāli.[7] We also read about the worship of the sun god Suriya, of the moon god, of Sakka, etc. Though the Buddha abhorred the brahminical blood sacrifices, and denied the value of the complicated rituals that accompanied these ceremonies, yet there is no doubt that from the very beginning Buddhist laymen brought flowers and food to the gods, as indeed is still the custom today in Ceylon, Burma, Thailand, etc.

In the teachings of all the old religions, sacrifices and gifts are to persuade the gods to grant the fulfilment of definite wishes to the suppliant. This also we find in the Pāli Canon, where gods and spirits are mentioned to whom monks may take refuge if necessary.[8] The moon or holy trees are petitioned to grant the birth of a son, etc.[9]

Buddha is supposed to have told two ministers who were his hosts: 'Wherever a wise man has taken up his abode, there he brings gifts to the gods of this place. Respected and revered by him, he in turn is respected and revered by the gods. They tremble for him as a mother trembles for her own son (they are well disposed towards him). He who enjoys the grace of the gods, sees only the good.'[10] Buddha also explains: 'The son of good family uses his wealth to present gifts, and reveres the gods worthy of gifts (balipatiggāhikā), respects and worships them. They in their turn are then gracious and say to him: Live long, attain a ripe old age.'[11] If they are gracious, he may expect increase rather than decrease. Similarly it is said that the Vajjian may expect increase and not decrease as long as they revere the cult places (cetiya) of the gods, and bring gifts (bali) there [5].

The power of the gods, however, is limited to the fulfilment of worldly petitions; to create the world, to change its order, to bestow a good rebirth on a suppliant, or to grant him liberation, is not within their power. In Vedic times the gods were still identified with certain objects, and only later were considered heavenly dispensers of them. In the Pāli Canon the abstraction of the gods from their substrates in nature is so advanced that only in rare and isolated instances does a relation remain. The physical moon is the movable palace (vimāna) of Candima, god of the moon, who can stay its course at will.[12] Both he and Suriya the sun-god are subject to Sakka, and have to interrupt their travels should he so order them.[13] Both are in constant fear of the demon Rāhu who tries to swallow them up. The Samyutta-Nikāya tells the story of how Rāhu gives up this intention at the request of the Buddha [31].

Another relation between gods and the elements of nature also exists. *Devas* are mentioned who have clouds for bodies, and who cause heat, cold, thunder, wind and rain.[14] Various feats of the rain god Pajjunna, the Vedic Parjanya, are told; in the seventy-fifth *Jātaka* he acts at the behest of Indra [18]. Usually it is but stated: A Deva causes rain.[15] And a commentary to the *Theragāthā*[16] shows that the gods may also stop the rain. King Bimbisāra had ordered the monk Girimānanda to appear before him. However, he forgot about this, and had the gods not stopped the rainstorm, the waiting monk would have been soaked.

Gods who are most closely connected with natural objects are the tree-spirits which are said to converse with *bikkhus* [32]. Everyone who has been to Ceylon knows that mountains, too, have gods: Mahāsumana,[17] already mentioned in the *Mahā-vamsa*, lives on Adam's Peak. The four world guardians entrust the goddess Manimekhalā with the stewardship of the seas, and the saving of the shipwrecked.[18] In the *Dīgha-Nikāya* we find that the gods may also be connected with a certain locality —the site of the future town Pātaliputra was seized by gods.[19]

Though some relationship between gods and nature is not totally lacking, it is very slight compared with the great Hindu systems. In the systems of *Shankara* and *Madhva*, and even in the *Sānkhya*[20] system, the elements and sense organs need divine *abhimāna-devatās* (guardians) to be able to function at all.

Two *Jātaka* stories illustrate the dissociation of the god concept from its nature substrate. *Jātaka* 144 [19] tells of a Brahmin who is a devotee of the fire god Agni, and who tends his fire. One day he was about to sacrifice a bull to the god. Lacking salt for Agni's food he went to a village to get some. On his return to the place of sacrifice he saw that hunters had come along, eaten the meat, and left only the tail. The Brahmin was enraged. 'If Agni is not even capable of protecting his own property, how can I expect protection from him?' he said, burnt the tail, and extinguished the fire. He had lost his belief in the sacred fire as the manifestation of Agni. *Jātaka* 543 [21] contains stanzas directed against the cult of the Brahmins: 'There are some who venerate fire as a god; the *milakkhas* (barbarians) take water to be a god. All are ignorant. All are wrong. Fire (*aggi*) is not a god, neither is water. Fire (*vessānara*) has no sense-organs, and its body is without consciousness; yet it goes about its task like one who possesses knowledge. How then can a devotee of Agni go the good way (to heaven) if his deeds be evil?' The *Milinda-pañha* expressly states that water is not a sentient being.[21] Arguments about water being without a soul (*jīva*), and without a permanent self, are directed chiefly against the Jains who believe that water contains innumerable living beings, and therefore boil it to avoid swallowing them.

Thus the gods lost their relationship with the nature substrates—so strong in Vedic times—and in turn became beings in their own right. As such, they have various functions.

They are helpers in need, grant worldly goods to petitioners or protect them in danger, as already discussed.

They act within the framework of a moral world order by rewarding good deeds and punishing evil ones. In particular in accordance with Vedic ideas, the gods vanquish the *asuras* (demons) in the everlasting battles. Occasionally the gods also plead for the good life. A *devatā* (female *deva*) upbraids the Bhikkhus of Kosala for their soft and undisciplined life, and thus causes them to mend their ways [33].

One of their functions is to proclaim the Buddha's glory, and always to venerate him.

The Buddhist gods have essentially the same function as the Christian and Islamic angels and saints. The only difference is that the Buddhist *devatās*, in conformity with the old tradition, are still called gods in spite of all the changes and developments. Western monotheistic religions do not speak of gods even where saints clearly have their origin in certain figures of the pagan pantheon.

The Buddhist gods differ from those of various other religions by being subject to birth and death. This, however, is not specifically Buddhist but rather a general Indian view. The *Upanishads* taught that gods come into being due to their good *karma*, and that after this is exhausted, they continue their round in *Samsāra*. The Pāli Canon frequently treats of the karmic causes which effect rebirth as a specific god or into a specific class of gods. Thus the eight properties are listed which a virtuous woman must have in order to be reborn among the *Manāpakāyikas* who are renowned for their beauty.[22] The *Samyutta-Nikāya* states the seven vows by fulfilment of which a man becomes Sakka, king of the gods [35]. A whole book of the Canon, the *Vimāna-vatthu*, lists the good deeds by means of which a devotee was reborn as a *deva* in a magnificent palace.

Devas are not born from the womb, but come into being suddenly by 'manifestation' (*upapāta*), at an age of between four and ten. Contrary to ordinary men, the gods know three things the moment they come into being: what their previous existence was, where they have been reincarnated, and by means of which merits they achieved their existence as gods.[23] Gods know of no illness until they die. Their approaching death is indicated by the following five signs: their garments become dirty; the flowers they wear wither; sweat collects in their armpits; their bodies lose their shining colour; and they fidget restlessly on their seats. The cause of death is variously the exhaustion of their allotted life span, or of their transcendental merits, or of their food; also their forgetfulness with regard to nourishment, or again the annoyance that arises in them when another god has greater splendour.[24] After their heavenly existence, most gods are reborn on earth; however, the highest gods may even during their heavenly existence become *arahats*, and need not return to earth.

The gods are classified into a great number of groups, some with very fanciful names, e.g. *Satullapa*, i.e. the hundred criers,[25] or *Para-nimmita-vasavattinas* [3], those who depend for the objects of their desires on the mental creations of other gods who—according to the commentary—feed them like cooks with their thought-creations. Both *Dīgha-Nikāya* and *Majjhima-Nikāya* give the names of many such classes of gods.[26] Dogmatists have classified these into a hierarchy of some twenty stages, with details about their length of life, sexual habits, etc.[27] There are, however, only three main divisions, gods of the *Kāmāvacara* (the realm of sense pleasures), of the *Rūpāvacara* (the realm of pure forms), and of the *Arūpāvacara* (the formless realm). The basis for this classification is that the gods of the lower realms still own a body and are partial to sense pleasures, whereas the gods of the higher realms become increasingly spiritualized.[28] And so the Buddhist heavens represent all the higher spheres of other religions, from the sensual paradise of the Mohammedans to the Christian supra-sensual planes of bliss, and the contemplative raptures of infinity-mysticism.

Most of the Vedic gods still appear individually in the Pāli Canon: Agni, Indra (Shakra), Varuna, Prajāpati and Brahmā, Sūriya, Candra (Soma), Ishāna (Vishnu), Shrī, Skanda, Samudra, Yama; the four *Mahārājas*—Dhritarāshtra in the East, Virūdhaka in the South, Virūpāksha in the West, and Vaishrāvana (Kuvera) in the North. In addition there are the lower gods, the *yakshas*, *nāgas* (snake spirits), *garudas* and *suparnas* (bird spirits), *gandharvas* (heavenly musicians); also the gods of rivers, earth, mountains, and air;[29] and there are the opponents of the gods, the demonic *asuras*, *rākshasas* and *kumbhandas*. Later Pāli literature also mentions Kāma (Makaradhvaja), Puradeva (the city god of Anurādhapura), etc. Ganesha is missing in Pāli literature, but figures in Buddhist Sanskrit texts and in Far Eastern literature.[30]

The Mahāyāna patriarch Nāgārjuna writes: 'Three chiefs there are among the gods: Shakra . . . lord of the two classes of gods (the *Cāturmahārājikas* and the *Trāyastrimsha*); then king Māra . . . lord of the *Kāmadhātu*, the six realms of desire (of the *Cāturmahārājikas* and *Trāyastrimshas*, *Yāmas*, *Tushitas*, *Nirmānaratis* and *Parinirmitavashavartins*); and finally the *Devarāja* Mahābrahmā in *Brahmaloka* (in the Brahmā world).[31] These three chiefs of the gods, Shakra, Māra and Brahmā, figure widely in both the Hīnayāna and the Mahāyāna literature.

Shakra (Pāli: Sakka) is in Vedic literature one of the names of Indra (Pāli: Inda), king of the gods. Buddhist texts almost exclusively use the former; the *Samyutta-Nikāya* plays on the etymology of the word when it explains it as 'he who "appropriately" (*sakkacam*, Sanskrit: *satkritya*) gave alms'.[32] This obviously false derivation nevertheless portrays well the nature of the Buddhist 'King of the Thirty-Three Gods'. And so the gigantic slayer of the dragon, the fierce warrior with his enormous appetite and his love of the intoxicating soma juice, has now become a generous, pious, and gentle god. Moreover, he magnanimously forgives his enemies after capturing them [34]. Reverently he pays homage to the Buddha, is taught by the

Buddha, and at all occasions praises the Buddha's glory. In the *Jātaka* stories he often grants a son to a barren woman, or fulfils the various petitions of his devotees. The Canon shows him as the protector of the community of monks. Singhalese chronicles constantly praise him as the guardian and benefactor of Buddhism.

When his good *karma* is exhausted, and a Shakra must abdicate, another Shakra steps at once into his place. As the position of a Shakra is the result of good works, it is possible that in the course of reincarnation a person may become Shakra repeatedly. The pious Sunatta became Shakra no less than thirty-six times (*Anguttara-Nikāya*) [6], and Buddha, too, during his karmic, previous lives achieved a similar number of rebirths as Shakra (*Jātaka Stories*).

If Shakra illustrates the ideal of the virtuous king, Māra (occasionally also called 'king' or 'god') represents the exact opposite. He is the evil demon who rules over the worlds of sensuous pleasures, is 'the lord of this world', and corresponds to the Christian devil.[33] As such he is often represented as the tempter of the Buddha or of other *arahats*, usually supported by his daughters and by a host of armed evil spirits. One of the numerous Māra legends is of special interest.[34] The *Majjhima-Nikāya* [23] tells us that Māra had got into the belly of the virtuous disciple Mogallāna, and caused great pain (just as Luther diagnosed his gall-stones as an affliction of the devil). But Mogallāna ordered Māra to be off; and further told him that in a previous life he himself had been a Māra called Dūsī, had harmed a disciple of a previous Buddha, and had been punished for it by thousands of years in hell. The present Māra, son of Dūsī's sister Kālī, was thus in a sense his, Mogallāna's, nephew. At that, the evil one was embarrassed and sped away, and the venerable monk recovered.

Contrary to Shakra and Brahmā, Māra has no allotted dwelling-place in Buddhist cosmology. It rather seems that he was expected to move around or roam in all the realms of desire, ever on the look-out for likely victims. An often repeated expression[35] states that a Buddha has recognized the world together with all its gods, with Māra and Brahmā. And so we may conclude that Māra belongs to the world system as much as do Brahmā and the other gods.

Among the gods who are in contact with the world, Brahmā is the most important.[36] Brahmā has not yet reached the highest state attainable to beings in *Samsāra*, for above his are other worlds; their inhabitants are in continuous meditation and attain deeper spiritual states. However, these beings do not actively engage in the affairs of this world, and so need not be discussed here.

Brahmā is often called Sahampati. This is supposed to be the name of the Brahmā who reigned at the time of the Buddha (*Samyutta-Nikāya*).[37] The derivation of it is as follows. In former times—to be exact, at the time when Kassapa was Buddha—Sahampati was the monk Sahaka, and by merit of his virtuous conduct was reborn as Brahmā. In another derivation[38] Sahampati is 'lord of the world of suffering' (from the root *sah*—to endure suffering). Further he is the ruler of a world which is subdivided into numerous levels and belongs to the world of pure form (*rūpāvacara*). And this world is inhabited by the *Brahmā-kāyika-devas* who are equally grouped into many sub-classes, but they are all beings with fine-material bodies, and are free of passions.

The appellations of Brahmā in the *Dīgha-Nikāya* are the same as those of *Ishvara* in the theist schools, i.e. 'Almighty, Creator and Ruler of the World, Father of all that was and will be' [11]. In the Buddhist view, these attributes are erroneous, for Brahmā is not an eternal being as the ignorant believe him to be. Nor is he omniscient, for when the monk Kevaddha asks him where the four elements of earth, water, fire and air finally cease without leaving a trace, he has to admit—after long hesitation—that he does not know [13].

Buddhists also deny the brahminical view of liberation being attained by union with Brahmā: Existence in the Brahmā world can in no wise be compared with Nirvāna. Much of what in Buddhist texts is said about Brahmā obviously serves the purpose of presenting brahminical views as inadequate, and to use them as stepping-stones within the Buddhist system. So Brahmā is mostly a humble devotee of the Buddha, and diligent in proclaiming his teaching.

Brahmā is the highest god in the Buddhist teaching, which thus retains a view which classical Hinduism no longer knows. In the latter, Brahmā only holds the humble position of a demigod, compared with Vishnu and Shiva, who have risen to the order of world rulers.

Belief in most of the above gods may be assumed since the beginning of Buddhism. A further reason for this assumption is that the Buddha's disciples and adherents of brahminical doctrines and cults did not live in separate communities. And the laity seem to have freely participated in the rites and festivals of both religions. The same still happens today in all countries where Buddhism is but one of the local religions. The gods have been more or less acknowledged by all Buddhists, at all times—see the evidence in the Pāli Canon, the *Abhidharmakosha*, and the older Mahāyāna texts—and as such belong so to speak, to the foundation of the doctrinal building, upon which later generations have erected new structures.

In the course of centuries, the Buddhist pantheon in India was further enriched by the arrival of new gods from the area of the Ganges, and also by gods hardly known before but now attaining eminence. The new gods also influenced Buddhist thinking. This applies to Vishnu, to Shiva, and to many other gods belonging to this group.[39] Divers local gods also were accepted into the Buddhist system. Tantric Buddhism, too, introduced many new gods, Acala, Hevajra, Heruka, etc., but especially also goddesses like Tārā, Māmakī, Nairātmā and so forth.[40] This development was caused by two newly emerging considerations; due to the stronger Hindu influence since the beginning of the latter half of the first millennium, the Buddhist gods became again more intimately connected with specific nature substrates, or with the normal events of life, and thus differ from the former *Abhimānadevatās*. And further they are often portrayed as manifestations of Bodhisattvas and Buddhas, or are related to them as their servants.

When Buddhism was introduced to the vast expanses of Asia by zealous proselytizers, and became established there, the local gods were naturally incorporated. In consequence of all this, the Buddhist pantheon is unique in its richness and variety, especially in Japan.

The *devas* have their origin in local creeds and are venerated by the pious because somehow or other they grant worldly goods. Besides them, however, Buddhist teaching knows countless other gods who have little or no connection with ordinary men. These gods are more or less unknown to brahminical thought and owe their existence to contemplation or speculation. Besides the *devas* of the *Kāmāvacara* realm, these are *devas* with whom the meditator can establish contact at any of the eight stages of meditative absorption, but they mostly appear to be but anonymous members of a certain class rather than individual beings; only the Brahmās of the lowest meditation stage have individual features. (In the *Mahāyāna* we find for the first time higher individualized beings residing in one of the higher realms of meditation. Thus Vairocana Buddha in his visible manifestation dwells in the *Akanishta* realm of pure form.) The gods of the meditative realms are again classified into two groups—those of the lower 16 (also 17)[41] classes may be reached within the four ordinary stages of meditation; they have pure, i.e. fine-material, bodies, and are free of all passions. They lack the senses of taste and smell which are unnecessary as they no longer take physical food and are nourished by 'joy'. The gods of the formless realm (*arūpāvacara*) have no bodies,[42] at least according to the orthodox view. Consequently they do not possess even fine-material sense organs and are pure mental formations in whom *Samjñā* and *Cetanā* (conscious volition as the *Samskāra par excellence*)[43] are present. In the *Abhidharma-kosha*[44] formulation, the gods of the formless realm possess as *Indriyas* only *Jīvita*, *Manas* and *Upekshā* (equanimity). Accordingly these realms are non-spatial, and though it is said that the *Arūpā* realm is situated above the *Rūpādhātu*, this is to be understood figuratively only.[45] Or, in its Kantian expression: 'The other world is not another place, but rather another view.'

Rebirth in the formless realms is not desirable in spite of their immateriality, for the gods there practise throughout many world cycles meditation on the infinity of space, of consciousness, and of nothingness, and realize the limits of perception and non-perception, but have little chance to tread the path of liberation.

All these gods may be seen in advanced meditation by the virtuous meditator, for it is assumed that the attainment of a specific plane of meditation enables one to become conscious of beings with whom contact was previously impossible. In the *Anguttara-Nikāya* the Buddha tells how in his meditations before his enlightenment he at first only perceived the shining light of supra-sensual entities; however, in constant and tireless continuance of his meditations he came to see the forms of the gods distinctly, then could even talk with them, and finally came to know their place in the hierarchical order, their type of food and their length of life, their *karma*, and their former and future rebirths [7]. This quotation constitutes a valuable hint as to how the belief in those various gods started. They owe their existence to meditative experiences which then by means of rationalistic systematization were formalized by the dogmatic theoreticians.

In my view there is no doubt whatsoever that Buddha and all his adherents believed in the concrete existence of these gods, just as do most Buddhists even today. It is an unpardonable mistake for a historian to assume that only later tradition has incorporated them into the teaching in order to pander to the masses. However, Buddhism differs from the doctrines of many other religions by regarding the gods as part of *Samsāra*, and as impermanent. Like all other beings, the Buddhist gods are subject to the karmic law of cause and effect, and natural law sets a beginning and an end for their status as gods. They are neither almighty nor omniscient, nor can they grant liberation.

In all this they take second place to the Buddha, and even after the more advanced of his disciples. So it is understandable that the Pāli Canon does not go into details about the gods, though they are constantly referred to. *Devatās* are first and foremost objects of veneration to the laity, but not to monks. On the graded path to liberation, the latter have already attained to a spiritual state which by far exceeds that of all the gods. Veneration of the gods in the older period is considered a fairly primitive form of religiosity compared with that that is directed towards liberation, which is the intrinsic aim of man. One who treads the path of liberation, or has become an *arahat* will, according to the *Majjhima-Nikāya*,[46] no more depend spiritually on the gods, and ponder about them than he does about the elements, living beings, higher states of consciousness, that which is perceived by the senses, unity, multiplicity, or Nirvāna.

Nāgārjuna goes still further:

> The gods are all eternal scoundrels,
> Incapable of dissolving the suffering of impermanence.
> Those who serve them and venerate them
> May even in this world sink into a sea of sorrow.
> Those who despise them and blaspheme
> May in this world enjoy all kinds of fortune.
> We know the gods are false and have no concrete being;
> Therefore the wise man believes them not.
> The fate of the world depends on causes and conditions;
> Therefore the wise man does not rely on gods.[47]

Though these verses deviate somewhat from Buddhist toler-
ance (as Lamotte remarks) they are meant to express in the
strongest possible terms that man is independent of the gods
with regard to both his fate and his liberation; and that the
wise disciple who has attained the required level of enlightenment need not worry about the gods.

2 PARALLELS FROM COMPARATIVE RELIGION

The Western reader is astonished and surprised when he learns
that in Buddhism the gods are impermanent beings. This is
mainly due to the false perspective from which he sees the
devas. He wonders how they come to have a beginning and an
end in time, for he cannot shed the unconscious tendency to
equate individual *devas* or all of them as a group, with the
Christian God. Yet, *devas* correspond rather to the angels and
saints who themselves are subject to something higher—in
theistic religions, the Almighty God, and in Buddhism the
world law. Buddhist *devas* share with the angels and saints of
Western religions also the feature of not having possessed their
high status since from all eternity. The angels were created by
God at the time of creation; saints attained to their status only
after their lives on earth. One of the various differences is that
unlike angels and saints, the Indian gods lose their status again
at a later stage, whereas the former retain it by divine decree
for all time.

All over the world we find in widely differing mythologies
the belief that the gods came into being at a specific point in

31

time. Mostly we hear that, like men, gods have a father and a mother. In other mythologies they issue from the body of another god; thus an Indian myth tells that Shiva was born from the wrinkles on Vishnu's eyebrows. Japanese Shintoism has gods issuing even from inanimate objects: from a broken sword, from jewellery that was chewed to bits, from the putre-fying body of a goddess.[1] Many myths also tell of gods who had originally been human beings, but because of their acquired merits had found a place in heaven. Their veneration started subsequently, either by consensus of opinion, or also for example by command of the Chinese emperor or other authori-ties.

In most religions we find the view that the gods had either come into being at a specific point in time, or at a specific point in time had started to be or behave as gods, saints, etc., but that, once attained, they will keep their rank or status for ever. In the classical Greek and Roman view the main dif-ference between gods and men is that the former are immortal. Schiller expresses this aptly:

> All mortal being is but smoke;
> With the rising column of flame
> Vanish king and sage and beggar,
> But the gods remain the same.

The cause of the immortality of the gods is their partaking of ambrosia (in Homer, even the gods' horses are fed on it). Other Indo-European religions have similar conceptions of a potion of immortality. The Gilgamesh epic tells of a plant of immortality; Shivaite and Taoist magicians and the medieval alchemists believed that in certain compound mixtures they had discovered the elixir of immortality. In the Egyptian con-ception Osiris was revived by a certain process of mummifica-tion and by the use of magical spells and rites, and hence by analogy a dead mortal, too, may be returned to life if his corpse is treated likewise. Elsewhere it is assumed that special initia-tions into mystery-cults guarantee immortality in a better world where a man may live for ever in the company of higher beings. The great Western religions derive the immortality of angels, saints, etc., from the will of God; and man, too, continues to exist after the resurrection only because God wills it so.

Though gods are said to be physically more perfect than man, and are frequently supposed to have an etheric, subtle body and finer organs, some myths also know of physical defects. The Germanic god Tyr lost his hand in a fight with the wolf Fenrir, and Wotan lost one of his eyes; the Indian god Ganesha lost one of his tusks.

In primitive religious beliefs gods may die. *Völuspa*, the famous Viking poem, prophesies the end of the gods; but the general view is optimistic, for after the gods have died, the world will again rise in shining glory. Death and rebirth are common to the myths of Osiris, Adonis, and other gods, and derive from cyclic events in nature.

Many religions see no contradiction in the supposed existence of beings who had a beginning but thereafter continue for ever. But since the *Upanishads* the Indians with their philosophical minds arrived at the logical view that something that has a beginning must inevitably also have an end. Only that which has always been so can be permanent and changeless. This belief is expressed in the doctrine of the immortal soul which moves on into ever new bodies. And from the beginning the idea of reincarnation also included the gods. The old view that there will always be an Indra, etc., while the world is in existence, was adjusted to the new ideas of the impermanence of the individual in *Samsāra*, and the gods were declared to be cosmic officials holding certain positions and having certain duties. These offices, for example, that of a heavenly general, or of a chaplain, remain constant though the individual entity that carries out the duties of Indra or Agni, etc., changes. Buddhism has incorporated this doctrine, though it does not teach the existence of a permanent soul as do Brahmin and Jain doctrines. It rather holds that what travels from one existence to the next is a stream of impersonal forces—the factors of being (*dharma*); these come into being and dissolve again in functional dependence on each other.

In many religious systems, the gods have but limited power which does not extend above their official duties. Particularly departmentalized were the Roman gods. Hermann Usener shows that of the innumerable separate gods each one has a

C

special function. For example in agriculture, there is one god for planting, another for sowing, a third for the sprouting of the seed, others again for ripening, harvesting, threshing, grinding flour, etc. The Japanese know guardian gods for the different parts of the house, for kitchen, kettle, and even the toilet.

The relationship of the gods to each other is conceived in various ways. They may be thought to be all members of one family of gods, or again of one heavenly realm; or they hold the various ranks and positions of a hierarchy the complexity of which the theologians have worked out with loving care. While some systems are satisfied simply to acknowledge the many gods as such, others see in them the servants and bondsmen of the one, incomparably superior, highest god or world ruler, and again others venerate, in and through the gods' particular aspects, the one divine *Ens realissimum*.

Seen from the historical point of view, a continuous process of change takes place within this host of divine beings. New gods appear, old ones are forgotten, many originally different gods are later taken to be phases or aspects of one only; or else one is divided into several others.

It is also typical that the gods are conceived in an earthly, mostly human image. They have human properties, both virtues and vices. One of the strangest manifestations in the history of religion is that though the gods are devoutly revered by the pious, the old mythologies invest them with various vices. Seen from the present-day moral point of view, they seem thoroughly inappropriate to set a standard of behaviour—an embarrassing point for the Greek philosophers. Especially with regard to sex the gods are supposed to be all too human. Examples are the manifold incest myths of the primitives, of the Japanese, and of the Indians (Brahmā); then the many amorous adventures, both hetero- and homosexual, of Jove, Apollo, etc. And the jealousy of the gods, their rivalries among themselves, and so on—all confirm clearly the saying, 'Man portrays himself in his gods'.

In this short survey we have seen that the Buddhist teaching of impermanent gods with restricted power is not so exceptional, and may be found in some form or other in various widely differing religions.

II. NO CREATOR OR RULER OF WORLDS

I BUDDHIST ARGUMENTS AGAINST THEISM

The old, developed religions of India acknowledge a multitude of impermanent gods, all of then subject to *karma*. Buddhism and Jainism, and the classic systems of Mīmāmsā and Sānkhya, consider all the gods without exception as karmically conditioned beings. Many orthodox Hindu and Brahmin sects, however, teach one uncreated, permanent world ruler (*Īshvara*) who is above all the impermanent gods. He exists eternally, and rules the cosmos and all individual beings. His adherents attempted to prove his existence by philosophical arguments, or by appeal to Vedic revelation, or to other scriptures considered to be authoritative. And Buddhist apologetics at all times tried to justify their different, atheist point of view. I present below the relevant arguments of Buddhist masters and texts, arranged not in chronological order but according to their logical development.[1]

Buddhism is a philosophy of becoming; consequently it cannot acknowledge the existence of an eternal, permanent and personal god. If there is nothing that is permanent in the world, if unconditioned substances do not exist, and if each personality is but a continuously flowing stream of changing *dharmas*, then no *Īshvara* can exist, no matter whether he is conceived as Brahmā, Vishnu, Shiva, or whatever. Therefore it is said (*Abhidharmakosha*): 'The assumption that an *Īshvara* is the cause (of the world, etc.) is based on the false belief in an eternal self (*ātman*, i.e. permanent spiritual substance or personality). This belief is untenable as soon as it is recognized that everything is (impermanent and therefore) subject to suffering.'[2]

Buddha says (*Anguttara-Nikāya*): 'As far as the suns and moons extend their courses and the regions of the sky shine in splendour, there is a thousandfold world system. In each single one of these there are a thousand suns, moons, Meru Mountains, four times a thousand continents and oceans, a thousand heavens of all stages of the realm of sense pleasure, a thousand Brahmā worlds. As far as a thousandfold world system reaches, the Great Brahmā is the highest being. But even the Great Brahmā is subject to coming-to-be and ceasing-to-be.'[3]

Like many of the Western schools, the theist ones of India taught a dual theology: they proclaimed God to be immutable and ineffable, and yet attributed certain properties to him. Buddha rejected both (*Dīgha-Nikāya*): 'The Brahmins themselves admit that none of them has seen Brahmā with his own eyes. So, in effect, they teach: To him whom we neither know nor see, to union with him we show the way, and this way is the only and direct way to attainment. This is as if one wanted to erect a staircase to the upper floor of a palace on a place one has never seen and the size of which one does not know. Or as if one said: I love the most beautiful woman in this or that country and want to make her my own. But if asked for her name, or her looks, her caste, or where she lives, one does not know. Is this not loose and foolish talk (*appātihīrakatam bhāsitam*) [14]?[4]

If God is too great for our perception, his properties, too, exceed our apprehension, and we can neither describe his being nor attribute creation to him [14].

Further, it is a contraction in terms to suppose that from something incomprehensible to us there can derive something we can conceive. And it is therefore better to stick to what we know—for example the elements—when we consider a first cause [41].

Buddhism considers *Ishvara* merely as a product of speculative thinking which actually contributes nothing to an explanation of the world and denies his existence just as much as that of a soul. Of the latter it is said (*Abhidharmakosha*) that the origin of thoughts, etc., is sufficiently explained by *Manas* and the *Samskāras*; there is no need to postulate a soul as well—this being as superfluous as a quack (*kuhaka-vaidya*) who is using an effective medicine, but adds to it by uttering the Mantras '*phut! svāhā!*' to suggestively influence and impress the patient.[5]

Theists who equate *Ishvara* with a specific god, Vishnu, Shiva, etc., and so present a positive theology, attribute to him human qualities like hate, pride, etc., that do not befit an almighty being. And how low and coarse is the god image when the *Mahābhārata* says of Shiva: 'Because he burns up, because he is severe, is cruel, and full of fire, and because he gorges himself on meat, blood, and marrow, therefore he is called Rudra.'[6] The world ruler grants the wishes of those whom he loves, but those whom he hates he makes to suffer or destroys them. This proves he does not possess the qualities of a Bodhisattva, as are appropriate for a higher being. For a Bodhisattva benefits all beings and will even give up his own life for their welfare—even for enemies that try to kill him.

A further argument against theism is that the different schools regard different gods as the creator and ruler of the world: the Brahmins, Brahmā; the Vishnuites, Vishnu, etc. Who, then, is correct? Nāgārjuna[7] comments that this difference of opinion is caused by Brahmā, Vishnu, etc., who in their arrogant ignorance consider themselves to be *Īshvara,* and thus also mislead men.

But the main attack of Buddhist philosophers is directed against the teaching of a creation by god. The following arguments have been extracted from the *Abhidharmakosha,*[8] the *Sphutārthā,*[9] and the *Bodhicaryāvatāra* [14].

If all is reduced to God as the sole cause, all would have had to be created at the same moment (*yugapat sarvena jagatā bhavitavyam*).[10] But things in the world arise in succession, and also in dependence on each other. The theist counters this by asserting that God creates the one, and causes the other to cease at his will (*chanda*). Against this the Buddhist maintains that it is then impossible to speak of a single decision of God as the one and only cause of creation, since in this case many decisions are required. Were God the sole cause of all things, all would come into existence simultaneously.

This argument is typically Buddhist, for the law of dependent origination teaches the conditioned arising of one *dharma* from a multitude of other *dharmas*. But as most Hindu schools see in the world process the eternal play of God, the argument loses some of its force—and would be far more apt if directed against the Persian-Jewish-Christian-Islamic theory of a final end of all things.

The theist reply to the above is that God creates things,

37

situations, etc., successively because he considers the relation-ships (*apekshana*). But if God does this, then he is again not the sole cause of everything; for then there are other causes, too, which in their turn depend on still other ones.

The main difficulty for the theists consists in their assumption that God is the creator of everything, while at the same time also accepting the theory of *karma*. According to the latter, each existence is the result of good or evil deeds in a previous existence. The inexorable consequence of this is that the world-cycle has no beginning. In this, the brahminical systems are in agreement with Buddhism (*Shākyaputrīya nyāya*). However, Buddhist thinking reduces everything to the law of *karma*, and is thus more consistent. The reciprocal causality of karmic law and the actions of God in the world cannot logically coexist.

If the theist does not *a priori* deny all natural causality, for example that sprouting depends on a seed, then he has to admit these natural causes as auxiliaries (*sahakārikārana*) to God. The latter, however, is then but a pious statement (*bhaktivāda*), for it can be demonstrated that for a seed to sprout, a field, water, etc. are essential; or that consciousness of seeing can only exist when and where an eye, colour, and perception by an organ of thinking co-operate. In all this, no active intervention of God can be observed. The fact is that sprouting, or the con-sciousness of seeing, only come about if and when the essential requirements are fulfilled. And so the assumption of a god additional to natural process is completely superfluous. Shāntideva [41] therefore holds that if God must make considerations in order to create—as the potter needs clay to produce a pot—then he is not the lord of everything. The followers of the *Nyāya-Vaisheshika* sect are known as extremists of theism, and their system particularly shows the insufficiency of the theist position. They hold the five elements, space, the soul, etc., to be eternal. Cognition, pain and pleasure are not derived from God; and they accept the law of *karma*. But in that case, God has no actual function to fulfil in either the natural or the moral world. And the theories of the Vedāntins are just as un-satisfactory, i.e. that God has transformed himself and become the elements, space, and individual souls, and through them caused the order of the world and beings to come into existence.

For the elements are not one but five, they are without intelligence and activity, and as they are not worthy of veneration either—how can they be God? Space does not act and so cannot be God; nor can the soul be God for it does not exist as a continuous, permanent principle (this latter according to the Buddhist doctrine of *Anātma-vāda*).

The doctrine of creation by God is only tenable on the assumption of an original creation (*ādisarga*), of one single origin. It is just this which is impossible according to the doctrine of *karma* which teaches that the beings in the present world are conditioned by their *karma* carried over from a former existence. And further, God cannot have been the original creator of the world because no point in time is imaginable at which God existed but not yet a world (at least in the latent form of *karma* carried over).

The remarkable point in these arguments against the theists is that a consistent development is missing in them. If the world is traced back to God as the single cause, one cannot settle it at this point, but rather must ask further: from what cause has God arisen? This is a question frequently asked by modern Buddhist apologists.*

Speaking as a Buddhist, the whole problem of the creation *ex nihilo* solves itself. According to the theory of causality, nothing can come about by one single cause so that the co-operation of a multitude of causes is necessary to produce something.

Again from the Buddhist point of view, it is difficult for theism to give a motive for the act of creation. If God created the world for his own pleasure, then it would seem that he delights in the existential suffering of his creatures, in their being subject to illness and the pains of hell, etc. And if God is almighty, then why has he made such a poor job of the world? And the final problem is: 'If God is the sole cause of all that happens, then the effort of man is vain.'[12]

In the earliest literature Buddha is said to have stressed the incompatibility of the theory of a good and almighty god with the vileness of the world, and with the doctrine of the freedom of the will. A summary from the *Anguttara-Nikāya* states [2]:

* 'Asked how life developed, he (the Buddhist) is bound to counter with the question: How did God develop?' (Prof. G. P. Malalasekera.)[11]

39

'Some ascetics and Brahmins hold: "Whatever comes to man, happiness or suffering, or neither, all is caused by the will of the creator (*issara-nimmāna*)." But I say: "So then because of the will of their creator and god, human beings become murderers, thieves, unchaste, liars, slanderers, covetous, malicious and heretical." And those who rely on the creation of a supreme god lack the freewill to do what is to be done, and to refrain from doing what is not to be done.'[13]

The *Bhūridatta-Jātaka* poses the question why God does not make all men happy, and why he does not bring order into the world (*ujju-karoti*). 'The lord of creation is unjust because though justice exists, he created injustice as well' [21].

Though Brahminical teaching is based on the Vedas and other canonical texts, it is of no value for the words of the Brahmins are mere lying chatter (*asatpra-lāpa*).[14] The *Milinda-pañha* calls them empty and without a real core [28]. In the *Vajrasūcī*—supposed to be by Ashvaghosha—the Brahminical scriptures are ridiculed.[15]

According to the *Majjhima-Nikāya* Buddha said: 'The Brahmins have handed on the old traditions down the generations, just as a basket is handed on; and they say: "This is true, and all else is false." But is there but one among them, even back to their old masters, who can say: "This I know myself?" They are all like a lot of blind men, walking one behind the other, and none of them sees in front, at the back, or in the middle' [25]. The Buddha contrasts Brahminical wisdom based on revelation with an insight which, according to him, can be won by everyone who has developed the necessary prerequisites.

Buddhism, however, is not satisfied in merely contradicting theist doctrines, but also developed a theory as to how the erroneous belief in a creator-god (Brahmā) came about. The oldest version of this theory is already contained in the *Dīgha-Nikāya*. I give this text with some interspersed comments.[16] It starts with a description of the cyclic periods of world creation and destruction:

After a long period of time, the world comes to an end. When this happens, all creatures escape—mainly into (the realm of) shining beings (*ābhassara*, i.e. gods of a higher realm that is not destroyed at the end of the world). There they live, having bodies composed of *'manas'*;* their nourishment is joy, they shine by their inherent splendour, fly in the air, and live in glory, for a very long time.

After a long period, the world then begins anew. When this happens, first the empty Brahmā palace appears. Then a being departs from the assembly of the 'shining ones' because his allotted life span is over, or because his own accumulated merits (to which he owes his existence in the realm of the 'shining ones') are exhausted. He subsequently appears in the empty Brahmā palace of the newly emerging world. There he lives with a *'manas'* body (see above), his nourishment is joy, he shines by his inherent splendour, flies in the air, and lives in glory for a very long time.

However, after that being has lived in the Brahmā palace for a very long time he becomes lonely, and there arises in him the restless desire: 'Oh, if only other beings, too, might come into existence!' Then other beings begin to depart from the realm of the 'shining ones', because their appropriate span of life is ended, or because their accumulated merits are exhausted. They also appear in the Brahmā palace, and keep the first-comer company. They, too, live there with *'manas'* bodies, their nourishment is joy, they shine by their inherent splendour, fly in the air, and live for a very long time.

Then the one who came first into the empty Brahmā palace thinks: 'I am Brahmā, the Great Brahmā, the Almighty, not subject to anybody, from whose eyes nothing remains hidden, undisputed ruler, the effective one, the creator, the highest lord who rules everything according to his pleasure, the father of all that has been and will be. I have created all these beings here. For in me there arose the thought: 'Oh, if only other beings, too, would come into existence!' That was the desire of my heart, and lo! they came into existence'. And in the beings that appeared after him the thought arises: 'This is the venerable Brahmā, the Great Brahmā, the Almighty. . . . He, the venerable Brahmā, created us all. For we found him here, and ourselves appeared after him.'

This is a very interesting statement, for it assumes that even the first dwellers on earth already had a monotheistic religion

---

* i.e. the organ of thinking composed of finest-material matter.

of some primitive form. However, it traces this monotheism back not to an original revelation, but to an error of assumption by both God and men.

Studying the above arguments against a personal creator and ruler, we find that the authoritative Indian texts of Buddhism show a clear and well-argued, negative attitude towards the idea of God. And so Buddhism with its strict denial of a divine creator and world ruler must be said to be atheist.

There remains, however, the question whether Buddhism was atheist from its beginning, or whether its founder, the historical Gautama, had another point of view. Some scholars attempted to clear Buddha of the accusation of atheism by suggesting that he never intentionally touched on the problem of God, that his purpose was only to teach the path of self-liberation, and that he therefore repudiated all metaphysical speculations.[17] Other scholars are of the opinion that Nirvāna or the eternal, cosmic law replaces God in Buddhist teaching. And others again suggest that Buddha did recognize a world ruler; or again, that from the very beginning his adherents saw in him a liberated, eternal being. All these widely differing attempts to prove the theism of Buddha[18] are so many speculations, and cannot be supported from the texts. They also lack historical foundation: if such a great difference is assumed between the teaching of the founder and that of the older texts of his religion, then detailed evidence has to be produced to show how this revolutionary change took place. Buddha himself left no writings; and his teachings were not taken down in shorthand or tape-recorded; for hundreds of years they were orally handed on until eventually they were written down. What Buddha himself taught can never be accurately ascertained. Yet, if one allows any authority to the transmitted canonical scriptures, one will also have to admit that in all probability Buddha's view did not vary greatly from that which is presented by all the later literature on the problem of God.

There is no need to go still deeper into this question, for our survey deals exclusively with the doctrines of historical Buddhism as they are reflected in the scriptures. A botanist engaged in writing a treatise on the oak tree will place his main interest on the fully developed tree; he will not be content with a monograph on the acorn plus speculations as to how far the acorn might differ from the tree.

That Buddhism was an 'a-theist' religion from the beginning is supported by the evidence of other non-theist religions in India.

2 PARALLELS FROM COMPARATIVE RELIGION

The Jains represent an atheistic pluralism. The teaching of this religion has much in common with Buddhism, but differs from the latter by assuming eternal, individual souls, and eternal matter. The basic, original relationship between the beginningless souls and the atoms, is the cause of all suffering in the world. Separation of these two unconnected entities is the prerequisite for liberation. And this can only be attained by personal effort. No god can help or aid a man towards it, for there is no *Ishvara* who rules the world or who could break the chain of *Samsāra* by an act of grace. And in Jain doctrine it is a heresy (*mithyādrishti*) to believe in an eternal, omniscient, omnipresent god who created the world (*kartā*, i.e. maker) and again destroys it (*hartā*, i.e. destroyer), for such a belief blocks the path towards liberation. Nor does the Jain teaching need such a god for it denies the cyclic origin and destruction of the world. The Jain arguments against the existence of an *Ishvara* are partly the same as the Buddhist ones: the incompatability of a good God with the evils of the world; the anthropomorphiza-tion of God by ascribing to him the properties of love and hate; the limitations of his omnipotence by the law of *karma*; the disagreement on whether Vishnu or Shiva is the cosmic lord, etc.[1]

In addition, the following arguments are brought out: the assumption that only an intelligent being could have created and ordered the world is a weak one, because matter, too, is subject to inherent laws. There is further the possibility that not one but many gods created the world—just as hundreds of ants erect one structure. Further, if a creator is assumed, then it must also be assumed that he has a body—on the analogy that a potter, too, has a body; and from this there arises the question why nobody can see the body of God. And because everything on earth that possesses a body has a beginning and an end, God, too, must be impermanent. If, however, it is

43

asserted that God is a purely spiritual being, then it seems impossible that he can create material things. According to the Jain teaching, only a pure spirit can be thought of as a liberator; and as such he has neither the possibility nor the wish to be active in the world.

If God is considered omnipresent, then he must also be present in unclean places, for example, in the hells. And how can it even be conceived that a good and kind being—God in the view of the theists—creates such terrible places of punishment, and causes sinners to suffer the most frightful tortures?

The various theist schools rely on the authority of their scriptures, considering them as divine revelations. However, those scriptures cannot have been produced by an omniscient being, for they contain many contradictions. Nor does it seem proper for an exalted being to continuously proclaim his own virtues. And so there is no convincing evidence whatsoever to suggest the existence of a creator and ruler of the world. The idea of a God is based on imagination which has no more reality than the idea of the son of a barren woman.

The orthodox Brahmins consider Buddhist and Jain teachings heretical, because they are not based on Vedic revelation. However, religious atheism exists also within Brahmin orthodoxy— it is very typical that of the six orthodox, philosophical systems two are specifically atheist—*Mīmāmsā* and the classic *Sānkhya*.

No other Hindu religious system lays more claim to possessing correct view than *Mīmāmsā*, the teaching of service. It purports to be nothing but a commentary on and a defence of the holy scriptures. The Vedas have neither been revealed by a god, nor have they been produced by man, but are an eternal, spiritual substance, and exist in and by themselves. They are, so to speak, the ethical and ritual order of the world expressed in words, and are the embodiment of *dharma* binding for all periods of time, the sum total of all religious duties from which nobody is exempt.

Kumārila, one of the main representatives of this teaching (eighth century) tries to substantiate the basic dogma, and to defend it against all attacks. For anybody who does not already believe in Vedic revelation, his arguments are no more convincing than those cited for the verbal inspiration of the Bible, or for the immutability of the Koran.

Those who believe in a God accept Prajāpati as creator and lord of all creatures. Kumārila declares this teaching as unfounded, for human beings did not exist before the creation; so there was nobody who witnessed the act, and might have reported it to others. If it be claimed, however, that God subsequently revealed to man how he created the world, this does not constitute a proof; God might have told this story only to illustrate his supposed almightiness. Nor can it possibly be assumed that God created the world out of love for the not yet existing creatures, for then he would have created happy beings only. If God is absolutely pure and perfect, how comes it that the world he created and rules is impure and imperfect? The theory that all evil and all delusion (*avidyā*) is founded on *māyā* is of little avail here, for if *māyā* can produce the whole manifold universe by itself and without the will of God, then there exists in fact a dualism of two original beings opposed to each other. And further, if delusion is an original being independent of Brahmā, then it can never be dissolved and liberation is impossible.

All the texts quoted so far assume that the world was not created once and for all at the beginning of time, but that world cycles periodically alternate with destruction. This corresponds to the belief of most Hindus. This assumption, however, contradicts all experience and should be discarded. (The Mīmāmsakas teach, as do the Jains, that the world as a whole is eternal and permanent.) This theory makes the existence of a world creator superfluous, for the karmic laws which condition the beginning of a new world would limit God's omnipotence. For these and other reasons the assumption of a ruler of the world is untenable. The authority of the Vedas is more convincingly secured by giving up the uncertain supposition of an omniscient creator, and admitting instead the theory of the eternal Vedas. The latter is not contradicted by various places in the Vedas dealing with a creation, etc., for these quotations in the holy scriptures only aim to stress the importance of certain rites, and to induce men to carry them out.[2]

In its classic form *sānkhya* is also atheist. The reasons for the denial of a creator are discussed by Vācaspatimishra in his commentary to Īshvarakrishna's *Kārikā*: God cannot be the creator of the world, for he cannot have been influenced by either of the two motives of rational behaviour, i.e. selfishness and kindness. Selfishness is impossible because God is eternally perfect, and all his desires are fulfilled anyway; and he cannot have acted out of kindness because all his creatures are most unhappy in his world. It is therefore much more reasonable to assume the world process is founded on the action of matter (*prakriti*); without being itself conscious but as regulated by *karma*, it is the cause of everything, just as the flowing of milk is the cause of the calf's growing.[3]

As shown above, at the time of classical Indian philosophy (AD 500–1000) there existed a number of teachings besides Buddhism. Though all of them assumed many impermanent gods, and were strictly religious in thought, they nevertheless repudiated theism and produced well-considered arguments against it.

Subsequently, due to the development of theist, pan-entheist, and theopantist trends, religious atheism became almost extinct in India. With a nation as conservative as the Indian it can, however, be noticed that once-important spiritual trends somehow still remain. And so, religious atheism has never been completely absent from philosophical speculations. During the first half of the nineteenth century the ascetic Bakhtāvar renewed—under the patronage of the Rājā of Hāthras—the Buddhist *Shūnyavāda* in his *Sūnisār* (the Essence of Emptiness) in a solipsistic-idealistic way. There is no God, and no outside world, and everything one perceives, imagines, or thinks, is but a reflection of one's own I.[4]

At the beginning of our century, and under the influence of modern Western thought, there arose a religious sect in the Punjāb which links a militant atheism with social reform, spiritualism, Yoga, and a Guru (founder) cult. In my book *Religious Reform Movements in Modern India* I have discussed this Dev-Samāj as an 'atheist church of the super-man'.[5] Of Auguste Comte's *Religion de l'humanité* it has been said that it is a Catholicism from which the Christian constituents have been removed; the Dev-Sāmaj could be defined as a modernized Hinduism without *varnāshramadharma*, transmigration, and any belief in transcendental gods.

Outside India as well there are beliefs and creeds which acknowledge the existence of numerous but limited gods, but deny the assumption of a personal overlord. A survey of these religions must take into account that some primitives—according to Diedrich Westermann—see in the highest god nothing but an impersonal force of fate; the same applies to some African and American Indian creeds. David Hume in his *Natural History of Religion* (1757) calls the various forms of pre-Christian paganism 'a kind of superstitious atheism', because they did not believe in a personal lord and ruler but rather in gods of limited but still considerable power whom they considered to be 'slaves of fate and of natural events'.[6] In China the conception of the highest god is a very vague one. Heinrich Hackmann says of Shang Ti, the 'highest lord': 'He never becomes a true and complete god. He remains a "power" more related to the concept of fate (Chinese: *Ming*, which often replaces him) than to that of a god'.[7] In the course of time, the concept of a personal lord and ruler became ever weaker in Chinese philosophy, and all but vanished from metaphysical thought. The Sung philosophers, especially Chu-hsi (AD 1130–1200) 'have purposely and systematically expurgated the transcendental remains from the explanation of the origin and the meaning of the world, which now consists of matter and the principle of force that shapes it. Buddhist atheism has doubtlessly helped to influence this new philosophy' (Otto Franke).[8] In the next chapter we shall see in somewhat more detail that many religions hold an impersonal force as the highest principle It is not our task here to trace this in the history of Western philosophy. An example from it is Arthur Schopenhauer whose metaphysical system, imbued with the idea of all-oneness, of a moral world order, and of liberation, must be considered a special expression of religious atheism.

III. THE LAW OF THE WORLD

I THE BUDDHIST DHARMA

'Just as "There is no God beside God, and Mohammed is his prophet" represents the essence of Islam, or the Trinity that of Christianity, and the Sabbath that of Judaism, so reincarnation is the essence of Hinduism. A person who does not believe in it is not a Hindu, nor is he accepted as one of them.'[1] With this statement the great Mohammedan scholar Alberuni (fifth chapter of his work *India—A D 1030*) shows the essential difference between the Western theistic religions and Hinduism.

The central dogma, common to Hinduism, Jainism and Buddhism, is the assumption of a moral world order manifesting itself throughout the cosmos. Its expression is the automatic law of cause and effect implicit in all activities, and thus the conditioning factor for reincarnation. The manifold divergences between the three Indian religions with their various schools and sects are only secondary compared with this fundamental world concept which unites them, and differentiates them from the Western religions. This also explains why both during the Indian Middle Ages and at present the various trends of Hinduism, Jainism and Buddhism consider themselves as parts of a whole, and believe they have the same foundation. It also explains the remarkable phenomenon that theists, pan-entheists, and a-theists, the devotees of Vishnu and Shiva, the adherents of the Vedas, and the heterodox believers usually lived peacefully side by side, whereas in the West considerably smaller differences in the concepts of God and soul led to devastating wars.

Modern Hinduism is very conscious of the fundamental importance of the teaching of a moral world order. This is shown by the address of the Premier of Madras, Rajagopalachari, delivered to the University of Patna on 'The Importance of Hindu Philosophy in a Modern State'. The *Overseas Hindustan Times* writes: 'Vedanta philosophy, Mr Rajagopalachari explained, is better adapted to modern times than other religions because it is founded on the order of Law. Other religions are based on fear and punishment which can be commanded by some highest authority. Hindu philosophy is based on the rule of the Law, and not on the whims of a ruler. Nor is the Law issued by an authority which rules by force. Hindu philosophy originates in natural law as recognized by science.'[2]

The Indian teaching of a moral world order which is manifested by karmic causality, is obviously best represented in those religions which do not assume an *Ishvara*, and so are not forced to define somehow the relation of an omnipotent god to an all-embracing world law. Buddhism is, next to Jainism, specially instructive for an understanding of *dharma*, that is the highest, impersonal principle of the universe in which our concepts of natural law and moral world order meet.

Dharma (from the root *dhar*, to bear or carry, and related to the Latin *firmus*) is the unshakable, firm bearer of all that happens in the world, the norm which rules all great and small events of the natural and the moral life. It manifests itself in the infinite multitude of those forces which are also called *dharmas* by the Buddhists: these are the factors of being which condition each other (*samskāra*), and which produce by their interplay the outer and inner world of an individual. They give rise to the laws of coming-to-be and ceasing-to-be, and of causal interdependence; they are also active in the norms, rules, commandments, duties, rights, as well as in the teaching of liberation. And they are implicit in the world-transcending, final aim of all striving, in Nirvāna, which is also called the highest *dharma*.

In the theist view, the transcendent God by means of his omnipotence dissolves the duality of natural and moral happenings, for he uses nature as a means towards a final, moral goal.

In Buddhism, the law immanent in the world produces the harmony between the natural course of events and the demands of moral consciousness. It shapes the world as well as individuals by its automatic action of cause and effect. All morally positive or negative actions are subject to it, so that each good action reaps its own reward, and each evil one meets its punishment. The whole cosmos is nothing but the continuous manifestation of the inexorable consequences of the moral or immoral actions

D   49

of its countless living beings. And so the universe with its realms of heavens, hells, and worlds resembles a *perpetuum mobile* driven by *dharma* and continuously wound up by *karma*. It has ever been in movement and can never come to rest, even though the single streams of life in it (the individuals) may cease on exhaustion of their *karma*. The Pāli Canon states repeatedly and explicitly that the great laws of existence are immanent in the nature of the world, and independent of the mission of a Buddha.

The *Anguttara-Nikāya* says: 'Whether *tathāgatas* have arisen or not, certain is this fundamental Law (*dhātu*, principle), this rule of the Law (*dhamma-tthitatā*), this lawful necessity (*dhamma-niyāmatā*): All conditioned factors of being (*sankhārā*) are impermanent, all conditioned factors of being are subject to suffering, all *dhammas* (i.e. the conditioned *sankhāras* and the unconditioned *dhamma*, that is Nirvāna) are "without self" (*annattā*, without permanent substance). This the *tathāgata* perceives and knows; and after he has perceived and recognized it, he teaches it, shows it reveals it, lays it open, explains it, preaches it, comments on it, and proclaims it.'[3]

The *Samyutta-Nikāya* says the same of the Law of Conditioned Origination (*paticcasamuppāda*),[4] that great law which Gautama discovered even before he was enlightened, when he still was a Bodhisattva,[5] and which the Buddhists at all times considered to be the most precious jewel (*ratna*) of all knowledge.

The three 'seals' or hall-marks of existence, *Anicca*, *Anattā*, and *Dukkha*, and the causal chain with its twelve links are the basis of all Buddhist conceptions and of all hopes for liberation. Contrary to almost all other religious and philosophical systems, Buddhism knows neither a first cause of the world, nor an all-embracing spiritual substance giving rise to all that is. It is rather that something comes into being in dependence on and conditioned by something else. A first beginning is as impossible as is a definite end. The Buddhist, therefore, regards all attempts to explain the world or the individual by means of one or more 'eternal substances' (such as God, soul, original matter, atoms, etc.) just as useless as if one tried 'to tie the reflection of the moon to the water with the hair of a tortoise'.[6] There are no permanent entities of any sort; and all that exists is conditioned and will again pass away. Philosophically analysed, the whole universe and everything in it reveals itself as a strictly ordered sequence of dynamic processes, as a play of the forces of *dharma*. The theory that each individual event is functionally dependent, is now further refined in that only a multiplicity of factors can bring about a new one, a single one being insufficient to do so. Thus there is no arising from one single 'original' cause from which something develops, but only a new coming into existence by mutual co-ordination of a multitude of conditions. And so the cosmic law manifests itself ultimately as a continuous and irrefragable 'condition(al)ism'. There are no isolated factors, and all things are connected with each other. Personality, too, is an ever-changing stream of *dharmas* which arise from multiple conditions, are active for a short time, and again cease, to make room for others.

The so-called personality is, in fact, but a bundle of *dharmas*. The conditions which govern the existence and suchness of a seeming personality are not—as we have seen—just physical or intellectual processes, but are above all of a moral nature. The moral quality of the actions performed by body, speech and thought during earthly existence conditions the next rebirth including everything that goes with it (surroundings, heredity, ability, etc.). In this respect each being is 'self-originated'; its form is due to the combination of those forces it has created itself in a former existence. The world law shows itself in that all the myriads of individual fates together form one whole. Harmoniously attuned to each other, they constitute the continuously flowing history of the world—without beginning, and without an end.

Because the world law is fixed in its ordered norm, a Buddha can predict with utter certainty what is possible and what not. This *thānakusalatā* is counted as one of the special powers of a Buddha (Sanskrit: *sthānāsthānajñāna-bala*)[7] in the *Dīgha-Nikāya*. Also in the *Anguttara-Nikāya* [1] where Buddha says: It is impossible (*atthāna*), it cannot come to be (*anavakāsa*), that one of right view considers a conditioned factor of being (*samkhāra*) as eternal, as not subject to suffering, or as a permanent substance; that he kills his parents, or *arahats*; that simultaneously two Buddhas arise; that a woman can become Buddha or cosmic lord;[8] that somebody does not reap the consequences of his good and evil actions. The *Atthāna-Jātaka*[9] lists a series of natural impossibilities.

Those things cannot occur because the immanent law and order make them impossible. And again we see in this the contrast with the theistic view according to which nothing is impossible for the Almighty.*

The cosmic law in Buddhism is often similar to the personal God of theist religions, for it conditions the origin, existence, and end of the world, rewards good deeds and punishes evil ones. But it is never revered as the creative or directive principle of the world: to the Buddhist, the cosmic law is a dire necessity rather than a semi-divine entity. Yet within limits, *dharma* is the subject of a cult, in its aspect of leading from the world to transcendence of it. The teaching of the Path of Liberation, the *dharma* revealed by Buddha, forms together with Buddha and *Sangha* the *Tri-ratna*. And it is repeatedly said in the literature of this teaching that it is 'lovely in its origin, lovely in its progress, and lovely in its consummation (*kalyāna*)': this *dharma* is *sanditthika, akālika, ehipassika, opanayika paccattam, veditabba viññūhi*, i.e. it is 'already active in this present existence, not bound to any time, open for everybody, leading to the goal, and to be grasped at once by the wise'.[10] In Shāntideva's *Shikshā-samuccaya* we find a similar though more elaborate statement to that in this extract from the *Dharma-sangīti-Sūtra*:

'Buddhas are born from the *dharma* (*dharmaja*), have the *dharma* as their light (*prabhā*), and as their realm (*gocara*). All wholesome things (*sukhāni*) whether worldly or supramundane, are born from the *dharma*, originated from the *dharma* (*nisphanna*). . . . *Dharma* is the same for all beings; it does not differentiate between low, middle, or high. *Dharma* has no con-

---

* Genesis 18,14: 'Is there anything impossible for the Lord?' Jeremiah 32,17: 'Oh Lord, You created Heaven and earth by Your great power and by the stretch of Your arm, and nothing is impossible unto You.' Jeremiah 32,27: 'I am the Lord, God of all flesh; how should anything be impossible unto Me?' Zachariah 8,6: 'Thus speaks the Lord of Hosts: If that seems too miraculous for the rest of the people, does it follow it should be too miraculous for Me?' Mark 10,27: 'And Jesus looked at them and said: For men it is impossible, but not for God, because for God all things are possible.' Luke 1,37: 'Each word that comes from God has power.' Luke 18,27: 'But He [Jesus] said: What is impossible for men is yet possible for God.'

nection with pleasure (*sukha*), and is impartial (*apaksha-patita*). *Dharma* is timeless, not related to time, and says to everybody: "Come and look" (*aihipashyika*); it must be experienced by oneself. . . . It is present both in the pure and in the impure (*kshata*), in *arahats* and in ordinary men (*prithagjana*), and acts by day and night (*pravartate*). *Dharma* is immeasurable like space (*ākāsha*), it neither increases nor does it decrease. It is not protected by living beings but rather protects them. *Dharma* is invincible. . . . It is not afraid of *samsāra* (*anunīta*), nor does it favour *nirvāna*, for the *dharma* is always constant (*sadā nirvikalpa*)."[1]

This teaching is venerated as a means of escape from suffering in the world. The *Dīgha-Nikāya* expresses this by a wealth of synonyms all of which mean veneration (*dhammam sakkaronto . . . garukaronto . . . mānento . . . pūjento . . . apacāyamāno*).[12] This quotation is also important in that it shows how the meanings of 'cosmic law' and 'way of liberation' are united into one whole.

Dharma, as the central concept of Buddhism, has been compared with the *brahma* of the *Upanishads*. The coincidences are, indeed, conspicuous: both are the premise for the existence of this world; and both, if seen into and recognized, lead from this world to liberation. Such a comparison, however, should not ignore the still very considerable differences between the two systems. *Dharma* is not the substantial ground of being, nor is it the quintessence of all that exists, and with which the enlightened one unites.[13]

2 PARALLELS FROM COMPARATIVE RELIGION

In various religions all over the world, we find not a persona god but an impersonal force governing the fate of the world and· of all who dwell in it. When man first questioned why the various gods are limited in their power, and why they may not interfere with the activities of other gods, the inevitable conclusion was the assumption that something even more powerful than the gods reigns over them. The first tentative attempts in this direction speak of this power in a way that shows that there was as yet no clear conceptual differentiation between a personal god and an impersonal force. But with advancing thought, there was a parting of the ways between those who chose a personal cosmic ruler, and those who preferred an impersonal cosmic principle as the explanation of the world. The following cross-section through the history of religions in classical times will show this.

The Greeks and Romans developed a series of conceptions concerning an impersonal power of fate which governs all and everything, and which is the ultimate cause of all worldly and heavenly events. Homer often mentions Moira, but his views of it tend to fluctuate. Sometimes it is a dark fate by which even the gods are bound. Or else it is considered as 'conceived personally, and either identified with the divine will, especially that of the highest god; and if not identified with it, then subject to it. Both these theories stand side by side, and it is futile to try to organize them into a consistent dogma.'[1] Other similar concepts were, for the Greeks, *adrasteia, aisa, ananke, dike, pronoia, nemises, tyche,* and especially *heimarmene;*[2] for the Romans, *fatum* and *fortuna.* The pre-Socratic schools see the whole world process as a law of natural necessity which is immanent in the cosmos. The Stoics taught that the ineffable *heimarmene* predestines everything, and that even the actions of the gods are subject to it. But the philosophers differ widely in the details of their definitions of the concept of fate.[3]

The Celts, too, had a strong belief in an inescapable fate to which all beings are subject. The concept of fate is especially pronounced in the Germanic races, but the assumptions of the relationship of fate and gods vary. Mostly, however, they too are powerless against fate. Hermann Schneider quotes from the *Norse Sagas*: 'When King Hrolf Kraki learned that his peasant host whom he had treated badly was in truth Odin, his men lamented their bad fate, being sure the god would seek vengeance. But the king said: "Fate [Norse: *audna*] rules the life of man, and not this evil god." '[4]

In India also there are a very few trends which accord to fate (*dishta,* the directed; *daiva,* the divine) the guidance of the world process. And related to them are those teachings which assert the inescapable predestination of all events, rather than attributing them to the fickleness of fate, and therefore hold 'necessity' (*niyati*) to be the ultimate principle. The sect of Ājīvikas, founded by Gosāla, a contemporary of the Buddha, seems to have adhered to this belief.

In pre-Islamic times, the Arabs believed in an impersonal fate that rules everything. The prophet combats just this belief when he says in the Koran: 'They say: There is but our worldly life; we die, and we live, and time (*dahr*) only destroys us.'[5] Werner Caskel has shown in great detail that ancient Arabic poetry employs widely differing expressions such as 'doom' (*al-himām*), 'meaning' (*al-qadar*, in the sense of 'to be meant to . .'), fate (*al-dahr, az-zamān, al-aijām*), etc., to describe a power that rules supreme and is not subject to another's will. The later monotheism has changed these concepts, 'for it seems that Mohammed drew on something known in his formulation of the concept *qadar* as the activity of Allah'. However, even in later thought, Allah has 'an inherent trend of blind self-will which seems to connect him with *dahr*'.[6]

The concepts of fate and time are often identified. Among the Greeks and Indians, time is occasionally the world principle. This applies especially to the sect of Zarvanites which developed within the religion of Zoroaster. The Zarvanites tried to solve the dualism existing between the good god Ahuramazda (Ormazd) and the evil god Angramainyu (Ahriman) by the assumption of 'unlimited time' (*zarvan akarana*) as the ultimate cause. Time also appears as a power that directs the whole cosmos and all its manifestations—either directly (as with Varāhamihira) or indirectly as in the various astrological systems of Europe and Asia. The latter assert the dependence of all individual fates on the heavenly bodies that follow their courses in eternal and harmonious order.

All the above teachings are based on an impersonal power which in its essence is beyond both good and evil. In contrast to these there exist Chinese and Indian ideas which assume a moral world order, and so ascribe to the impersonal, highest world principle the function of establishing a just balance between the ethical behaviour of the individual and the fate meted out to him.

The metaphysical views of the Chinese have changed greatly in the course of time, but widely differing trends have often existed simultaneously. This is not the place to examine whether in olden times a belief existed in a personal overlord (*shang-ti*) or in a personally conceived heavenly god (*T'ien*), and to what extent theistic thought has asserted itself in China throughout its history until the present day. Yet it must be stressed that in China—even if a creator of all that happens was admitted—this was done in an unusually abstract and unmythological way, differing widely from the belief in gods of, say, the Indians, Israelites, or others. The Chinese heavenly ruler seldom intervenes on behalf of an individual, and seems rather the personification of an eternal world order which 'without speaking' proceeds peacefully and in accordance with the law.

The conception of *Tao*—as we find it in Lao-tsu's *Tao-Te-Ching*, supposedly seventh century BC—is particularly impersonal. *Tao* is 'the "way" of what happens in the world, the life process of the universe in its innumerable effects and forms, the original force which keeps in constant movement both the cosmos and each single, tiniest particle in it. It is the ceaseless change of coming-to-be and ceasing-to-be, the course of nature which is invisible, inaudible, formless, and inconceivable, is beyond time and space, without a beginning and without an end. And yet it is active, everywhere, and everywhere its activity is recognized.'[7] This activity of the *Tao* is good, because it is the natural way. If man acts in accordance with *Tao*, and is pervaded by it, if he does not stray from it by selfish or self-willed greed, then by such spontaneous, instinct-guided action which is not self-acting but rather a non-acting (*wu-wei*), he attains the peace of quietness.

The teaching of *Tao* goes back to very early times; Lao-tsu expressed it in its most profound form. Later Taoism has expanded it by various other connotations, but also harmed it through fantastic speculations and superstitious practices.

Tradition assumes Lao-tsu to be an older contemporary of Confucius (572–479 BC). Confucius, too, tried to give new expression to the old teachings. But unlike Lao-tsu, Master Kung was no mystic who saw the highest good in self-sufficient contemplation. As a rationalist, his main concern was with an ordered life in state and society. Though it is often stated that Confucius was a philosopher and moralist, not a religious teacher, this is not quite true. Such a judgment is based on the assumption of a religion being exclusively the more or less emotional type of occidental creeds. In a history of religions, however, we must consider all forms of religious expression, and not just those with which we happen to be personally

56

familiar. A zoologist, too, does not limit himself to the Europ-
pean fauna only, but must take into consideration that of other
continents as well.

Confucius did not lay down a concise, dogmatic teaching
about gods and spirits and their relation to men, nor about the
nature of life after death, supernatural events, etc. But there
is no justification for considering him irreligious on these
grounds. From it we can only conclude—as indeed is demonstrated by the historical facts within other fields of comparative
religion—that the urge to formulate certain metaphysical concepts, hopes or desires, and to express them in mythical forms,
may and does vary greatly with different types of mentality.

Confucius' thought was formed in accordance with his time
and his country; he accepted the ancestor-cult as obligatory,
believed in the efficacy of sacrifices and rites, and therefore in
the necessity of their observance. This shows sufficiently that
he is not to be considered only as an ethical or political theorist,
but also as a religious thinker. Though he is not the founder of
a new religion, he certainly is the renovator of an existing one.
His achievement is not in a new creation but rather in his
giving a profound meaning to many of the traditional concepts,
and in the elimination of archaic customs no longer fitting to
an advanced morality. This was obviously done with the
intention of reinstating in their pristine purity the ancient
beliefs and rites that had become degenerate.

To Confucius, heaven was the one and highest world principle.
He took heaven to be a personal being, but saw in it not so
much a god who arbitrarily, by means of miracles and revelations, interferes with the course of history and with individual
life; rather he considered it to be the regulator of the eternal,
cosmic moral law which rules all things in heaven and on earth,
and keeps them in order.

Theistic conceptions still exist in Confucius' own teaching,
though they are but slight compared with Western and Indian
religions. In the course of time, however, they became ever
more slender till they finally almost disappeared in the development of the Confucian system.

The so-called 'Neo-Confucianism' of Chu-hsi (1130–1200) was
the official philosophy until the end of the Chinese Empire.
Its doctrine is pronouncedly atheist. It utterly repudiates the

assumption of a heavenly god, though it duly acknowledges the cults of gods and ancestors. The old concepts are reinterpreted accordingly. Chu-hsi says: 'The sky is the blue which revolves above our heads. In this blue there is no lord of heaven who rules the world. There is no person who counts the sins of men. Though such has been asserted, it is untenable. And yet it cannot be said that the world is without a lord for it is governed by law, an unconscious and fateful lord. The law does not exist outside of matter which it moves. It does not exist as a separate entity, and cannot exist as such.'[8]

From such and other statements, Wieger and others took the teachings of Chu-hsi as an atheistic materialism on a par with that of Haeckel. Other scholars again tried to place Chu-hsi nearer to theism.[9] But in fact, the Chinese philosopher commands a position of his own. He denies a personal, transcendental god, but sees a moral law immanent in nature. 'This moral law is the birthright of man, of every living being. It is the natural occupation, always the same, indivisible, given since beginningless time, eternally unchangeable, for it is as much the cosmic as it is the moral law; it is the axis around which the cosmos revolves, it is in itself the cosmos. This is, indeed, a unique concept, and of such shattering clarity and strength as even Plato does not approximate.'[10]

The teaching of Chu-hsi is religious, partly because it sanctions customary cults, etc., and mainly because it sees an ethical order active in the world. It is also atheistic because it emphatically denies a creator who is above the world and issues commandments. Its ethics are autonomous, as they are in Buddhism. Man has to devote himself to moral tasks by his own reason and strength because he has recognized the moral order immanent in the world; not because he has been commanded by a transcendental god, or because negligence is an act of disobedience to the cosmic lord and a slight to his majesty.

In India, the concept of a world law immanent in everything is already expressed in the *Rigveda*. There it is called *Rita*. The word means, according to Grassmann, eternal order, law, truth, right, holiness, holy work, sacrifice, etc.[11] Herman Oldenberg described the essence of *Rita* specifically as 'the processes which give rise to the assumption of order by their constant regularity or recurrence; they obey *Rita*, or their occurrence is *Rita*."The rivers flow *Rita*," "The heaven-born dawn rose by *Rita*." . . . In the deeds of men *Rita* acts as the moral law which . . . enjoins truth and the treading of the straight path. . . . The man who harms his fellows by deceit or evil magic is opposed to the honest man who "aspires to *Rita*". "The path is easy to walk, without brambles, for him who follows *Rita*." Where *Rita* manifests, the cult is specially prominent. . . . (This is in accord with) the assumption that the great laws of the cosmos live in the sacrificial process. Just as the rivers flow in obedience to *Rita*, and the dawns return at their allotted times,[12] so also it happens by "harnessing" *Rita* that Agni is kindled for the sacrifice.'[13] And so *Rita* is the order of the world which appears equally in nature, in moral life, and in the cult.

Heinrich Lüders in his *Varuna*, published posthumously by L. Alsdorf, states that 'everywhere in the Vedas, *Rita* stands for and means truth'.[14] But though *Rita* is doubtless to be translated as 'truth' in most instances, two other considerations contradict this exclusive statement.

One is that Indian abstract ideas often differ from ours. The conceptual sphere they occupy is different from our own. It is therefore not possible simply to translate the same word throughout the text by the same English word.

Further, the Indians associated with the concept of 'truth' not only 'the coincidence between an asserted and a concrete fact', but also considered it as a metaphysical concept, as shown in the above quotations from Oldenberg. *Rita* can only be correctly rendered by circumscribing and narrowing down the wide meaning of 'truth'. But it then turns out that the Indians understood truth precisely as coincidence with the cosmic-ethic-ritual order of the world. Grassmann rightly observes that the concepts of 'permanent order' and 'eternal truth' are 'often inseparable'. That the Vedic Aryans distinguished shades of meaning between *Rita* and truth (*satya*) is proved by the following quotations: 'Your law shall be truth, heaven and earth!' or: 'Law and truth were born from the kindled *Tapas*.'[15]

The same contradictory tendencies we encountered in the Homeric *moira* we also find in the Vedic conception of *Rita*. Sometimes it is the all-embracing power that rules even the gods. And sometimes it is said that *Rita* is the creation or an instrument of Varuna, or of other gods. In this we can see—as it were in the making—those two wide streams in Indian religious history which still continue today; the belief that an impersonal world law is the highest principle; and the other, that a personal god transcends it.

In the *Rigveda* the 'net' (*prasiti*) of the law is said to be above heaven, space, and the various gods.[16] This is of interest, partly because it seems to show that *Rita* is higher than the other gods, but mainly because it clearly shows how the Aryans themselves considered *Rita*: as a subtle substance embracing the universe. Since the archaic mind assigns a concrete material existence to concepts which we have long since learned to consider as purely abstract, there is also a place or locality from which *Rita* unfurls its all-embracing activity. This locality was considered to be the 'farthest away' (*parāvat*),[17] there where the horses of the sun-god are unharnessed,[18] etc. We see that the idea of a law that pervades everything still clings to quite material conceptions; it is like a fine fluid which sprays from a certain place and spreads everywhere. Empedocles has a parallel to it: 'That which is the law for all is spread throughout the farthest ether and pervades the immeasurable glory.'[19] In my book *The Philosophy of the Indians* I have referred to similar theories held by the Stoics.[20]

During the time of the *Brahmāna* texts, the impersonal world law is the necessary premise for sacrificial mysticism. Sacrifice as the basis of a frictionless functioning of life and the events therein is conceivable as such only because the sacred acts prescribed in the Vedas or by their commentators have always the same result (*phala*, fruit). The numerous magical manipulations that must be executed daily or on special occasions are subject to a strict order which is itself based on the order of the world (*rita, vrata, dharman*). The gods who are addressed by the sacrifices, or to whom gifts are brought, are mere tools for the attainment of the reward expected from the efficaciousness of the sacrifice. In this theurgic attitude towards the gods, they become so to speak pawns in the hands of the priest, and are no longer the supernatural lords who are free within the framework of their limitations to act as they please. And so the conceptual world of the *Brahmānas* in their exaggerated esteem of the sacrifice was given philosophical expression in the later *mīmāmsā* which as shown above (p. 44) no longer recognized a personal overlord.

The cosmic-ethical-ritualistic law is generally called *dharma* in the *Upanishads*, and its theory was changed profoundly and developed further. For in these oldest philosophical treatises there appears for the first time in a Sanskrit text, and already clearly formulated, a teaching destined to become the central dogma of all Indian religions: the law of the cause and result of action (*karman*), of reincarnation in new existential forms, and of the necessity and possibility of liberation. Though the teaching of reincarnation is found in various forms, even in primitive cultures, and was known to Celts, Germans, Greeks and Romans, and even to individual Jewish, Christian, and Mohammedan heretics, yet nowhere else has it become the general foundation of all metaphysical systems. And it further seems that no Indian school—except the modern reform-movements of Brāhma- and Dev-Samāj—ever as much as questioned it. So persuasive is the influence of this belief that even non-Hindus, i.e. individual Christians, Mohammedans, and Parsees, have adopted it.*

Having discussed it elsewhere,[21] I need not go into details here about the origin of this teaching, nor about the forms it developed in the various schools. Nor is this the place to demonstrate how in India the doctrine of *Karma* combined with theistic, pan-en-theistic, and atheistic forms of belief. It is only of interest in this connection that this teaching is considered by the Jains, the Mīmāmsakas and the Sānkhyas as a sufficient explanation of the world which makes the assumption of a creator and ruler superfluous. To them, the doctrine of *karma* is the most complete form of evidence for a moral world order. Belief in such a doctrine, provided it is fully developed, requires three correlates:

First, man must have free will, for without it the moral life is impossible.

Then, a just relationship must exist between good behaviour

---

* The present professor of philosophy at the university of Baroda, A. R. Wadia, reports: 'The feeling of injustice branded my soul, and while still a boy I started pondering, but found it difficult to believe that there could be a just God when there was so much poverty and evil in the world. Had I not found the Hindu teaching of *Karma*, I doubtless would have become an atheist. This Hindu belief is not confirmed by the Parsee teaching, but centuries of connection with Hinduism have made it a constituent of it.'[22]

and human welfare, i.e. there must be the reward of good actions, and punishment of evil ones.

Finally, the individual must have the possibility of continuing his development even after his present existence comes to an end.

The teaching of the cause-effect causality of all deeds appears in the *Upanishads* as an impersonal world law, amalgamated with the teaching of the impersonal Brahma as the cosmic ground of being and of all moral order. The fusion of these two teachings shows clearly how very strongly all Indian philosophy was influenced by this conception of impersonal power.

The suggestions in this chapter were designed to show that the most widely differing cultures may consider the principle that rules the world as impersonal, and that in this respect Buddhism is not an exception.

I leave to others better qualified the interesting task of showing how in Western philosophy, too, both personal and impersonal theories of the ground of being exist side by side and succeed each other.

Nor is it the purpose of the scientific study of religion to indulge in speculations as to whether these impersonal connotations are original, or whether they should be considered as degenerations of a hypothetical original monotheism.[23] For in the present state of our knowledge nothing can be asserted about the beginnings of religious life. A critical consideration of the existing material can only lead to the conclusion that in the known history of all religions personal and impersonal conceptions of the world-ruling principle exist side by side.

IV. THE BRINGERS OF ENLIGHTENMENT

I BUDDHIST CONCEPTIONS OF THE BUDDHAS

Buddhism assumes neither a god who rules the world, nor a personal, immortal soul; as such, it is the most impersonal religion on earth. Though it recognizes countless impermanent gods who fulfil the functions of helpers in need and of distributors of gifts, these in no wise correspond to the ethical ideals which the fully developed religions realize in a personal god and his earthly manifestations. This lack, perceived by many of its believers since earliest times, has been compensated by the veneration of divine human beings.

In the (sixth) *Devadhamma-jātaka* we are told that the future Buddha in his incarnation as Prince Mahimsāsa, in the company of his two brothers, happened upon a pond in which lived a demon (*yakkha*). By decree of the god Vessavana this demon was only permitted to eat such men as did not know what is divine (*devadhamma*, i.e. possessing the qualities of a (true) god). When the brothers entered the pond to bathe, the *yakkha* duly asked them whether they knew which beings are divine. One brother answered: 'sun and moon'; the other: 'the four points of the compass'. These answers were insufficient, and so the *yakkha* dragged them down and brought them to his dwelling. When Mahimsāsa noticed that his brothers did not return, he also went to the pond. But when the demon asked him the same question, he answered:

> 'He who is dedicated to pure virtue,
> Whom shame and shyness let not sin,
> Who in the world is good and holy,
> Is known to be to gods akin.'[1]

When the *yakkha* heard this, he released his two captives, became converted himself, and henceforth committed no more evil deeds but lived the good life.

In a way that is typical of early Buddhism, this charming story shows how the concept of the divine has been fully translated from a former cosmic interpretation to a now entirely ethical understanding. At the same time it also bears witness to the fact that in India at all times common opinion accorded to the 'holy' man a semi-divine position well above the mere human level. Whoever has seen the cult with which many Hindu sects even today surround their Guru, and knows how many miraculous deeds are told of the holy men even of the recent past, cannot be surprised that the religious fervour of the Indians seized upon the holy men of the past so strongly that they seem to be gods to a foreigner unacquainted with dogmatic niceties.

For this reason both ancient authors and modern travellers almost always describe Buddha as a god. Significant properties of a god are, indeed, ascribed to him: he has supernatural powers (omniscience); he works miracles; hymns and legends praise him as being in possession of countless virtues; and in the temples, the pious bring gifts to his statues.

And yet the Buddhist idea of Buddha is not that of a god in the sense of any other religion. Buddha is not an *Īshvara* ruling the world, not a future lord of the cosmos; neither is he a human incarnation of an eternal creator and ruler. Though the Hindus have conceived him to be an *avatāra* of Vishnu, this is purely a brahminical speculation which has never been acceptable to Buddhists. Neither is Buddha one of the Buddhist *devas*—which Buddha himself is said to have denied [4]. This is made clear right from the beginning, for Buddha was born of a woman, and did not appear spontaneously by *upapāta* (manifestation) as the *devas* are supposed to do. In the Buddhist view, Buddha is a man who transcends all human limitations; he is not a *deva* but an *ati-deva*, a super-god, or better still, a lofty being *sui generis*.

Buddhist texts, especially the later ones, report many miracles that Buddha is said to have performed. For this reason, some of the early scholars did not regard him as a historical personality, and explained his life as a solar myth, etc. When research in Buddhist literature showed that the oldest levels of transmission contain comparatively little of such deifying tendencies, most scholars found the above hypothesis untenable. The fact that the life of Napoleon, too, could easily be taken as a solar myth shows how precarious such speculations are. The present accepted view takes Buddha as a historical person who like other religious founders is surrounded by a garland of legends which became ever more elaborate. This view is the most likely, and the historian finds many analogies in India where at all times religious founders or leaders have appeared who were all similarly 'deified'. This applies not only to the remote or even recent past, for example, Mahāvīra, Shankara, Kabīr, Caitanya, Vallabha, etc., but is also continuously enacted in the present. All kinds of stories are told of Rāmakrishna, Gāndhī, or of the Gurus of modern sects such as the Rādhāsvāmīs!

The form of Buddha, together with all the many miracles with which it became adorned in the course of the centuries, may be compared with a statue overloaded with countless garments and ornaments, but which is itself not contained in the drapings but possesses a true, original core to which one may still penetrate provided one does not get sidetracked by the many elaborations.[2]

Today there is agreement between most scholars on the historical person of the Buddha, and on the fact that his form is adorned by countless legends. But the question as to what extent anything is to be considered historical, and to what extent legendary, is answered in many different ways. This is partly due to the different evaluation of the source-material. Can the Pāli texts of the Singhalese Theravādins be taken as representative of the oldest tradition which approaches the actual time of the Buddha? Or at least a part of the texts contained in the *Vinaya* and *Sutta Pitaka*? Or do we have to assume that the scriptures of other old schools, and of the Mahāyāna, which are scarcely extant in Indian languates but abundant in Chinese and Tibetan translations, give us a more correct and broader picture of the Buddha and his activity? This question must obviously be solved individually in each case. But the assumption that only the Pāli scriptures can give us an adequate idea of the historical person of the Buddha is untenable, because the Pāli Canon is only the work of one sect beside which many others existed at the time. The value of the Pāli Canon is, in fact, that it is the only complete body of literature preserved, and at least in many instances shows a

E

simpler picture of the Buddha, and one which is not yet completely overwhelmed by the halo of myth.

Any attempt to reconstruct the mythical history of the Buddha from the image of the Mahāyāna (or from the antecedent scriptures of the Mahāsānghikas, etc.) is faced by three obstacles.

The Pāli scriptures do not take issue with the views of other schools, whereas Mahāyāna presupposes the doctrines equivalent to the Pāli Canon. With regard to their content, the Pāli scriptures are older at least to a considerable extent.

Next, Buddhism arose contemporaneously with Jainism, and in the same part of India. The Buddha image which is transmitted in the Pāli Canon is in general agreement with the Jain image of their *tīrthankaras*. This is not the case in the Mahāyāna.

Thirdly, the objection raised against the Pāli Canon, that such a teaching could not possibly have attracted the Indian masses because they were accustomed by the Brahmins to elaborate cults and an exuberant mythology—rather on a par with those of the Mahāyāna and its predecessors—is not correct. Jainism shows that a doctrine of the strictest abstraction could be very influential. The mistake in this evaluation is that the European critic immediately assumes that all religions must have started like Christianity, Islam, etc., from a popular movement. However, all Indian founders or leaders of sects which enjoy great popularity to this day, such as Rāmānuja, Madhva, Vallabha, etc., were learned theologians. But this proves that at all times it was possible in India for religious forms of great import to take shape, the complicated teachings of which were accessible only to scholars and an educated class; and yet these sects, too, gained many adherents. But it was only an élite capable of evaluation that thoroughly studied the dogmatic discussions; the masses were more attracted by the suggestive personality of the founder and the emotional content of his message.

It is therefore going much too far to reject the research of Oldenberg, Rhys Davids, and others as too 'rationalistic'. Individual reservations about their interpretations of the old texts do not entitle us henceforth to ignore the historical core of the tradition, or to attempt to prise it free from the tangle of surrounding legends. It seems to me that the following items are indicative of just such an original core.

The dates of the Buddha are known—approximately 560–480 BC.[3] This is in accord with the chronological tradition, but more important are the non-Buddhist texts where well-authenticated persons, such as the kings of the time, and founders of other sects, for example Mahāvīra and Gosāla, are cited as the contemporaries of Buddha.

There is an old tradition which was already extant at the time of King Ashoka (died 232 BC) as to the places where Buddha was born, became enlightened, where he preached his first sermon, and entered Nirvāna.

And finally there are certain events in Buddha's life which could not have become part of the texts unless loyalty to a truthful transmission had compelled their inclusion. I refer to actual facts which one would not expect to find in the life of a holy man—such as that the Buddha was married and had a son (it might have been tempting to portray him as an upholder of eternal chastity),* that he entered the ascetic life without the permission of his father (which is against the Indian tradition of filial piety), that he studied under Brahman teachers (and so attained his insight not solely by his own powers of penetration). Also that at first he followed the false way of exaggerated asceticism, and only gradually discovered his own path. Then, his first adherents left him; and in spite of his elation about his attainment of *bodhi*, he was unable to convert the Ājīvika Upaka [38]. Likewise, dysentery caused by his partaking of pork was the reason for his death.

Buddha's own adherents and disciples considered him to be a man of superhuman rank. The reasons for this are partly the strongly suggestive impact of his dignified personality, and partly the ready belief of those who saw in him the great master, the revealer of the mysteries of the world, and the leader along the way of enlightenment. It is beyond doubt that Buddha, in common with Zoroaster, Mahāvīra, Jesus, Mohammed, and the other religious heroes, had great self-confidence and a very developed sense of the value of his achievement.

* Thus Mahāvīra is said by the Digambaras, a very strict sect of the Jains, to have led an ascetic life from boyhood. But for the Shvetāmbaras he was a married man before his renunciation, and had a daughter.

Whether the *Mahāvagga* is supposed to contain his own words or not [38], they are on a par with that of other religious founders.

Even in the oldest Buddhist communities, the Buddha was offered so much admiration and veneration, that later ages inevitably removed him more and more into a supernatural sphere. The psychological reasons for such a development are plausible enough.

For a world-enlightened one, and a bringer of enlightenment to the world, everything had to assume enormous dimensions in order to show Buddha's greatness. Thus his father, probably only the head of an aristocratic republic, becomes a mighty king; Buddha has thirty-two nurses as a child, and, as prince, eighty-four thousand dancing girls. Later, when he preached, an assembly of thousands listened to his teaching, etc. Once he converts eighty thousand village headmen at one time. And to highlight the greatness of his renunciation, the luxury he is said to have renounced is highly exaggerated.

The importance of Buddha is also illustrated by numerous stories designed to point out his eminence. He is of supernatural birth; astrologers and a Himalayan sage prophesy his future fame; his birth, enlightenment, and death all fall on the same day of the year; his death is accompanied by strange terrestrial and atmospheric events, etc.

In the earliest times there was as yet no great interest in many events in the Buddha's life which seemed important to later generations. And as there was no reliable information available, it was reverently invented. The stories of his youth may be taken as belonging to this group; they elaborate his capabilities as a sportsman (archery), and his knowledge of all the alphabets (in all likelihood, Buddha could neither read nor write), etc. Some legends may have arisen from the necessity to link localities, which had only later become important, with the biography of the founder: Buddha prophesies the future greatness of Pātaliputra, he visits Ceylon, etc.

In the heroic legends of all times, the inner events in the life of the hero are concretized as factual events in the world. Queen Māyā's dream of the elephant that penetrates her side[4] is interpreted by later, dogmatic formulation as the Bodhisattva entering the womb of his mother in the shape of an animal. The

68

prince's pondering on impermanence takes shape in the beautiful story of the four excursions (which, by the way, was originally not told of him, but of the Buddha Vipassī); the inner struggles are dramatized in the form of dialogues with Māra; the symbolic expression of the 'turning of the wheel of *dharma*' is coarsened by the introduction of a precious wheel, etc.

The religious person loves everything that is miraculous and sees in it concrete proof and justification of his belief. Every biographer tends to surround his saint with the aura of a thaumaturge. And so, from the still rather simple water miracle [15][5] to the story of the inexhaustible rice cake,[6] and the miracle of the mango tree,[7] from the air journeys to Ceylon[8] to the fantasies of the *Lotus of the Good Law*, the hagiographers overreach themselves until in the latest texts they reach the limit of exaggeration.

In a country that at all times was deeply pious, it is only natural that the great gods and all the heavenly hosts appear again and again in the course of the life of a saint, to act as a heavenly choir in proclaiming his great deeds, to serve him, etc.

In many religions, the extraordinary importance of the founder is also emphasized by asserting his pre-existence. In an atheistic doctrine that teaches the reincarnation of all living beings, this can only be expressed by stories about previous, impermanent existences of the founder. This greatly enlarges his biography, in the words of Alfred Foucher, from a tragedy in five acts to a 'dramatized legend in a thousand and one pictures'.[9] In the Pāli Canon we read that the Buddha himself had an early knowledge of his previous existences and achieved complete knowledge of them in the night-watch before his enlightenment. In some of his sayings he brings up details of his previous existences. These *Jātakas* form one of the most popular themes of Buddhist literature. They serve a dual purpose: they have to demonstrate the presence of a moral order in the world, and they specially stress that even the greatest of all living beings did not possess his venerable position inherently, but like every man worked himself to it in the course of aeons. As *samsāra* is without beginning, the earliest existences of the Buddha are lost in the remote past. Only ninety-one world cycles before ours, to wit 38,971 million years ago, was the veil of obscurity lifted!

Gautama's experiences in previous lives serve as explanations for the events in this life. The verses of the *Apadāna*,[10] ascribed to Pubbakamma-piloti, interpret the illnesses he contracted, etc., as the karmic results of sins committed in a previous existence.[11]

Buddhism is a religion of the 'eternal world law'. Unlike the Western religions of 'historic revelation', it does not teach one single world process of six thousand years which started with a creation from nothing, and which will end with the destruction of the world. The Buddhist believes in a *samsāra* without beginning—and would, therefore, consider as both incomprehensible and unjust the assertion that Gautama Buddha was the one and only human being who had found the Noble Path to liberation and proclaimed it. Buddhist dogmatism accordingly assumes that before the Shākya prince there were others who spread the teaching that 'is lovely in its origin, lovely in its progress, and lovely in its consummation'. In Pāli literature the Buddha was convinced that he had had predecessors. Perhaps we may see in this a remote memory of other men who taught the 'theory of the *dharma*' before the Buddha; Jacobi, Stcherbatsky and Sten Konow were of this opinion. The possibility for such an assumption exists; it is probable that the teachings about the factors of being, and of the non-existence of a permanent self, developed by a number of steps, taking a middle position between the primitive doctrines of the Brāhmana texts, and the profound and philosophic expositions of Gautama. However, we know nothing about their existence owing to the lack of reliable sources. What the texts tell about previous Buddhas is strictly schematic and entirely mythical. In this context it is, however, important to note that in spite of the intention to highlight the supernatural grandeur of Buddha, the whole of the Buddhist tradition never once asserts the single appearance or uniqueness of a Buddha.

According to dogma, a Buddha is an *arahat* who for and in himself 'has completely (*sarvathā*) destroyed all darkness (i.e. ignorance/delusion) so that it cannot arise again; and who has extricated the world (of living beings) from the morass of *samsāra*' (in the beginning of the *abhidharmakosha*). His attributes are manifold: the revered (*bhagavat*), the thus-come (*tathāgata*), the venerable (*arahat*), the completely and perfectly enlightened (*samyaksambuddha*), the one possessing (perfect) knowledge and virtue (*vidyā-carana-sampanna*), who has walked a wholesome path (*sugata*), the knower of the world (*lokavid*), the unsurpassable (*anuttara*), the leader of man-bulls to be tamed (*purusha-damya-sārathi*), the lord of men and gods (*shāshtā devamanushyānām*), the awakened (*buddha*). These attributes appear constantly in the Canon,[12] and have all been interpreted in Indian fashion, i.e. with a wealth of artificial etymologies. For example: he is called *arahat* because he destroyed the spokes (*ara*) of the wheel of life (*hata*) [39], etc.

Typical of the Buddha's physical appearance are the thirty-two marks of beauty (*lakshana*).[13] These are, according to Foucher,[14] of pre-Buddhist origin.

From Buddha's body—said to have been a golden yellow—an aura of six colours* emanates (Pāli: *chabanna ramsi*; Sankrit: *rashmi*).[15]

The decline of the light rays that Buddha radiates from the different parts of his body is treated exhaustively in the *Mahāprajñā-pāramitāshāstra*.[16] A long extract contained in the *Ratnolka-dhārani* gives an extensive description of the rays radiating from Bodhisattvas.[17]

Special importance is accorded to the footprints of the Buddha. These so-called *pada-cetiyas* (Pāli for holy places of footprints) show a wheel of a thousand spokes.[18] Buddha may show them as he pleases, to one individual only, or to all men.

In the *Mahāvastu*[19] Buddha is said to have five types of eyes, to wit the physical eye (*māmsa-cakshus*), the divine eye (*divya*), the eye of insight-wisdom (*prajñā-*), the eye of *dharma*, and the eye of Buddha.

The powers of Buddha have been systematically treated by Buddhist teachers.[20] His physical strength is ten times greater than that of the *chaddanta*-elephant which belongs to the tenth and highest of the species of elephants. His spiritual powers are frequently listed in the Pāli Canon,[21] and extolled by the dogmatists.[22] They are concerned with the knowledge of the

---

* Colonel H. S. Olcott created the so-called 'Buddhist flag' from these six colours. At the time of my visit to Colombo and Kandy on the occasion of the Mahātmā Gāndhi lectures, these could be seen everywhere beside the old lion flag of the Kandy kings, and the Union Jack.

possible, the natural properties of individuals, karmic effects, and of means leading to liberation. All these spiritual powers of the Buddha far exceed those of ordinary men and are subsumed in the concept of omniscience (*sarva-jñatva*).[23] However, according to orthodox opinion, and contrary to the belief of the Mahāsānghikas,[24] this does not mean that everything is consciously known by him at the same point of time, but only that when he ponders on something he is capable of getting to know it.[25] This omniscience the Exalted One attained with the destruction of all the unwholesome (*akusala*) roots in himself.[26] This is a necessary corollary of enlightenment. In its essence it is as infinite as space, as the multitude of world systems, or as the number of living beings.[27]

The enlightenment of Buddha is something without effort, spontaneously emerging. It is not something that can be learned.[28] Though the Exalted One had teachers for worldly affairs, his transcendent enlightenment grew in himself; therefore a Buddha is called a *svayambhū* (one who has attained by himself alone).[29] It is especially stressed[30] that the Buddha did not receive his knowledge from the god Brahmā as otherwise could be assumed from his attribute as *brahmā-cārin* which might be misunderstood as 'following Brahma'.[31]

An argument against the Buddha's omniscience is—so the dogmatic philosophers say—that he did not establish the Sangha rules in one go but instructed his monks in them little by little. This is, however, easily explained by the *Milinda-pañha*,[32] in that the Enlightened One did not wish to frighten away his first disciples by many rules. Therefore he issued them as occasion arose. A stronger objection is this: why did the Buddha allow his cousin Devadatta to enter the order, knowing he would cause a schism in the Sangha and try to assassinate him? The same text[33] explains this as Buddha's foresight that had Devadatta been refused admittance he would have committed still greater crimes. It is said that by entering the order in spite of his many evil deeds, he yet could not help but imbibe Buddhist truths to the extent that in the hour of his death he took his refuge in the Exalted One. Purified by his punishments in the hells as a result of his crimes, he will—so it is said—later find the right way, and finally attain liberation as the Pratyekabuddha Atthissaro.[34]

By assigning omniscience to the Buddha, the Buddhists give him an attribute that in theistic religions is reserved for God alone. One more item places the Buddha on an equal footing with a cosmic lord: it is taught that he attained to the highest state of moral perfection. His thoughts are always good (*kushalaikānta*).[35] He is without anger or hate,[36] full of compassion,[37] always striving to protect all beings from what is unwholesome and to guide them toward the wholesome.[38] If occasionally he uses hard words, he does this to help men, like a father who scolds his children for their own good.[39]

Buddha is both spiritually and ethically the most perfect being (*anuttara*),[40] and yet he differs profoundly from a theistic God by not being almighty. Though he possesses many miraculous powers, he is not the creator, guardian, or lord of the world; he has not decreed its laws, nor is he able to alter them. He cannot stop the change of all things, nor can he dissolve the law of causality that adheres to actions.[41] Thus he is not the judge of the world who rewards good and punishes evil. He is not even the discoverer of the teaching he proclaims.[42] He is like the sun who brightens the valleys and mountains but does not create them. By means of his eye of wisdom he has rediscovered[43] and again proclaimed the path of liberation, shown by previous enlightened ones, which had been forgotten.

In the view of the Hīnayāna schools Buddha is not a god but a super-man. He is—as he himself is supposed to have said— the beautiful lotus blossom that grew from the swamp of the world and stands above it [4].

He but shows the way [27] to Nirvāna and cannot induce anybody to tread it. 'You yourselves must strive with diligence, Buddhas do but point the way', he says [9] to his disciples.

Reverence is due to a worldly teacher, is due in a still higher degree to a spiritual teacher, but is especially due to a monk who has 'renounced the world for good' (*acalā pabbajjā*).[44] How much more due is it to the Buddha who not only unites the functions of a teacher and an ascetic but stands unique in the world like the sun among the planets.[45]

The veneration of the Buddha is expressed in outward forms (bringing of flowers to his image) which all cults have in common. But the implicit idea is that the heart of the believer becomes purified and that his *karma* improves. As Buddha is completely extinguished in Nirvāna and has no more relationship with the world, he cannot perceive the veneration of his believers, nor can he reward them for it. The old cult (and the theory at least of present-day Theravādins) thus derives from an 'as-if' conception, and does not expect any reaction from the Buddha.

Veneration of the physical relics of the Enlightened One serves the same purpose; they may incite the pious who worship them to ponder the teaching also, and thus awaken wholesome factors in them. For this reason the *Milinda-pañha*[46] compares the relics with the wooden sticks with which a new fire can be kindled, or with a fan by which wind may be summoned artificially—even though a great fire has died down, or a great wind has blown itself out (i.e. after Buddha entered Nirvāna). And so the cult of relics is said to be productive of three blessings: liberation, rebirth in heaven, or rebirth as man.[47] If miracles do occur at the Stupas containing relics of an *arahat* who has entered Nirvāna, this is not by means of the *arahat's* activity but because a living *arahat*, a god (*devatā*), or a pious man may call them forth.[48] Though veneration of relics is recommended for the laity,[49] monks are supposed rather to devote themselves to spiritual exercises.

The person of the Buddha became cloaked in an ever denser tangle of legends (for example his journeys to Ceylon and Burma); yet the Exalted One has always remained a man for the Theravādins and Sarvāstivādins—though a man of supernatural stature, of unique moral qualities, and in possession of inconceivable spiritual and moral powers. The dogmatic statement of the Buddha's body being just as unclean as that of everybody else shows this beyond doubt. The *Vibhāshā*[50] reasons that like that of all other beings, the body of the Liberated One came into existence through the 'factors of being', i.e. ignorance and thirst for life; had he been utterly free of all *āsravas*, women could not have loved him, nor could his enemies have hated him.[51] Contrary to this view, the Mahāsānghikas and Sautrāntikas held that the body of one exalted above the world must necessarily be pure.[52] The Andhakas and Uttarapāthakas interpreted this in a crudely material sense and stated that in the case of the Buddha everything, even his excrements, was perfumed.[53] The Theravādins countered this with the argument that like other men the Buddha had lived on rice, and hence the above statement was impossible. The Andhakas had such a high opinion of the Buddha's proclaiming the *dharma* that they had come to believe he had preached in a supernatural manner, and on supernatural themes only.[54]

Some of the Hīnayāna works show a tendency to lift the Buddha, even during his earthly life, above all concreteness into wholly transcendental spheres. The later Mahāyāna works exclusively emphasized this aspect, so that these intermediary Hīnayāna texts constitute, so to speak, a bridge between the Small and the Great Vehicle. Especially interesting in this intermediary literature is the *Mahāvastu* (The Book of Great Events). It is a large but unclassified compilation of old and new material that claims to relate to the literature on discipline (*vinaya*) for Lokottaravādin monks (transcendentalists), a Mahāsānghika branch of the Madhyadesha (i.e. the northern part of central India). In fact, however, the book in its extant form contains little on the subject of *vinaya*, but rather the most diverse legends. Apart from a few exceptions, its dogmatic content is Hīnayānist, though with such a varied content and with the many contradictions the book contains, it is impossible to trace a clearly defined dogmatic content throughout.

In the above context, a short quotation[55] from it is interesting. There it is said of the Buddhas that their bodies, their walking, standing, sitting, and reclining, their behaviour and their virtue, are transcendent (*lokottara*), 'other-worldly'. That they wash their feet in compliance with the 'customs of the world' (*lokānuvartanā*) even though they are always clean as lotus petals. Likewise, they sit down in the shade though they do not suffer from the heat of the sun. And they eat though they feel no hunger, in order to provide the pious with an opportunity for almsgiving. They cut their hair though it is unnecessary to do so, and they wear garments though without them they would be equally clothed. They do not grow old but only seem to do so. Though able to cancel the action of their *karma*, they allow it to run its course. And though they do not come into manifestation through the union of man and woman, yet they act as if they had parents. And though they attained complete enlightenment *kotis* (one *koti* is ten millions) of world cycles

75

ago, they yet behave as if they were ignorant and still had to attain it.

All such 'docetic' tendencies reach their full flowering in the great Mahāyāna work of the *Sad-dharma-puṇḍarīka*, the 'Lotus of the Good Law'. Since this was already translated into Chinese between A D 265 and 313, it must have appeared at the latest in the second century of our era.[56] In it, Shākyamuni is a completely supernatural being who shows his powers by a multitude of miracles and the like. His earthly existence as the historical *arahat* who entered Nirvāna after eighty years of successful teaching, is but an illusion produced by him for the purpose of converting human beings. For he has attained to Buddhahood immeasurable periods of time ago, and will continue to instruct men for twice as many hundred-thousand myriads of *kotis* of world cycles until he finally reaches the completion of his life. Or so we are told in the fifteenth chapter. Theoretically the classic scheme is thus retained, i.e. that each Buddha has first to attain liberation, and that he finally enters Nirvāna. This, however, is of no importance for the practical religious life, for Buddha will bring liberation to all beings for inconceivable periods of time. Similar conceptions of the infinite life span of the Buddha are developed in the second chapter of the *Suvarna-prabhāsa Sūtra* (the 'shimmer of gold' Sūtra).

If the Buddha is still alive, he also has, of course, the possibility of liberating the pious who turn to him as their refuge. He is the great bringer of enlightenment who constantly pours out the nectar of his teaching in forms suited to the various beings [47]. He looks after his believers, for even if they are oppressed by evil people he sends them helpful spirits to protect them. And to those who study the scriptures he appears as a figure of light to explain the true meaning to them [48].

The picture which the *Lotus Sūtra* draws of Shākyamuni's activity shares some common traits with the Christian God image. Yet the Buddha cannot be compared with the Lord of theistic religions. It is explicitly stated that there are innumerable Buddhas; and further, that Shākyamuni has not been the world liberator from the beginning but has attained to this office in time—though it may have been immeasurably long ago. And finally, the activity of Shākyamuni is limited to the soteriological field alone; he has no influence on the creation, rule, or continuation of *karma* in the world.

The words which have been taken to prove 'infiltration of the God image into the *Lotus Sūtra*' have a quite different meaning. Louis de la Vallée Poussin rightly says 'There is no place in the "Lotus" (*Sūtra*) which cannot be adequately interpreted in the orthodox, i.e. non-theistic manner. Shākyamuni may be called *Svayambhū* (one who has attained by himself) because like all Buddhas, he too, became Buddha without having received the teaching from anybody else. . . . He is not the father of the world in the sense of the creator of human beings, but because of his teaching he is the father of the holy ones, the future Buddhas'.[57] In theory the Buddha differs radically from the theistic God; in religious practice, however, and within the realm of sentiments on which the *Lotus Sūtra* is based, he obviously shares some features with a gracious 'Father in Heaven' who is the protector of men in need.

With such a connotation of the Buddha, the cult naturally gains a meaning different from that of the Theravādins: the pious revere Buddha for direct or indirect help. The increasing complexity of rituals within the Great Vehicle is the natural consequence of this conceptual change.

To the best of our knowledge, Buddhism has at all times taught that Gautama was but one in a series of enlightened ones who have appeared in the world, and will continue to appear. This view is consequential on the premise that a world functioning as a process has neither beginning nor end. Such a system presents great difficulties to the assumption of the unique appearance of a saviour in its Christian connotation. Though the old teaching—in conformity with Hindus, Jains, Christians, Muslims—shows its geographical limitations by the assumption that Buddhas appear in India only, in Jambud-vīpa,[58] this does not *a priori* exclude the premise that Buddha may also appear in other of the innumerable world systems—an assumption which must be foreign to all those religions that hold our earth to be the one and only 'world'. According to the old teaching, the number of Buddhas is limited because within one world cycle (*loka-dhātu*) there cannot appear more than one Buddha at one time [1].[59]

The *Milinda-pañha* explains[60] this as follows: the virtues of a Buddha are so great that the world cannot simultaneously produce more than one perfected being. All that is really great on earth is unique—as examples are given the world ocean, the world mountain Sumeru, the god Brahmā, etc. Further, that the simultaneous appearance of two Buddhas in the world might lead to strife amongst their followers; and finally that the earth might not be able to support more than the virtue of one Buddha. Vasubandhu further remarks that the respect for a Buddha and thus the impression he makes upon men, will be greater if his appearances are rare.[61]

According to him, Buddhas can appear only in those world periods during which the average life-span of man, though decreasing, will be from eighty thousand to one hundred years. They cannot become manifest in those periods during which the expected life span either increases above eighty thousand or decreases to below one hundred years, for then the necessary premises for instructions about suffering, etc. are lacking. The Theravādins say that three Buddhas have already appeared in our world cycle, and one more is still to come.[62] The oldest texts[63] refer to three more predecessors of Gautama, and according to the *Buddhavamsa* Gautama had twenty-four predecessors, the first of whom was Dīpankara; the same work (Chapter 27), however, lists another three Buddhas before Dīpankara.

The *Anāgata-vamsa* mentions a further nine future Buddhas additional to Metteya who is already mentioned in the *Dīgha-Nikāya* [17]. Still later literature cites more and more Buddhas —the *Lalita-vistara* fifty-four, the *Mahāvastu* more than a hundred. The *Abhidharmakosha* mentions a fantastic number of Buddhas, all of whom Gautama is said to have venerated during his previous existences; some names are given.[64] Significantly the name of the first Buddha venerated by the later Shākyamuni and under whom he vowed to become himself a Buddha, was also Shākyamuni.

In the *Mahāvastu*[65] the World-Honoured One says of himself that during his previous lives he venerated three hundred *kotis* of Buddhas called Shākyamuni and eight hundred Dīpankaras. This is only to illustrate how even in some Hīnayāna schools the number of Buddhas grew like an avalanche. But the possibility for such an increase is provided by the theory that all these Buddhas had their fields of action in one or other of the countless world systems.[66]

So the Small Vehicle already provides the basis for the Mahāyāna doctrine that the Buddhas are 'countless as the grains of sand in the Ganges'. This assumption is the logical consequence of the belief that each living being ought to strive to become a Buddha, and that many have already attained this goal. Further, the active spirit of the Mahāyāna saw the true task of the good life in the service of deluded humanity; so the concept of the Buddhas gradually changed—they were no longer regarded as *arahats* extinguished in Nirvāna and having no more share in the events of the world. They remained and acted in the world, motivated by compassion. The philosophical premise for this assumption is the contention that Buddhas defer their Nirvāna for the sake of all living beings; or that before entering Nirvāna they leave behind in the world a supernatural manifestation of their personality which fulfils the function of a liberator. Finally, the theory of *Apratishthita-nirvāna* or 'dynamic Nirvāna' (see below) opens up the possibility of assigning activity even to Buddhas who have entered Nirvāna.

No other Mahāyāna Buddha has attained to such popularity as Amitābha. The *Sukhāvatī-vyūha* tells us that long ago he was a pious monk called Dharmākara,[67] and that under Lokeshvararāja Buddha he vowed to become a Buddha himself. He also vowed to defer his Buddhahood until by his power he could rule a happy land in which there was no evil. For a long time he acted as a Bodhisattva for the benefit of living beings, and in the end by means of his virtues and merit he created the happy land Sukhāvatī which lies to the west of our world. Now he lives there and continuously proclaims the great teaching. Into his realm he receives all who piously call upon him in the hour of their death, and in it he causes them to mature without effort so that they attain Nirvāna.

The important new view which filtered into Buddhism by means of the Amitābha cult is the assumption that those human beings who by their own effort cannot reach liberation, attain their goal by the easier way of belief in the help of a merciful Buddha. The old teaching already stressed the point that faith (*shraddhā*) in the Buddha is the premise for that change of heart which makes possible the willing acceptance and understanding of the words of the Enlightened One—it may be compared with the dawn that precedes sunrise. The purifying power of spiritual contemplation of the Buddha is said to effect rebirth among the gods even for one who lived an evil life for a hundred years, provided he calls on the Perfected One in the hour of his death.[68] This is explained by the analogy of a ship that may carry a great load of stones across the water, whereas each stone alone would sink. Yet this and other signs of a tendency to expect liberation by the grace of a supernatural being rather than by renunciation and work on one's own inner being, would hardly suffice to explain the arising of such a basically un-Buddhistic view. It must be assumed that Hindu *Bhakti* theology exercised the main influence, the more so as it seems that the belief in Amitābha arose at just the time when the *Bhagavadgītā*, the epitome of the love of God, first cast its spell over the Hindus.

Since Amitābha is completely unknown in the older Indian tradition, the idea of this god of light may have been imported from the peripheral regions of the Buddhist missions under Iranian influence. However that may be, it is certain that Amitābha developed in the course of time, from small and tentative beginnings to become one of the grandest figures in the Buddhist pantheon, often surpassing Shākyamuni or even utterly outshining him. This teaching of merciful compassion became fully developed not in India but in China and especially in Japan.

There is no doubt that Amitābha-'pietism' (so called by Takakusu[69]) presents a form of Buddhism totally different from the old teachings with regard to dogmatic, philosophical and emotional content. And yet and notwithstanding the analogies that exist with the salvation teachings of the Vishnuites and Christians, it is quite mistaken to consider it a Buddhist belief in a God of theistic conception. For like the Buddha of the *Lotus Sūtra*, Amitābha is not the creator, giver of laws, ruler, and judge of this impermanent world. He is a saviour who uses all his wisdom and power exclusively to help living beings and to liberate them from *Samsāra*. The 'Western Paradise' created by him is a purely ideal realm which is connected with the things of this world only in the poetical descriptions of it, and in fact is utterly beyond all that is of this world.

Amitābha is but one of many Buddhas who have a supernatural world prepared for their believers.[70] The common point
of all the Buddhas is their noble task of altruistic service to all
that breathes; but they differ from each other in caste, size,
and length of life.[71] Though there are many different Buddhas,
according to Mahāyāna teaching they also are only one, for the
same spiritual principle is active in all of them; and so all are
one in the *Dharmakāya*.

The theory of the three 'bodies' (*tri-kāya*) stems from the
attempt to harmonize and unify the various aspects of a
Buddha, i.e. that of a mortal man; that of the ruler of a
heavenly realm; and that of a metaphysical concept beyond all
multiplicity. This theory continuously engaged the thinkers of
the various Mahāyāna schools, and has been formulated in
different ways. The basic considerations are threefold.

As long as a Buddha lives on earth with the physical form
of a human being, he is but a magical transformation (*nirmāna*)
and a limited reflection of the supernatural Buddha. His physical
body is a *Nirmāna-kāya*, is not real but has been adopted out of
compassion in order to lead living beings to liberation.[72] In
an extremely docetic way this theory has sometimes been interpreted as meaning that the Buddha has a purely illusory appearance. When he equally illusorily entered Nirvāna, no physical
relics can have remained.

The real, true Buddha is the Buddha of a supernatural
world who is provided with a *Sambhoga-kāya*. Literally, *samb-
hoga* means enjoyment. So the *Sambhoga-kāya* is the glorious,
supernatural body attained by a Buddha on the basis of religious merits accumulated in previous lives. He acts in majestic
glory, continuously teaching, in a supernatural world which in
some texts is conceived as an idealization of the Vulture Peak
on which Gautama is said to have taught. Other texts take this
place to be the highest sphere of the 'realm of pure form',
akanishta; or into a supernatural paradise (*sukhāvatī*, etc.). In
this form Buddha may be seen by higher beings such as Bodhisattvas, and by the pious in meditation. Later on this body is
taken as two, one of enjoyment for the Buddha himself, the
other for the enjoyment of the Bodhisattvas who behold and
revere it.

The *Dharma-kāya* is that aspect of the Buddha that is ex-

F

perienced as the 'religious *per se*' which is beyond all personal limitations, and 'empty' of any definable properties.

These three aspects of the Buddha, as an earthly, a heavenly, and an absolute being are analogous to the three aspects of reality as presented by the teachings of the 'consciousness-only' school, i.e. the imaginary, the relative, and the absolute.

Of these three 'bodies' the *Dharma-kāya* is of special importance for our investigation. It may be useful first to consider the changes it underwent in the course of time.

The word *Dharmakāya* appears already in the Pāli Canon (see note 13). In the *Vyākhyā* of the *Abhidharmakosha* the word *dharmakāya* is already interpreted differently: *anasrāva-dharma-santāno dharma-kāyah, āshraya-pravrittir vā.*[73] De La Vallée Poussin translates this: 'The *Dharmakāya* is the series of the pure *dharmas*, or a rejuvenation of the psychophysical organism of the personality.' As appears in another context,[74] this means that if one who treads the path of liberation has completely seen into and understood the truth in meditation, then the series of his *dharma*-patterns, the stream of 'factors of being' which constitute his (seeming) individuality, has become *anasrāva*; their substrate, i.e. his body (*āshraya-kāya*) undergoes a fundamental change: he ceases to be a bundle of drives, and all passions are burnt out.[75] If it is said that all Buddhas are the same in regard to *sambhāra, dharma-kāya*, and (*jagatas*) *arthacarya*,[76] this only signifies for the Hinayāna that they have attained a body free from the drives of passion, have accumulated merit, and act to benefit the world.

In the *Samyutta-Nikāya* the Buddha says: *'yo dhammam passati, so mam passati, yo mam passati, so dhammam passati'*, 'Who sees the teaching (*dhamma*), he sees me; who sees me, he sees the teaching (*dhamma*)'.[77] And once more he confirmed the identification of his personality with his teaching of liberation, when just before his death he exhorted his disciples to take the *Dhamma* and *Vinaya* taught by him as their master after he departed [16]. And so the body of the Buddha continuing after his death was seen in his words, or in the scriptures expressing these words.[78]

Two of the roots of the *Dharmakāya* may derive from the two assumptions that Buddha after his enlightenment had a body free from all worldly passions, and that his teaching of the way of liberation continues unchanged after his death. Their further development into the idea of a metaphysical body of the Buddha was only possible after a further Mahāyāna theory had arisen, i.e. that nothing belonging to the impermanent world has true reality. This resulted in a search for a monistic principle which comprised the essence of transcendence active in all *Tathāgatas*. Hence it was concluded that an unoriginated, permanent, transcendent, supra-individual one-ness in all beings strives to bring about their liberation.

This *Dharmakāya* is considered the same as *bodhi*, Nirvāna, *shūnyatā* and *tathatā* (thusness). But it is also taken as the liberating force in the universe, as the 'Buddha-germ' (*tathāgatagarbha*) inherent in all beings, and which, if developed, becomes complete enlightenment and hence Buddhahood. Thus the *Dharmakāya* represents two aspects, the static void, and the active principle of liberation as it is manifested in all Buddhas. Though the latter reveals itself in the world again and again, those who can grasp it are few: 'When the sun rises, the blind do not see him; when the thunder rolls, the deaf do not hear it. Thus the *Dharmakāya*, too, continuously radiates its light and proclaims the *dharma* (law, teaching); but beings who have accumulated debts of evil deeds for innumerable Kalpas, do not see it, nor can they hear its voice.'[79]

Vasubandhu explains this teaching of all beings resting in the *Dharmakāya* by the following analogy. 'Just as there are no material forms outside space, so there are no beings outside the *Dharmakāya*.'[80] And in the *Mahāyānasangraha-shāstra*, Asanga clearly states that the *Dharmakāya* is essentially the all-one, the absolute. André Bareau translates: 'Existence (*bhava*) and non-existence (*abhava*) are marked by non-duality (*advaita*); this is because all *dharmas* are without existence (*avidyamāna*); what exists really is only their hallmarks which are emptiness (*shūnyatā*).'[81]

In such quotations, both the manifested world and Nirvāna are embraced and inter-related by Buddha. Other Mahāyāna works, however, take Buddha and suchness to be the imaginings of man still caught in the web of multiplicity. Candrakīrti cites the following stanza in his commentary to Nāgārjuna's *Madhyamakakārikā*:[82] 'The *tathāgata* is but an image (*pratibimba*) of the wholesome *dharma* that is free of all evils (*anās-*

rava). (From the highest point of view) there is no *tathatā* (suchness) and no *tathāgata*, and in the whole world there can be seen but an image *(bimba)*.'

In effect these two quotations state that there exists in truth only the non-dual voidness, and that *tathatā* and *tathāgata* or the *Dharmakāya* are but incomplete names for the ineffable.

If the *Dharmakāya* as the ideal of truth and liberation is here wholly raised to the transcendental and supra-personal level, other sects identify it with the Buddha who is specially revered by them. To a certain extent this constitutes a parallel to the teachings of some Vaishnavas and Shaivas who consider the impersonal Brahma in the formulation of Yājñavalkya as Vishnu or Shiva. For the Japanese Jōdo and Shin schools Amitābha (Amida) is the central Buddha. As *Dharmakāya* he is the infinite, the ultimate and only, inconceivable reality, the thus-ness *(tathatā)*. In relation to space, the infinite is immeasurable light; in relation to time it is immeasurable life *(Amitābha* and *Amitāyus*, two names of Buddha). Seen from the aspect of skilful means *(upāya)*, the infinite is the dispenser of insight and love. 'Amitābha is thus our universal self. And our desire for knowledge and illimitable life proves that as a stone in obedience to the law of gravity strives towards the centre of the earth, so we feel ourselves eternally attracted to and are eternally being drawn towards the infinite being, Amida Buddha, who is the heart of the world.'[83]

Here the belief in a world saviour whom man approaches in pious reverence, and whose active grace can be experienced with each pious thought, connects with theopantist speculations. Amitābha Buddha is doubtless a supernatural, divine being; yet he must not be equated with the theistic god, for he has not created this world of suffering, nor does he rule it.

Identification of the *Dharmakāya* with a specific Buddha has in the Chinese *T'ien-t'ai* sect led to an equation of the three 'bodies' with three different Buddhas; the *Dharmakāya* is Mahāvairocana, 'the great, sun-like Buddha', the *Sambhogakāya* is Rocano who represents the totality of all purity; and the *Nirmānakāya* is the historical Shākyamuni.[84]

Closely related to Indian pan-en-theism is the Mantra school (Shingon) which is based on the esoteric teaching brought to China between 716 and 719 by the Indian teachers Shubhakarasimha, Vajrabodhi and Amoghavajra.[85] According to this teaching the three bodies are but the All-Buddha Mahāvairocana. The *Dharmakāya* is no transcendental, ideal being but Mahāvairocana himself. He has as substance (*dhātu*) the six elements of earth, water, fire, air, space, and consciousness. The marks (*lakshana*) of his appearance are *mandalas* (mystic circles which are used in the cult), his mystical, supernatural powers (*adhishthāna*) are the three 'secrets' used in his rites, i.e. action of body (gestures, *mudra*), speech (*mantra*) and mind (meditation). Esoteric Shingon claims to have been revealed directly by the *Dharmakāya*, and holds that the teachings of the other Buddhist sects were proclaimed by a *Sambhoga-* or *Nirmāna-kāya*.[86]

The Hindu view is that on the one hand God is contained in the whole cosmos and pervades it; on the other hand he surpasses it as a personal being and lives in a supernatural world. Analogous to this is the doctrine that though Mahāvairocana is omnipresent, he yet has his seat in a palace located on the highest level of the realm of pure form (*rūpa-loka*), in the Akanishta heaven. He is also called *Maheshvara* (great lord), a definitely divine attribute.[87]

Though the old view still subsists[88] that Mahāvairocana attained his insight only in the course of time, this is without practical significance for he is the enlightened liberator from the beginning of time. The aim of the sun-Buddha's activity is to cause living beings, including plants and stones, to participate in his cosmic life, and he achieves this by arousing their insight: his wisdom and compassion cause the pious to become united with Vairocana during meditation, and Vairocana to become united with them,[89] so that at the end of spiritual development there occurs a complete 'becoming Buddha'. This signifies a becoming conscious of something that existed from the beginning but until then was veiled by illusion. Kōbō-Daishi, the founder of the Japanese Shingon school, is said to have once assumed the form of Mahāvairocana for a short time.

The Shingon sect considers itself as belonging to the 'diamond vehicle' (*vajra-yāna*), the spiritual movement that grew out of late Buddhism, i.e. the Mahāyāna of about the middle of the first century AD. It constitutes a form of 'tantrism', i.e. the trend conspicuous in Indian religion which by developing ideas

85

already existing in the sacrificial mysticism of the Brahmins, strives for worldly and transcendental liberation by means of rites, magic formulae, etc. Though Shingon exclusively uses the terminology of dogmatic Buddhism and repudiates brahminical doctrines—the denial of a world creator, and of an *ātman*[90]—it has yet accepted into its system numerous Hindu forms of thought and cult together with many Hindu gods and goddesses.

In its essence, however, it has until now remained a 'pure' Tantra as it lacks the sexual-metaphysical element of the Shakti cult which in India penetrated all Tantric schools to an extent that often defies classification. As I have shown in another context, Japanese esoteric Buddhism has to be regarded as the remnant of an older, not yet eroticized Tantric school. The still extant Vajrayāna texts from India, Nepal, and Java all seem influenced by Shakti ideas.

The essence of the Shakti cult is that it attributes special importance to the female element and to sex. It therefore pairs the divine Buddhas and Bodhisattvas with female partners in whose embrace they enjoy the bliss of non-dual all-oneness. For the eroticized Vajrayāna[91] the ultimate cosmic principle is voidness (*shūnyatā*); this is named Vajra for it is as hard, indestructible and imperishable as a diamond. In the view of the 'consciousness-only' school the essence of the Vajra is mind only, i.e. an insight in which subject and object have become one.

Just like the *Dharmakāya* in the schools discussed above, the highest reality in Vajrayāna is personified as a Buddha who is usually called *Vajra-sattva* (the 'diamond being'). Vajrayāna knows of still another aspect of the Buddha which is beyond the three 'bodies': the *Mahāsukhakāya* or 'body of great bliss'. In the embrace of his Shakti the Buddha has renounced the consciousness of his personality in order to experience together with her the mutual bliss of *sama-rasa*. With this, the Buddha becomes the highest god of a system based on the polarity of male and female which finds the ultimate unity realized in the union of the sexes. This sexual dualism pervades the whole universe; in the highest spiritual realm it reveals itself in the static female principle of *prajña* (insight-wisdom), and the dynamic, male principle of *upāya* (the skilful means in trans-

86

mitting the teaching). And just as a Buddha is only perfected
when he combines highest wisdom with the ability to transmit
it and thus to liberate living beings, so an awakened one has
only attained the goal when his activity has entered the womb
of pure insight.

The *Vajrasattva* of the Buddhist Tantra shares his attributes
with those of the cosmic lord of the brahminical systems: he is
unoriginated and imperishable, omnipresent, all-pervading, the
subtle germ of everything (*sarvo-go vyāpi, sūkshma-bījam*),[92]
and is also the creator, destroyer and ruler (*kartā hartā jagat-
patih*). In some texts he is directly taken as a divinity identical
with the self of the worshipper: '*ātmaiva devatā*—the self, just
that is divinity (that of the meditator)'.[93]

In the beginning of the *Guhyasamāja* and in other texts we
are told that the All-Buddha creates the *tathāgatas* and their
Shaktis by his meditation.* In Europe, these Buddhas first
became known by the name of *dhyānibuddhas* (meditating
Buddhas; but actually they are Buddhas brought forth in
meditation). In mandalas they are generally portrayed as
below.

North
Amoghasiddhi

West	*Centre*	*East*
Amitābha	Vairocana	Akshobhya

South
Ratnasambhava

These *tathāgatas* are connected with the five *skandhas*, with
the five elements, with certain parts of the human body, with
certain colours, etc.[96] As retinue each one has a specific Shakti,
a specific Bodhisattva, and other beings. And so the *Vajra-
Buddha* appears as the creator of a spiritual world which helps

---

* The view that one Buddha miraculously causes other Buddhas to emerge
from him is already extant in the *Mahāvastu*,[94] where we are told that Gautama
created numerous appearances of himself (*nirmita*) in order to give joy to all
those who wanted to hold a sunshade over his head. And according to the
Mahāprajñāpāramitā-shāstra, the Bodhisattva Samantabhadra continuously
sends forth Buddha worlds (*buddha-loka-dhātu*), from all the pores of his skin,
with Buddhas and Bodhisattvas that fill the ten realms.[95]

the meditator in his struggle to gain insight, and which is represented and revered in the mandalas.

With this a basic Buddhist dogma, i.e. that a Buddha matures slowly, and that he reaches his enlightenment by his own effort alone, is abandoned even theoretically. *Vajrasattva*, the 'original Buddha' (*Ādi-buddha*), has been 'the awakened one' from the very beginning, and by his meditation brings forth all the other Buddhas. We do not know when this view first appeared. When Asanga (fourth century) in the *Sūtrālankāra* asserts that an *Ādi-Buddha*[97] cannot possibly exist, this does not prove that at that time there were Buddhists who believed in an *Ādi-Buddha*. His statement may be polemical, and directed against Yoga which assumes a soul *sui generis*, i.e. *Īshvara* who has always been enlightened.

The belief in an *Ādi-Buddha* arose and took shape in a series of hybrid systems which show strong brahminical influence. For example, Hindu gods take part in the process of creation.

One of these teachings is the *Kāla-cakra* system which contains the *Mūlatantra*, said to have been written in A D 965. Some information as to the content of these teachings is given in the text edition of a ritual work belonging to it, the *Sekōddhesha-tīkā* of Nadapāda (Naropa) by Mario E. Carelli;[98] a full edition of the *Kāla-cakra Tantra* is, however, necessary for a proper assessment of its contents. Tentatively it can be said that in it the *Ādibuddha* is called *Kālacakra* (wheel of time) because he unites in himself the insight of emptiness (i.e. that there is no real world outside the All-One) with compassion (which together with *upāya*, skilful means, leads men to awakening). The *Ādi-Buddha* leads those who recognize him beyond time-conditioned impermanence, which latter manifests itself in the—purely imaginary—turning of the wheel (*cakra*) of *samsāra*; he leads them to enter (*la* = *laya*) the ground of being (*kā* = *kārana*, cause, origin); or so a mystical interpretation of the individual syllables of the word '*kāla-cakra*' promises.[99]

We know texts and systems from India, Java, and Nepal, in which a Buddha is said to become indirectly the world creator. The *Kārandavyūha* starts with the story of how the *Ādi-Buddha* in his meditation created *Avalokiteshvara*, and further relates that from his eyes, forehead, shoulders, heart, etc., came forth sun, moon, Shiva, Brahmā, Nārāyana.[100] The Javanese *Sang-hyang Kamahāyanikan*[101] teaches a complicated system of emanation. From the 'not-two' (*advaya*) emanates the Buddha-principle *Divārūpa*, which in *Shākyamuni* takes on personal form. From his two sides issue respectively two *Dhyānibuddhas*, and Vairocana emerges from the centre, i.e. the face of Shākyamuni. Vairocana then creates Shiva, Brahmā, Vishnu, the elements, the solid bodies, and the whole world; and finally creates the five Shaktis of the *Dhyānibuddhas*. Like the *Kunjara-karna* legend, the above shows a pronouncedly monistic trend. Moreover, Vairocana is the universal being who exclaims: 'You are I—I am you.'

In these schools or better systems, the *Ādi-Buddha* has become a god in the sense of Indian pan-en-theism. But according to B. H. Hodgson,[102] the Aishvarikas, a Buddhist sect in Nepal, consider him theistically. For them, he is the creator of the world because in his meditation he created the *Dhyānibuddas* who then created the *Dhyānibodhisattvas* who created and rule the world. But the *Ādi-Buddha* himself, as '*deus otiosus*' dwells in remote vastness, and is far beyond anything mortal. These contentions present a certain 'deism' of a type which we can also find in primitive creation myths. But even in these systems there still remains a remnant of the trend common to all Buddhist schools from the very beginning, i.e. that a Buddha has nothing to do with actually ruling the world.

2 PARALLELS FROM COMPARATIVE RELIGION

In the following, I shall first present parallels to the various events in the biography of the Buddha, including those that are so well known that they have been omitted in the previous chapter. I shall then conclude with parallels between later, developed Buddhist teaching and the history of other religions.

Pre-existence

Many religions emphasize the uniqueness of their founder by positing his existence even before his earthly life. To Christian speculation about the *logos* corresponds in Islam the doctrine that Allāh created as the first of all things the 'Light of Mohammed', that light which after many generations of moving to and fro, finally manifested itself in the best of all human beings, in the centre of the world, in Mekka. In Iranian belief, the spiritual essence of Zarathustra was transmitted to his parents by angels before they physically conceived their son. Some such assumption of the embodiment of a supernatural being is also the premise of Hindu thought in which Krishna, Rāma, and other humans are regarded as *Avatāras* of Vishnu, or of some other god. This belief in divine incarnations is still widespread in India today, and the founders of the great schools, the Gurus of the *Rādhāsvāmis*, and other saints are regarded as incarnations of a god.

A parallel to such ideas is contained in the teaching of later Buddhism which sees in Shākyamuni the *Nirmānakāya* of a higher being, or that in Tibet where the Dalai Lama and other *Khubilgans* are held to be *Tulkus* of Avalokiteshvara, etc. Under the influence of Buddhism the Taoist church, too, developed similar ideas.

The teachings of early Buddhism on the pre-existence of Gautama are of a totally different kind. For though in his last life before he became Gautama he was a god in the Tushita heaven, this heavenly existence is but a tiny link within the beginningless chain of rebirths which preceded it. The Pāli Canon[1] repeatedly states that Gautama remembered his previous existences back to the ninety-first *Kalpa*, or even further. In the opening chapter of the *Nidānakathā*[2] he is said to have started on the path of liberation as a Bodhisattva four *asankhyeyas* and a hundred thousand world cycles ago. He had then been the rich Brahmin Sumedha, and decided to become an ascetic. The reason is this: when he lived in Rammanagara, he saw the inhabitants mending the streets in preparation for the arrival of the then Buddha Dīpankara, and he himself took part in this road-mending. But Dīpankara arrived while the work was still in progress. Sumedha lay down in the muddy road so that the Perfected One could walk on his body as on a carpet without getting dirty. At that moment he decided to become a Buddha himself. Dīpankara foretold the fulfilment of his wish on the grounds that Sumedha was a 'Buddha-germ', predestined to become a Buddha, a presumptive Buddha (*buddhabīja, buddhankura*).[3] From then on he continued to perfect his virtue under the following Buddhas until as king

Vessantara he reached the peak of self-abnegation and entered the Tushita heaven from where he again descended to his last existence on earth.

The stories of Gautama's previous lives correspond to what is told of the previous existences of the Jain founders (*Tīrthankaras*).[4] The Jain legends, however, are less ornate. The tracing of former incarnations of famous persons is a popular device in many Indian stories. In other cultures, such thought is rare, and if it exists at all then only in very restricted form (compare the stories about Pythagoras, Empedocles, etc.).

The Miraculous Birth

It is dear to the pious heart to see the birth of a saint surrounded by circumstances that differ from normal events. Frequently the father or the parents are supposed to be advanced in years, so that nothing short of a miracle could give them a child (Isaac, Confucius). It is also often assumed that great men are the offspring of gods, or that they have one divine parent (Egyptian and Babylonian kings, Greek heroes, Alexander, Augustus), or that their mother conceived them by some special means. The future saviour of the Iranians, Saoshyant, will be the son of a virgin who—while bathing in lake Kasava—will become impregnated with the semen of Zarathustra stored in the lake. The Hindus tell a similar legend with regard to the mother of Mohammed. Lao-tsu's mother, at the age of eighty-one, is said to have become pregnant from a ray of the sun. In North American Indian lore, the mother of a saviour frequently conceives by swallowing a small stone, etc.[5] Shankara's mother is believed to have conceived her great son by supernatural means from Shiva while her husband was on a pilgrimage. (In Calcutta I saw an Indian film which featured this event as a heavenly light penetrating into the mother's womb.) Christian legend, too, tells of the virgin birth as the result of an overshadowing by the spirit of God (Matthew 1,18–25; Luke 1,34). Both genealogies are traced through Joseph and may be taken as evidence that the myth of the virgin birth arose only later. Two Englishwomen, Lewis and Gibson, discovered an old Syrian manuscript on Mount Sinai; here it says (Matthew 1,16): 'Joseph, to whom the virgin Mirjam was engaged, begot Jesus.' At the time of the event, nothing was heard or known about the virgin birth. In Matthew 1,25, it is said of Joseph: 'And he did not know her [Mary] until she gave birth to her first son.' Luke 2,7 refers to Jesus as the first-born of Mary; Matthew 13,55; Mark 3,31 and 6,3 tell of the brothers and sisters of Jesus.

Though since the time of St Jerome many European authors have claimed that Buddha was the son of a virgin, this is not supported by the old texts. These—the *Nidānakathā* and *Lalitavistara*, for example—tell that Queen Māyā made a vow of chastity shortly before conceiving the future Buddha and asked her husband not to approach her. It can therefore be said that Māyā conceived the Buddha in a 'pure' way. For of the three factors required to produce an ordinary human being, i.e. sexual union of the parents, the mother's capacity to conceive, and the being ready for rebirth (*gandharva*) and therefore ready to enter the womb of the future mother,[6] the first factor is missing in the case of the Buddha. The *Nidānakathā* also relates Māyā's dream—the Bodhisattva in the shape of a white elephant penetrated her right side. Other texts present this dream as an objective event. The *Abhidharmakosha*[7] states that this was only a prophetic dream, for the Bodhisattva had long ago transcended the possibility of animal existences[8]; and he entered the 'usual gate of birth' in human form, in conformity with all other *gandharvas*.

The birth of Mahāvīra and others was also heralded by prophetic dreams. The mothers of Christian saints, too, had dreams announcing their conception—the mother of St Willibrord saw the moon penetrate her breast, the mother of St Theodore a star, and the mother of St Francis of Placentia had a vision of a bitch barking inside her body.[9]

When Māyā related her dream to her husband, the Brahmins interpreted it as announcing the birth of either a world ruler or a world liberator. In a similar way, their sons' future greatness was foretold to the mothers of Mohammed, Thomas Aquinas,[10] and other great men during their pregnancy. Queen Māyā's pregnancy lasted ten months, but she experienced none of the usual complaints or symptoms. The child in her womb was not polluted by her blood, etc. The same conceptions are found in Pseudo-Matthew, in many legends of medieval saints,[11] and similarly in Islamic literature. The light radiating from the Buddha while he was still in his mother's womb, and also at his birth, has a parallel in the Iranian religion where a shining halo (*hvarna*) surrounded the mother. The same is said to have occurred at the birth of Christ (Pseudo-Matthew), of Krishna, Moses, Apollonius of Tyana, and of Mohammed. Mohammed's mother Āmina is said to have described it as, 'When I gave birth to him there came forth from my womb a light that irradiated all the castles of Syria.'[12]

We find the same ideas in many Christian legends of the saints, 'from that of St Epiphanius of Pavia until the seventeenth century when Mechtild Fuazza wrote the biography of the woman mystic Aemilia Biecheria (Vercelli, d. 1314)'.[13] The *Lalitavistara* tells us that shortly before the birth of the Buddha, nature stayed its course, rivers stopped flowing, etc. The Book of James (*Protevangelium*)* contains a parallel to this.

At the moment the Buddha was born, he stood up, looked into the four directions and up and down, took seven steps and said: 'I am the first and greatest in the world. This is my last birth.' Mohammed, too, 'fell down on his knees, placed his hands on the earth, and looked up to heaven', which is said to have foretold his future role and his exalted mission.[14] Both Apollo and Prithu talked when they were born, whereas Bacchus, St Bonitus, St Furesus, and St Isaac of Cordova already talked while still in the womb.[15]

The sage Asita praising the infant Buddha has a parallel in the history of Simeon (Luke 2,25) and is found elsewhere.

Childhood Legends

The Buddha's religious vocation already became apparent in his early childhood. When he visited the temple, the statues of the gods rose and worshipped him. There are points corresponding to this in other religions. In the apocryphal Pseudo-Matthew, and in countless Acts of the Martyrs we read that the statues of gods fall down,[16] an idea that may have originated in Isaiah 19,1: 'Behold, the Lord rides on a fast cloud and comes to

* Cf. *The Apocryphal New Testament* translated by M. R. James, Oxford, 1924, p. 38 ff.

Egypt. And the gods of Egypt tremble. . . .' Islamic tradition
has it that the morning after Āmina conceived Mohammed, 'all
the world's idols had fallen down and were scattered on the
ground'. In this we see the same basic idea, now changed in
conformity with monotheistic conceptions.

The future Buddha proved himself better informed than even
his teachers—which again has a parallel in the apocryphal
Gospel of Thomas, Chapter 6. Apollonius, too, knew all languages without having ever learned them.[17]

Legend tells that from his childhood, Buddha prepared himself for his future mission. In the *Lalitavistara* it is said that once
after a long search, his father found the boy meditating under
a rose-apple tree. Mary and Joseph, too, searched for the boy
Jesus and discovered him in the temple where the teachers were
surprised by his learning. The young Mohammed was also
lost and was found near the Ka'ba.

The Vocation

All religious founders suddenly renounce their hitherto com-
fortable and sheltered life, and devote themselves to their
religious mission. Gautama was twenty-nine years of age when
he entered the homeless life; and after years of searching and
seeking he became the Enlightened One, the Buddha. Mahāvīra
left worldly life when he was thirty; after more than twelve
years he attained omniscience. Zarathustra left his father's
house at the age of twenty, and for years wandered about as a
mendicant until Ahura Mazda granted him his revelation. Jesus
was 'about thirty years of age' (Luke 3,23) when he was bap-
tized by John; whereupon he withdrew into the desert to fast
until he embarked on his mission. In his thirties, the prosperous
merchant Mohammed piously kept religious observances in a
cave near Mekka, and there had the visionary experience which
determined the whole of his later life.

The common point in all these legends is that before commenc-
ing their mission the heroes retreat from the world for a certain
period of time. It is notable that this point is also stressed by
religions which otherwise are not actually against worldly
affairs—Mazdaism and Islam are two good examples.

Another recurring trend in the biographies of religious founders is that after receiving the call, the founder is unwilling to

undertake his mission. Buddha decides only after Brahmā urges him to do so.[18] The same applies to Moses (Exodus 3,11 ff.) and Mohammed.[19]

Māra, the evil one, repeatedly tried to dissuade the Buddha, and especially just before his enlightenment urged him to cease his exertions. Zoroaster, too, was tempted by demons trying to make him renounce the true belief. Matthew 4,1 and Luke 4,1 tell of Satan tempting Jesus.

Miracles

Buddha,[20] Jesus and Mohammed, all admonished their disciples not to expect them to perform miracles; however, of each one a multitude of miracles is reported. But in contrast to Christianity and Islam, Buddhism has little to say about healing miracles. Buddha neither revived the grandchild of mother Migārā,[21] nor did he heal the monk Vakkali, who committed suicide on account of an unbearable illness.[22] Most of Buddha's miracles are of a magical type. Such are the taming of a snake-king, or of a wild elephant; the ability to transport himself through the air from one place to another, or of walking on the water (compare Matthew 14,25 f.), etc. A water miracle is also reported of St Hyacinth of Cracow and of St Sebald.[23] Orion received from Poseidon the ability to walk on the sea, and Iamblichus could fly over the earth.[24] In about 430, Faustus of Byzantium tells us that the holy bishop Daniel the Assyrian crossed rivers in his travelling boots without getting them wet.[25] The food miracle reported in the introduction to *Jātaka* 78 has parallels in both Christianity (Matthew 14,15 f; Mark 6,35 f; Luke 9,13 f.) and in Islam.[26] The power of a Buddhist *arahat* transcends what is natural and mortal—he grasps sun and moon, and caresses them.[27] Mohammed is said to have cut the moon in two, so that the inhabitants of Mekka could see the two halves.[28]

The Jews know of the ascent into heaven of Enoch, Moses, and Elijah; Christians and Muslims believe in the ascension of Jesus, the Hindus in that of Caitanya; and the Taoists assume it of Chang Tao Ling; all presume the ascension to herald permanent dwelling in a higher world.

Nothing like this is said of the Buddha, though he did ascend to the higher realms of the gods during meditation. The introduction to *Jātaka* 483 tells of a stay of some months' duration in the realm of the thirty-three gods, on which occasion Buddha is said to have proclaimed the *Abhidhamma*.[29] In the same *Jātaka* we are also told of how he descended a staircase of gold and silver in the company of the gods.

Mohammed, mounted on the miraculous animal Burāq, is said to have seen the 'wonders between heaven and earth' and Jerusalem as well, all in one night, whereupon he climbed up to the seventh heaven on a ladder, saw Allāh, and received supernatural wisdom from him. We may do well to interpret all these stories as visionary experiences, but they also illustrate characteristic differences between Buddhism and theistic religions. Buddha teaches the gods—the prophet receives revelation from God.

The above parallels of the Buddha legends with the biographies of other religious founders show that their lives—at least as far as recorded by their biographers—took a similar course. Studying the legends of the holy men of all creeds, it may be presumed that there is practically no event or miracle of the Buddha, especially in Mahāyāna literature, that has no parallel in the religious or sacred literature of the world.

The great courage of the saints and holy men, their patient endurance of terrible tortures, the invulnerability of their bodies, their knowledge of others' thoughts, their power to counter or cancel the natural order of things, the exorcism of demons, the ability to make manifest a variety of things such as scents, etc., the visions and revelations vouchsafed to them, their prophecies and magic revelations, their journeys into heavens and hells, all these are frequent and regular features in the legends of all religions. So are the stories of great adventures and ordeals, of the reward of the pious and the punishment of the unjust, of the conversion of robbers, the gratitude of animals, of grace-bestowing relics and footprints. These individual events take place accompanied by the music of heavenly choirs, while flowers rain from heaven and gifts fall. They occur in thunder and lightning, sudden and unmotivated rain or sunshine,* and while the earth quakes and other awe-

---

* The Congress Hall of the Sixth Buddhist Convention in Rangoon (Burma) was built consequent on a vision of the then Premier U Nu. Its inauguration is said to have been sanctified by the miracle of a rainfall on precisely that spot during the dry season. (Edward Conze, *Manchester Guardian*, May 11, 1954.)

inspiring events take place (mountains are ripped asunder, or they vanish, and trees bear fruit out of season, etc.).

Reading the essays of Peter Toldo, *Lives and Miracles of Medieval Saints*, or Stadler's *Almanach of Saints*, or again Heinrich Grüner's *Occidental Christian Legends*, and *Buddha in Occidental Legendé*, one finds a vast amount of parallels to Buddhist lore.[30] Innumerable legends of a similar kind may be found in other religious literature devoted to similar themes. The reason for this is that the circumstances and conditions of life of the great *homines religiosi* resemble each other in many ways, but mainly because the *milieu* and the mentality of the pious biographers tend to be the same. Some legends may have migrated from one country to another, but a comparison of recorded biographies of diverse religious forms shows that the human mind creates the same stories again and again out of similar motives. Their historical diffusion is considered more dubious today than many authors concerned with the problem have hitherto assumed.

In many religions the pious feel the need to place the founder in an exalted position beyond anything mortal. Shortly before the fall of the Manchu dynasty, even the sober Chinese made Confucius the equal of the gods of heaven and earth (September 30, 1906), though Confucius himself never claimed such elevated rank. Just as the Buddhists claim special properties for the Buddha, so do the Muslims for their prophet Mohammed—supreme physical beauty, moral perfection, infallibility, and being free from sin by the grace of God. Some sects even saw in him an emanation of the world mind. Others held that he was a man only in outward form, but immanently an angel. A further mark of his perfection of form is that flies never settled on his body.[31] The ideas of the 'docetic' Buddha mentioned above (p. 93) exactly correspond to the Christ image in some sects. 'The Christ of the Valentinians has by means of his fasts attained to such freedom that he no longer eats, digests, and defecates in the human way.'[32] The same Valentinus (AD 120–160) also taught that Jesus's physical body was not subject to the laws of nature, and consequently, that the embryo had passed through his mother's body 'like water through a hose'.

Satornil evolved the theory that the saviour was a man in appearance only, and that in truth he was unborn, without a body (*sine figura*), and not compounded of matter. Clement of Alexandria mentions an old legend which in the second century was recorded in the Acts of John; after Jesus was taken from the cross, John wanted to touch his body, but his hand touched nothing.

Some of the Gnostics believed that the crucifixion was but a visual fantasy. This is probably also what St Jerome means when he says: 'The blood of our Lord had not yet dried in Judaea when it was already said that his body was but a phantom.' Doctrines of this sort have tenaciously continued in heretical sects. The Albigensians are said to have believed that Christ, the Virgin Mary, Joseph, and John were angels in human form. In recent time docetic doctrines have again been expressed in the form of 'Christian Science'.

The Predecessors

In one way or another, each new teacher depends on others preceding him, and so the founder of a religion has to ratify his position with regard to them. Buddha is said to have studied under Brahmin teachers but was not satisfied by what he learned. Yet he insists on having rediscovered an age-old way, like somebody rediscovering an old path in the jungle leading to an ancient city—the way of the past Buddhas, leading to Nirvāna [36]. Buddha therefore only claims to have presented an old teaching in a form that fitted his own time. In Matthew 5,17, Jesus says he had not come to undo the Law or the prophets, but to fulfil them; John the Baptist is considered to be his immediate forerunner.

Confucius had no desire to instigate something new and only wanted to be the faithful keeper of the old teachings transmitted from the emperors of yore. In the Koran,[33] Mohammed mentions prophets preceding him, but he himself is considered to be the seal (*khātam*)that cuts the line of prophets for good. Even in the Parsee creed, the sage Haoma[34] is thought to be the herald of Zarathustra. In India the idea of a predecessor is expressed in the teaching of the *Tīrthankaras* before Mahāvīra, and in the *Avatāras* of the divers gods venerated by the various sects.

The assumption of world cycles and hence cyclic events makes it feasible for Brahmins, Buddhists and Jains to assert the appearance of future liberators. Buddha is said to have given a detailed account of the fate of his religion, its later decline,[35] and the impending appearance of the future Buddha Maitreya [17]. Parallel to it is the Jain doctrine of the future *Tīrthankaras*, and the Hindu doctrine of *kalki*.

Similar ideas are also present in the religions of the West though they are formulated differently owing to the assumption of one single world process. Such are the Parsee theory of the three *Saoshyants*, the Hebrew idea of the coming Messiah, the Christian concept of the paraclete, and Muslim ideas of the *Mahdi* and of the 'hidden Imām'.

The Founder Giving Precedence to Other Exalted Persons

In some Mahāyāna sects the person of Gautama Shākyamuni has retreated behind the forms of the mystic Buddhas Amitābha, Vairocana, etc. There is an Islamic parallel, for according to some Shi'ite sects Mohammed was deprived of his exceptional position as the 'seal of the prophets' and replaced by his son 'Ali. 'Some of them discovered that the angel Gabriel might mistakenly have brought the gift of God to Mohammed whereas it was intended for 'Ali.'[36] Others directly criticize the prophet because he assumed for himself the status that was the prerogative of 'Ali. A Syrian sect, the Nusirians, preserves many pre-Islamic features; they almost consider 'Ali a being of eternal and divine nature compared with whom Mohammed has but the inferior form of its 'veil'.

The Erotic Element Entering Religion

This is the most striking feature in the history of Buddhism. In the teachings of both the Small and the Great Vehicle, when the Buddhas entered the homeless life, their religious training included chastity. Yet the later Vajrayāna portrays those Buddhas in passionate embrace with their Shakti. In Peking I myself saw a Tibetan painting of the blue Akshobhya embraced by a white Shakti with red hair ('Buddha sleeps with an English lady', the guide cynically explained!). A similar picture from Nepal was acquired by the Ethnographical Museum in Geneva. One is inclined to consider as unique and unparalleled an idea that

99

couples the person of the founder of a religion that is averse to anything sexual, with erotic imagery. Yet even for this there are occidental parallels, and moreover fairly recent ones.*

If such events can take place even in modern Christian Europe, it is not really surprising when in Asian countries where old sexual cults still continue, the Buddhas were pictorially presented in the *Yab-Yum* (father-mother) position, and that the Buddhist doctrines of *prajñā* and *upāya* were interpreted erotically.

Introspection

All religions have produced mystics who saw beyond the person of the founder the supra-individual transcendental, and therefore use the founder's name to designate a purely inner event. Mahāyāna speaks of Buddhahood as a mystical experience.[37] Parallel to this are expressions of the Christian mystics, for example, Angelus Silesius:

If Christ were born a thousand times in Bethlehem
But liveth not in you—perdition is your fate.

Pearls are born inside of mussel shells
Fathered by dew—and you who disbelieve
Behold: The dew is where God's spirit dwells,
The pearl is Jesus Christ—your mussel-soul conceives.[38]

Jalāl-ed-din Rumi sings:

Behold in your own heart the wisdom of the prophet,
Without a book, nor teacher, nor instructor.[39]

* In the eighteenth century, the so-called 'Buttlar Group' believed the theologian Winter, the medical practitioner Appenfeller, and the female founder Eva von Buttlar with whom both men were in love, to be the incarnations of the Father, the Son, and the Holy Ghost. Another founder of such a sect, Johann Paul Philipp Rosenfeld who preached in the eighteenth century in the district of Brandenburg, was acclaimed as the 'living God', and his adherents brought him their daughters as 'brides of Christ'. Confined in a lunatic asylum, he had intercourse there with the fifteen-year-old daughter of the shepherd Gunto, in 1770, in the presence of her family who had all come to visit the holy man. The former Anglican priest Henry James Prince (1811–1899) was revered as the Holy Ghost in human form; in his church at Spaxton (Somerset) he deflowered the beautiful Miss Paterson in the presence and with the pious connivance of the whole of his community.

And Kabīr, the weaver:

> Rāma's house is in the East,
> And in the West dwells Allāh.
> Search in your heart, see into your heart,
> And behold both Rāma and Allāh.[40]

V. THE ABSOLUTE

I BUDDHIST DOCTRINES OF THE ABSOLUTE

The Asamskritas

In philosophical terminology, the word *'absolutum'* means something that exists by and of itself, that rests in itself and is not conditioned by anything else. The corresponding word in Buddhist terminology is *asamskrita* (Pāli: *asankhata*). It denotes a *dharma* (factor of being) that does not depend on anything else for its arising. As such, it differs from the 'conditioned *dharmas*', the *samskāras*, and it also differs from them by being permanent. It is free of the four marks of 'arising, continuing, changing, and ceasing-to-be', combined with which all conditioned *dharmas* arise.*

The *Abhidharmakosha* defines an *asamskrita* as something that does not arise,[1] which always is and does not change.[2] It is neither caused by anything, nor does it by itself constitute the cause of anything.[3] It is therefore always 'close by'[4] (in time, and in contradistinction to past and future). It does not belong to the *upādāna-skandhas* which may form an individuality.[5] It is, however, a reality that can be recognized.

Buddhist schools differ as to what may be considered *asamskritas*;[6] but all agree that Nirvāna is *asamskrita*. Some schools also use the term *pratisankhyā-nirodha*, i.e. the conscious and complete destruction (*nirodha*) of all future passions and suffering, the 'dissolution' of the connection (*visamyoga*) with the impure *dharmas* [40] which is effected in full consciousness (*pratisankhyā*). This *pratisankhyā* is a special *prajñā*, a wisdom-insight that is based on the complete understanding of the Four Noble Truths. The Theravāda school considers Nirvāna to be the only *asamskrita*, but other schools assume more than one.

In the light of the theory of the 'moment only', there also

---

* 'The concept "*dharma*" as such does not include the mark "coming-to-be and ceasing-to-be"; the process or act of arising and disappearing is abstracted from the *dharma* that carries out this process.' O. Rosenberg, *Probleme der buddhistischen Philosophie* (Heidelberg, 1924), p. 121.

takes place a continuous 'not arising' of *dharmas* though such a perception of the Four Noble Truths does not exist. For example, this happens when mindfulness is so concentrated on something that everything else is shut out from consciousness. The *Abhidharmakosha* cites two examples: when the eye and the thinking process are very much engaged with an object of sight (*rūpa*), other objects of sight, as well as of sound, etc., do not come into consciousness.[7] Secondly it is an *apratisankhyā-nirodha* when premature death cuts off a life so that the *dharmas* which could have arisen had it continued, do not now in fact arise.[8] It is also an *apratisankhyā-nirodha* of femininity (*strītva*) if a woman is reborn as a man in the next life.[9] The distinctive feature of such a *nirodha* is that the *dharmas* cannot arise because they lack the necessary premises. In that it differs from *pratisankhyā* (above) where the (impure) *dharmas* have consciously been destroyed and cannot arise again.

Some schools also regard empty space (*ākāsha*) as an *asam-skrita-dharma*. They define space as the 'complete absence of everything, and hence also of everything that might prevent the appearance of any *dharmas*'.[10]

Other schools regard the fundamental law of all existence, the chain of dependent origination (*pratītya-samutpāda*) as *asamskrita*, for it is unchangeable, and acts continuously. Consequently the eternal way (*mārga*) to liberation that is fixed for all time, and is taught in the Four Noble Truths (*satya*), was also considered an *asamskrita*. The path to liberation (*niyāma*) has further as natural corollary the *apratisankhyā-nirodha* of bad rebirth as an animal, etc.[11] Entering this *niyāma* guarantees the attainment of right view which brings liberation.[12]

There are also schools which count as *asamskrita* the attainment of higher levels of consciousness and existence in the formless realm (*arūpa*) which the meditator enters with the four contemplations (that of infinity of space, infinity of consciousness, of no-thing-ness, and of neither-perception-nor-non-perception). Also regarded as *asamskrita* is the extinction of discernment (of perceptions and conceptions) and feeling, the so-called *nirodha-samāpatti*, i.e. the temporary eclipse of all consciousness and mental activity, which constitutes a temporary displacement from the world of restless change. The equanimity (*āniñja*) of the fourth stage of meditation (*dhyāna*) is sometimes counted an *asamskrita*.

Besides the accepted *asamskritas* belonging to the relative truths of the world of appearance, the Yogācārins also know of a sixth *asamskrita* which is transcendent and all-embracing, i.e. 'suchness' (*tathatā*), the identity of all that is, the quintessence (*quidditas*) of everything. It is obvious that this *asamskrita* differs from all the others for it includes them all.

Some texts distinguish three types of *tathatā*: (1) the *quidditas* of the 'good' (i.e. wholesome) *dharmas* (*kushala-dharma-tathatā*); (2) the *quidditas* of the 'bad' *dharmas* (*akushala-dharma- tathatā*), and (3) the *quidditas* of the 'neutral' *dharmas* (*avyākrita-dharma-tathatā*).

The above differentiation departs again from the highest point of view, for only the *quidditas* of the wholesome *dharmas* corresponds to the absolute—as may be seen from the other synonyms for it, such as *nairātmya-bhāva* (the condition of no-self, i.e. non-substantiality), *shūnyatā-bhāva* (the condition of emptiness), *alakshana* (without distinguishing marks), *bhūta-koti* (peak of reality), *paramārtha* (highest reality-content), and *dharmadhātu* (element, i.e. foundation of the teaching). Other sects deny the above tri-partition and hold *tathatā* to be the only *asamskrita*.[13] Sthiramati makes it abundantly clear that *quidditas* 2 and 3 have fictional value only.[14] In truth there exists but the one *tathatā* as the ultimate reality.

The Mahāyāna systems present us with a peculiar ambiguity in the use of the term '*asamskrita*'. Some authors, texts, or schools employ it as defined by the Small Vehicle; others use it in the meaning of something transcendental so that it denotes the essence of all things (*dharmatā*, the *Dharmakāya* of Buddha, *Bodhi*, etc. Others again regard all *samskrita-* and *asamskrita-dharmas* as belonging to the 'world of appearance'; true reality is beyond both. For the old schools, an *asamskrita* was the absolute; for some Mahāyāna schools it presents but a 'relative absolute' (if one may call it thus), superseded by the true, absolute 'super-absolute'.

Below I give in abridged form Bareau's[15] table of the *asamskrita* of the various schools (the latter in parentheses).

1 *A samskrita* Nirvāna
   (Theravādins, Vatsiputrīyas, Sāmmitīyas)
3 *A samskritas* 2 *nirodha, ākāsha*
   (Sarvāstivādins, Sautrāntikas, Mādhyamikas)
4 *A samskritas* (a) 2 *nirodha, ākāsha, tathatā*
   (Vaibhāshikas of central India)
   (b) 2 *nirodha, niyāma, nirodhasamāpatti*
   (Andhakas)
5 *A samskritas* (a) 2 *nirodha, ākāsha, tathatā, pratītya-samutpāda*
   (Mahīshāsakas of the South)
   (b) 2 *nirodha, tathatā, pratītya-samutpāda, niyāma*
   (Pubbaseliyas)
6 *A samskritas* 2 *nirodha, ākāsha, tathatā, āneñjya, nirodhasamāpatti*
   (Yogācāras)
8 *A samskritas* 2 *nirodha, ākāsha,* 3 *tathatā, āneñjya, nirodhasamāpatti*
   (Yogācāras)
9 *A samskritas* (a) 2 *nirodha, ākāsha,* 3 *tathatā, pratītya-samutpāda, mārga-tathatā, āneñjya*
   (Mahīshāsakas of the North)
   (b) 2 *nirodha, tathatā, pratītya-samutpāda, mārga,* 4 *arūpa*
   (Mahāsānghikas of the North)
   (c) 2 *nirodha, dharmasthitatā, pratītya-samutpāda, niyāma,* 4 *arūpa*
   (Pubbaseliyas)

It would be out of place to go into the intricate connections between these schools, or into the history of their development. The interested reader is referred to Bareau (above) who tried to shed some light on this little-known field of study.

It is, however, important for the following expositions to know that in many of the older schools Nirvāna is by no means the only *asamskrita*. Further, that though the Mahāyāna schools developed the theory of 'all is one', they nevertheless retained the multiplicity of *asamskritas*. This fact indicates that even the Theravādins, Vātsīputrīyas and Sāmmitīyas who regard Nirvāna as the only *asamskrita*, did not understand it as something that exactly corresponds to the brahminical absolute, i.e. Brahmā.

The development of the concept of Nirvāna is of interest, for it is the only *asamskrita* which is acknowledged by all schools, and was from the first considered the *summum bonum* of all Buddhism.

Nirvāna

The Pāli Canon defines 'Nirvāna' as the complete and utter dissolution of the three unwholesome roots of greed, hate, and delusion.[16] It is said of the *tathāgata* that on entering Nirvāna[17] the *skandhas* (bundles) are completely dissolved, and are rooted out, so that they can never arise again. The five *skandhas* are: *rūpa, vedanā, samjñā, samskāra* and *vijñāna,* or respectively physical form, feeling, perception (both physical and mental), drives, and consciousness. Thus Nirvāna is the utter extinction of everything upon which a worldly existence is based, or of what gives rise to one. The famous quotation from the *Udāna* [37] describes it as something totally different from the material world, but also from the ideal worlds of the higher meditations —where there is no coming, no going, no striving, neither ceasing-to-be nor coming-to-be. It is without foundation, without beginning and without end. 'Difficult it is to perceive what is without a self, not easy to grasp is truth; the thirst is overcome by him who knows, and nothing exists for the meditator.' Nirvāna is also called the unborn (*ajāta*), the uncreate (*abhūta*), the unmade (*akata*), (by *samskāras,* i.e. volition karmically) unconditioned (*asankhata*); and finally it is said of Nirvāna that it is peace without movement or desire, and the end of all suffering.

From all this it appears that Nirvāna is utterly different from all that is earthly or even conceivable. It is without a substantial self (*anattā*),[18] perfect peace, a 'nothing' as compared with all visible configurations. It is something that can be expressed in the negative only, for it possesses no specific marks that language can encompass. It is figuratively described as the cool cave in the heat of everyday life, as the happy isle in the sea of *samsāra,* as the place of no death, which is not shaken by anything, etc. The Pāli Canon [8] even employs the paradox that Nirvāna is 'bliss' though there is neither a subject to enjoy it, nor the skandha *vedanā* (feeling); the bliss of Nirvāna consists indeed in not feeling anything. According to the *dharma* theory, Nirvāna is a reality *sui generis*, a *dharma* that becomes fully effective only when all impermanent *dharmas* no longer exist. Nor is it conceived as a state that may arise in a subject, it is rather a 'thing-ness', for which reason it is said that one 'touches' it (*phusati*).

Both Hīnayāna and Mahāyāna use the image of empty space as the best analogy to explain Nirvāna. Thus the *milinda-pañha* [29]: just as infinite space, Nirvāna has no original cause whatsoever, it is *ahetu-ja*. Neither is the conception of time of any use for it is uncreated and cannot be created, is neither past, present nor future. It is not subject to sense-perception, and yet it is not no-thing (*natthidhammam*), for it may be perceived by the purified mind of a liberated being.

From all this, Nirvāna is a mystery. It is also the diametrical opposite of the world of *samsāra*. It does not belong to the world, has no relationship with it, nor does it affect it. It might best be called the 'totally other'; this is, indeed, a much more suitable expression for Nirvāna than it is for the Christian God who, though being above the world, yet governs it and is thus in constant touch with it. If God were the 'totally other', he could never be the 'good friend' of the soul, and neither could the soul establish a relationship with him. C. G. Jung therefore rightly says: 'It is psychologically unthinkable that God is nothing but the "totally other", for the "totally other" is never the good friend of the soul, which God also is. Only paradoxical or antinomian statements about the God image are psychologically correct.'[19]

In Pāli literature, the expression '*nibbāna*' does not exclusively denote the transcendental that is beyond suffering, passion, egoism and impermanence—for it is also employed with reference to things and persons still existing in the visible world.

The commentary on the Dīgha-Nikāya[20] knows of a triple Nirvāna, i.e. the *kilesa-parinibbāna*, the complete extinction of all evil which took place with the enlightenment under the Bodhi-tree; *khandha-parinibbāna*, the extinction of the various groups of factors of being which was realized at the moment of the Buddha's death; and *dhātu-parinibbāna*, the complete disappearance of all Buddha relics. The latter happens when the teaching has become extinct, and all relics have miraculously united in the Mahābodhi sanctuary. There they form the golden body of the Buddha, together with the aura, and then they are all destroyed by fire. The second of the above Nirvānas corresponds to the transcendental state of liberation which the dying ascetic enters. The third Nirvāna concerning relics is the result of later speculation, and of no interest here. The *kilesa-nibbāna* corresponds to what is generally called 'Nirvāna with additions' (*saupādisesa*,[21] *sopadhishesha*)[22] or 'Nirvāna while still alive' (*ditth'eva dhamme, drishtadharma*). This is the condition of one who is already liberated, where the groups of *dharmas* forming an individuality still exist, but he has overcome all passions and no longer produces *karma* leading to rebirth; he only waits for complete extinction in death. The time-lapse between reaching 'Nirvāna with additions' and entering perfect *parinirvāna* may be a long one, as was the case with Gautama Buddha. In exceptional circumstances, however, the end of all passionate drives may coincide with the end of life.[23] In that instance the liberated one (in the *Puggala-paññatti*)[24] is called *samasīsin*, i.e. literally one whose 'two heads (i.e. ends) are the same'.

'Nirvāna with additions' corresponds roughly with *jīvanmukti*, 'salvation while alive' which is accepted by many Hindus.

The Hīnayāna schools assume but two types of Nirvāna, the first one in time, followed by the eternal one. Mahāyāna teaching accepts two further Nirvānas.

One of them is *Apratishthita-nirvāna*.[25] This is a kind of eternal *jīvanmukti* lasting beyond death. There is a vague analogy to the *Chāndogya Upanishad*[26] where the liberated one after his death continues to exist as an individual. In Buddhism this has been turned into a completely ethical concept. For according to some texts a liberator—even though he has left earth already—may continue to act for the good of all living beings. This Nirvāna is called *apratishthita* (without ceasing), and it might be translated as 'altruistic' or 'dynamic' Nirvāna. It is a state of inner quietness amid great outer activity, a condition that lacks all compounded or dependent karmic factors. It is a perfect, world-transcending freedom coupled with highest wisdom (*mahāprajñā*) and compassion (*mahā-karunā*) towards all beings.

Such a Buddha, though still living in the world, is yet beyond all that is of the world. He is no longer swayed by *samsāra* but acts within it for the benefit of all living beings. It is said that this 'dynamic' Nirvāna is incomparably superior to the 'static' Nirvāna that resembles the 'extinction of a lamp'. And so *arahats* who had attained the static Nirvāna may subsequently be recalled in order to attain the dynamic Nirvāna.

The other and thus the fourth Nirvāna is *anādikālika-prakriti-shuddha-nirvāna* (the Nirvāna that has been naturally pure since beginningless time). It is a tenet of those schools who see the world and all that is in it as appearance only, as nothing but a mirage. Accordingly *samsāra* does not really exist and only Nirvāna *is*; it is thus also immanent in each individual. All multiplicity, all passion, and all ignorance are but illusory, and veil the realization of Nirvāna. And so Nirvāna is the absolute, continuously present behind all phenomena and all causally conditioned being.

Historically later still are equations of Nirvāna with the 'pure land' of Buddha Amitābha, which originally was considered as an early stage of Nirvāna; also with Shaktic conceptions, the realization of Nirvāna in the ritual love-act. But these are of no interest for this book.

However the ramifications of the Nirvāna concept may vary, the basic idea is the same: it is an undefinable state, independent of all worldly ties, beyond all earthly passion, freedom from all egotistical, false ideas—in short, it is the exact opposite of everything known to conditioned, individual existence between birth and death.

Tathatā, Shūnyatā, Vijñaptimātratā

The Pāli Buddhism of the Theravādins knows of only one absolute—Nirvāna—which has no relation to the world of form. As such, it differs from the impermanent world as light differs from darkness. The question of a possible mutual premise for both *samsāra* and Nirvāna is never posited, nor answered. Buddha kept himself strictly to psychological facts, and on the ground of its being fruitless speculation refrained from all theories about a 'metaphysical depth' of the world of form. He also contradicted the Vedānta teaching of a self (*ātman*) that is manifest in both *samsāra* and the ground of being [10]. The latter especially he considered sheer foolish doctrine (*paripūro bāladhammo*) [22].

Not content with this concrete positivism, other schools evolved theories on the transcendental nature of the *dharma*, as did the Sarvāstivādins. Others regarded the causal nexus (*pratītya-samutpāda*) or the universal law (*dharma-sthitatā*) as *asamskritas* that remain uneffected by change. The Mahīshāsakas also accepted *tathatā* as *asamskrita*, the 'suchness' of the wholesome, unwholesome, and neutral *dharmas* (*kushala-, akushala-* and *avyākrita-dharma-tathatā*).[27] This facilitated the approach to a theory that saw a transcendental principle behind *samsāra* and Nirvāna. These theories found further support in the docetic tendencies just arising, which exalted the Buddha so that it was assumed that his *Dharmakāya* outlasts his death. The more one occupied oneself with the secrets of the transcendental being of the Perfected One, the closer one approached the assumption of an absolute above all time and change.

These speculations are again closely connected with the fundamental changes that influenced the conception of *dharma* in the Mahāyāna.

Early Buddhism denied true being to the individuality (*pudgala*) on the grounds that it represented only an impermanent stream. But now the texts of the *Perfection of Wisdom* (*prajñāpāramitā*) ask: 'The Hīnayāna schools teach that *dharmas* are conditioned—how then can they be regarded as ultimate realities if they arise in causal dependence on other *dharmas*, only to disappear again?' This question was especially relevant, for Hīnayāna philosophy had already arrived at the assumption that the impermanence of a karmically conditioned *dharma* is to be understood in the sense that it exists for one moment (*kshana*) only. 'The moment it comes into existence, it immediately disappears again' (*ātma-lābhād anantara-vināshi*).[28] Should it seemingly remain in existence, this is caused by another *dharma* of the same kind replacing it. This idea refers back to the Buddha who had taught the same with regard to mental processes.[29] So *dharmas* have momentary existence only, arise by being related to other *dharmas*, and only last while being kept in existence by the combined effect of their causes; but such *dharmas* cannot be said to have independent existence.

Thus the doctrine of *Pudgala-nairātmya*, i.e. the theory that the individual does not possess a permanent essence, had to be complemented by the doctrine of *Dharma-nairātmya*. According to the latter, the *dharmas* lack inherent content, they are empty (*shūnya*). Subtracting from each *dharma* the properties it has been supplied with by something else but does not own, all *dharmas* are seen as having but 'stolen goods' [42] and to possess no capital themselves. Therefore they cannot be regarded as true and real.

The main representative of the teaching of 'emptiness' (*shūnyavāda*), the great Nāgārjuna (second century AD), asserted in his essay on the *Perfection of Wisdom* (*mahāprajñā-pāramitā-shāstra*) and in his *Teaching Verses of the Middle Way* (*madhyamaka-kārikās*) that all *dharmas* are relative. His masterly analysis of all metaphysical concepts and doctrinal views—of earlier Buddhism as well as of other Indian systems—leads to the logical dissolution of them all. Though in popular parlance it is perfectly justified to talk about fire, there is no fire *per se* but only an appearance depending on the type of fuel.[30] Each so-called substance exists only by relation to its manifold qualities. The same applies to all concepts. 'Being' exists only as the opposite of 'not-being',[31] etc. So there is nothing that exists by itself, and everything is dependent on and related to each other. There is nowhere anything that has an isolated existence of its own, neither matter, nor soul, etc. Therefore all the *dharmas* are rather like magical beings produced by a magician, and they themselves again bring forth other magical beings [43]. With regard to their 'reality', they are an illusion, a mirage, a dream, and totally imaginary configurations.[32]

Excluding everything that is conditioned by something else, the world is seen to be empty. This does not only apply to the physical world as it appears to the eyes of the non-Buddhist or of the still unenlightened *prithag-jana* among the followers of the Exalted One, but holds good also with regard to liberated beings and the truth of Buddhism. Once this law of relativity has been recognized, it cannot stop short of the Buddha, the Way to Liberation, or Nirvāna. For they, too, are relative and of conditioned and thus temporary value only. As there are therefore no *samskritas*, consequently no *asamskritas* exist either—they are a pair of opposites. In truth there is neither *samsāra* nor Nirvāna, nor is there any difference between them (*na samsārasya nirvānāt kimcid asti visheshanam*) [46].

If everything we can discern is as unreal as a mirage [44], and empty of any essence of its own, what, then, does in fact exist? The reply is: emptiness, uncreated and permanent, unchangeable and indefinable, which is therefore called the 'unthinkable' (*acintyatā*). Thus Nāgārjuna arrives at the absolute that is free of everything, including, of course, all multiplicity (*sarva-prapañca-vinirmukta*; here the word *prapañca* is ambiguous: it may mean the multiplicity of the world of form—as is often the case in its Sanskrit usage—or it may express vague combinations full of fantasy as frequently occur in Buddhist texts).[33] Nāgārjuna's absolute is above all such discussion, and transcends being and non-being.

So we arrive at the final conclusion, the impossibility of making a concrete statement about anything in the world, for all things and all concepts are found to be mutually contradictory. The wise man will accordingly not engage in fruitless discussion and thus remain 'free from perturbations'. He can neither logically fathom nor adequately describe in words that which 'in truth neither disappears nor appears, is neither impermanent nor eternal, neither one nor many, and is without coming or going'. 'For the son of good family, the absolute is silence only' (*paramārtho hy āryānām tūshnīm-bhāvah*).[34]

Nāgārjuna stresses that the absolute as unfathomable emptiness has itself only a relative meaning and is thus not to be made the subject of speculations regarding the ground of being, etc. [45]. The attempt to misuse this emptiness for extraneous purposes is dangerous, like a poisonous snake when wrongly handled. It is of use in adequate doses but must not exceed the range within which it is valid. Again, it is like salt: a farmer ignorant about salt, upon hearing it praised as excellent by a townsman, swallowed a whole mouthful of it with the result that he did not experience any of the pleasant effect.[35] To discourage any misuse of emptiness, it is suggested that wrong conceptions of emptiness as a quasi-substance should be uprooted by meditating on the 'emptiness of emptiness' (*shūnyatā-shūnyatā*).[36]

On reading such expositions on emptiness, one is inclined to consider their author an acute sceptic, or a dyed-in-the-wool agnostic, but Nāgārjuna was a famous patriarch who had no small share in the shaping and spreading of the Mahāyāna. His book, lost in Sanskrit but admirably translated from the Chinese by Étienne Lamotte, is about the Perfection of Wisdom, and shows him to be a strictly Buddhist dogmatist who is thoroughly at home in the world of pious legends and astounding miracles. To him, the Buddha's teaching is THE way to enlightenment for everybody who is still caught in the world of multiplicity and the entanglements of dependent origination (*pratītya-samutpāda*). The path of liberation, however, leads the aspirant beyond the provisional 'seeming truth' (*samvriti-satya*) to absolute truth (*paramārtha-satya*) that culminates in the insight into *shūnyatā*.

Shūnyatā is frequently compared with infinite space. Like space, it is inconceivable, pure, and can only be expressed negatively (as absence, as that which remains after abstracting the contents of space, i.e. the heavenly bodies, etc.). On the other hand, the highest concepts of Buddhist thought are used as synonyms:[35] it is absolute truth (*paramārtha-tattva*), 'suchness' (*tathatā*), the true being of *dharma* (*dharmatā*), enlightenment (*bodhi*), Nirvāna, Buddhahood (*buddhatva*), and the *Dharma-kāya* of all the Buddhas. All this goes to show that to Nāgārjuna emptiness was not an abstract, philosophical concept but a factual, mystic experience that is far beyond the grasp of discursive thinking. By enveloping that which itself is 'without attributes' with all the attributes dear to the Buddhists, *shūnyatā* became a complex idea in which critical reasoning and sophisticated dialectics together with reverent faith and dark mysteriousness formed one whole. Its manifold aspects engendered both profound searching and religious feeling, and could also fulfil them.

It is obvious that even in India *shūnyatā* was variously interpreted by both the Buddhists and their opponents. European interpreters, too, differ widely. Western research, passionately concerned with the understanding of *shūnyatā*, has continuously wavered between the different conceptions. The two scholars most concerned with the problem of *shūnyatā*, Theodor Stcherbatsky and Louis de La Vallée Poussin, constantly, though often unconsciously, changed and revised their ideas in accordance with the points of view they tried to master.

Nāgārjuna is a thoroughly Buddhist philosopher, as is attested by his non-theism, his denial of permanent substances, his conditionalism, and his belief in an ineffable Nirvāna which has to be experienced by higher insight. Yet his teaching already contains traces of the elementary force of monistic thought which since Vedic times had cast an irresistible spell over the Indian mind. For Nāgārjuna's attempt to equate *samsāra*—governed by and dependent on the law of origination, and subject to a moral world law—on an admittedly higher plane with transcendental 'emptiness' which is beyond all duality (*advaya*), is but an infiltration of Vedantic thought into the structure of Buddhism. Strictly speaking, this does not as yet apply to Nāgārjuna, but is again and again stated in later Hindu polemics: 'That which the followers of the doctrine of emptiness (*shūnyavādins*) call 'empty' (*shūnya*), just this the followers of the doctrine of *Māyā* (māyin) call 'Brahmā' (*yacchūnya-vādinah shūnyam tad eva brahmā māyinah*).[38] For as far as we know, the *Vedānta* of Nāgārjuna's time did not yet possess the only subsequently perfected *Māyā* doctrine to which this *Madhva* expression corresponds. However, the trend towards an all-one doctrine has persisted since the *Upanishads* and was gaining ground, and the Brahmin Nāgārjuna could not remain entirely untouched by it.

The doctrine of *Shūnyatā* influenced Buddhist thinking to a great extent. This is best shown by the Hīnayāna systems which continued to develop the germs existing in early Buddhism, and extended them under the influence of the *Prajñā-pāramitā* texts and the doctrines formulated by Nāgārjuna. We know of the existence of Harivarman's (AD 250–350) Satyasiddhi school from Chinese sources. Within this school a *Sarva-shūnya-vāda* was formed on the lines of the Sautrāntika school. Junjirō Takakusu cites many instances where their views closely resemble those of Nāgārjuna.[39]

The *Vijñānavāda* of Asanga and Vasubandhu (AD 350?) is a further stage in the penetration of Vedantic ideas into Mahāyāna. *Vijñānavāda* tries by means of introspection to approach the deepest levels of the personality, and finds below the surface consciousness a store-consciousness (*ālaya-vijñāna*). This replaces the Indian *ātman* which the brahminical systems conceive as transmigrating between existences. However, it is not a permanent substance but a constant flux of *dharmas*, a receptacle of all impressions imprinted during the beginningless series of continuous existences. This 'consciousness-only' doctrine differs from both the earlier Buddhist systems, and the older *Vedānta* by considering consciousness the only reality. The outer world is but an 'imagined' (*parikalpita*) projection of thought. And the illusion of an 'I' and of a concrete world confronting this 'I' comes into being by consciousness splitting into a subjective and a seemingly objective (image) part. The delusion of the polarity of this image can be dissolved by Yoga exercises. Successful meditation results in a basic change (*parāvritti*) of personality which is productive of enlightenment. The eight consciousnesses are transformed into the perfect wisdom of the Buddha. By this, the aspirant is freed for good from all limitations caused by delusion, passion, *karma*, etc. He has entered *Apratishthita-nirvāna* (see above, p. 108) and is free to devote himself to the benefit of all living beings.

The *ālaya-vijñāna* is the source of all mental activity, the storehouse of all that has been experienced, and the cause of memory. It flows on through all rebirths, from time without beginning until Nirvāna. There it assumes its true, unlimited nature for intrinsically it is 'consciousness only'; after all adhering murkiness has disappeared, it contains neither subject nor object, and is as pure as space. And so the transcendent absolute which constitutes the quintessence of all being, and is therefore equated with enlightenment, Buddhahood, etc., is in the last analysis seen to be sheer mind. This highest absolute reality is the base and ground of everything, and is called *parinishpanna*, the 'complete'.

Between the utterly unreal and only 'imagined' (*parikalpita*) outer world, and undifferentiated mind which has the highest and only reality, there is the intermediate realm of the 'dependent' (*paratantra*) which has a conditional reality. This is the world of momentary *dharmas*, the causally conditioned combinations of which feed the imaginations of the *ālaya-vijñāna* but falsely appear to it as both an inner and an outer world. The 'dependent' is itself an aspect of the absolute, because it is consciousness that transforms itself into thoughts of things, feelings, and egos. The difference between this type of absolute and the complete one of *parinishpanna* is that the former is not pure and appears veiled by something else. Thus the world that we perceive in all its multiplicity does not completely differ from the absolute (for without it it could not exist), nor is it identical with it (for it is not pure like the absolute).

The following analogy, however inadequate, serves to illustrate the doctrine of the three kinds of reality. If one sees a rope in the dark and mistakes it for a snake, then the snake has 'imagined' reality (*parikalpita*), and is only an illusion. The rope which was mistaken for the snake, and thus is the cause for the arising of error, has as *dharma*-combination a conditional, dependent reality (*paratantra*). Only the hemp of which the rope is made has highest reality (*parinishpanna*). This analogy may be unsatisfactory but perhaps promotes understanding.

Stcherbatsky sees the peculiarity of the doctrine of the absolute with its grades of reality in that the Vijñānavādins assume two forms of the absolute. As *parinishpanna* it is the abstract, universal, eternal whole; as *paratantra* it reflects itself in point-instants, i.e. in the *dharmas* which each last for a moment only and which co-operate in functional dependence. 'So that there are two absolutes, the absolutely particular, and the absolutely universal; or it may be expressed as the deepest ground and the highest summit . . . in Kantian language we may perhaps say that the one is transcendental and the other is transcendent.'[40]

The still later development of Mahāyāna doctrines is not the subject of our enquiry here. Indian texts do not exist, and the doctrines have to be studied in Chinese and Tibetan translations.[41] The trend is to bring the seeming world of appearance into ever closer relationship with the absolute. Both are thought to be intimately interrelated. Individual beings are to the absolute as the waves are to the ocean. The ocean is not the wave, but as to its nature the wave is the ocean, which the wind of *karma* shapes into waves of individual form. To the open eye of the wise, all-pervading mind manifests itself in all that is, and is immanent in everything. Nor does this include gods, men and animals only, but each flower and every stone. All things have the Buddha nature. When I visited Mount

Kōya (in Japan), a Shingon priest told me that the life-principle of the cosmos and the liberating power of the absolute as personified in Mahāvairocana may be perceived even in the murmuring of a brook, or the sound of wind in trees, and that to the adept this is a continuous proclamation of the *dharma*. With the Asian sense of nature and mystic intuition, Chinese and Japanese painters have expressed this doctrine of the absolute manifest in phenomena in true aesthetic perfection, and given a new value to the seeming world of appearance.

In India with its totally different mentality, we find no such accentuated sense of beauty that could continue and remodel Buddhist thought. There the final stage of the doctrine of the absolute is Vajrayāna with its imprint of Shaktic ideas. Even in its doctrinal structure it approaches Hindusm. Though Buddhist terminology is adhered to throughout, the idea of an individual self (*ātman*) which is one with the imperishable *vajra* nevertheless gained more and more ground.* *Vajra* as the unchangeable absolute is 'hard as a diamond', and as shown above, has as Vajrasattva become identified with the *Ādi-Buddha*.

Considering the historical development of theories concerning the absolute we find that Buddhism at all times believed in an absolute that is 'separated' and totally different from the world and is beyond all karmic *conditionality*. In the Shūnyā-vada the transition is made from the above conception to that of an absolute behind all impermanent *dharmas*, as empty space is behind all changeable heavenly bodies. In Vijñānavāda the absolute becomes 'mind only', which in its highest and true form is beyond the opposition of subject and object, whereas in its lower form it manifests itself as a kind of derived, half-real truth. In still later systems the idea of the absolute contracts and shrinks ever more into the form of a concrete core of the world which is 'hard as a diamond'. Common to both Mahāyāna and Vajrayāna thought is the dual conception of the absolute—as a transcendent principle, and as the liberating

* S. B. Dasgupta[42] cites some examples. The word 'Self' as a synonym for the absolute or for the Buddha is already used in Mahāyāna texts. The *Mahā-parinirvāna-Sūtra* (translated into Chinese in about A D 400) states: 'The not-self is transmigration, the self is the *tathāgata* . . . each real, true, permanent, individual, basic, unchangeable being (i.e. *dharma*) is called "self" (*ga* = *ātman*)'.[43]

117

principle of the cosmos. As such it is identified with the *Dharma-kāya* or personified as a specific Buddha.

2 PARALLELS FROM COMPARATIVE RELIGION

Yasumitra gives a parallel to the doctrine of the three *asams-kritas* (of the Sarvāstivādins): 'The adherents of the Vaisheshika doctrine teach that there are many *asamskritas* (like) atoms, etc.' (*paramānv-ādayo behavo (a)-samskritā iti Vaisheshikāh*).[1] In this comparison of the atoms (earth, fire, water, and air) of the Vaisheshika doctrine with the *asamskritas*, the *tertium comparationis* consists in both the *asamskritas* and the atoms being eternal, permanent, and not amenable to sense-perception. Otherwise the two philosophical conceptions have no points of contact, for atoms are the smallest material building bricks and constitute all matter. Their uniting with and again parting from each other is the world process. This does not, of course, apply to the *asamskritas*. Nor may they be compared with other substances (*dravya*) of this Brahmin system such as souls, *manas*, or time. The only possible analogy is that the Vaisheshikas, too, considered ether (*ākāsha*) and space (*dish*) to be *dravyas*. But there is again a difference between the Buddhist and the Vaisheshika conception. The latter regard *ākāsha* as the concrete premise for the transmission of sound, and *dish* as the cause of our ideas on space because by means of it we differentiate the directions.

Nor can the *asamskritas* be compared with the concepts of other schools.[2] The *asamskrita* tables of the Buddhists are just the special features of one system which continues the archaic theories of the Brāhmanas according to which a quasi-existence is accorded to what we call processes and conditions.[3]

The only *asamskrita* having parallels in other Indian systems is Nirvāna. Buddha is said to have stressed the differences between the Nirvāna he taught, and that of other *samanas* and Brahmins [12] who believed in a Nirvāna to be realized already in the visible world. The latter fall into five groups; one of them considers Nirvāna to be reached when a self (*attā*) enjoys the pleasures of the five senses; the others see the realization of Nirvāna in the attainment of respectively the first, second, third or fourth stage of meditation. Buddha denies these doctrines on the ground of their suggesting the reality of a permanent soul (*sato sattasya*), and therefore not yet having penetrated to the true Nirvāna which is beyond the fourth stage of meditation.

The *Lankavatāra Sūtra* refutes all heretical ideas on Nirvāna.[4] As such it lists the theories of the Small Vehicle, but also those of various ascetics and of non-Buddhists (*tīrthika*), i.e. of the Jains, Vaisheshikas, Sānkhyas, Shaivas, and of numerous other sects. The error of all these views is that by means of words and concepts of their respective systems they somehow try to describe the transcendental, which cannot be expressed by the linguistic means of our world of seeming appearance.

The Nirvāna of the Pāli Canon has often been compared with transcendental theories of other religions. However, such a comparison can be fruitful only if it clearly defines on which points the various conceptions differ from the transcendental. Thus Nirvāna cannot be equated with the Christian God for it lacks most of the distinguishing marks of God: it is not a personality; it does not think, feel, or will; it did not create the world, nor does it rule it, etc. The one item which shows a certain similarity is the idea of the 'peace of God which passeth all understanding' (Philippians 4,7).

The analogies between Nirvāna and the impersonal *Brahmā* of the *Upanishads* are closer. However, Nirvāna is neither universal spirit identical with the individual soul, nor is it the ground of being of the whole world.[5] The Pāli Canon is not concerned with any speculations about a fundamental being which splits itself into the multiplicity of manifestation. It is therefore unjustified to assume 'that from the total impression of Buddhism, and especially from the undifferentiated and unconscious Nirvāna which constitutes the goal of liberation, may be concluded some such undifferentiated unity behind the empirical, individual world of manifestation'.[6] In my opinion the task of the Buddhist scholar is not to continue and develop the thoughts of the Buddha, but rather to present them just as they have come down to us. Otherwise, as the Bible does not inform us about God's activities before the creation, one might equally well engage in a wealth of speculations on what existed or happened during the infinite time before that event. No religious or philosophical system—not even the most detailed one—gives an answer to many questions that worry us who are born in different times and different mental climates. This is because either their founders had not as yet become consciously aware of them, or if they were aware, did not consider them as problems.

It is well known and needs no elaboration that Nirvāna in Mahāyāna formulation has many common features with Vedānta—especially with the doctrines which bear strong Buddhist influence, i.e. those of 'Yoga-vāsishtha', Gaupāda and Shankara.

A comparison of the Buddhist concept of Nirvāna (including both Small and Great Vehicle) with that of the liberation theories of other Indian soteriological systems shows that the expressions about the state of liberation differ widely. So do all attempts to give it a philosophical premise, or to classify it within a Vishnuite, Shivaite, Shakti, theist, pan-en-theist, or non-theist (Jain) system. Yet all of them have one point in common, for all of them postulate as the ultimate aim and goal a transcendental bliss, in which all passions that cloud the mind and all the suffering of impermanence are dissolved for good. The conceptions of the Nirvāna of the Small Vehicle, of Shūnyatā and of the Ālaya-vijñāna are of course closest to all those religions which regard as the highest good the disappearance of the split between subject and object, and the attainment of a 'higher consciousness' in undifferentiated unity.

This, however, does not apply to the mystical teaching of India only. In spite of all the existing differences one may also see a common feature in the mystical experiences of Lao-tsu and Chuan-tsu, of Plotinus, of Eckhart, and of Hallāj. The difference between Buddhism and the other mystical schools is that while the latter strive to dress their mystical experience in the garments of their religious forms, complete with theories of the origin of the world and the relationship between God and soul, Buddhism attempts to preserve the mystical experience in its pure and immediate nakedness.

The profound difference in the Nirvāna concept of the Small and the Great Vehicle is best illustrated by a comparison with other religions. In the teachings of the Small Vehicle, Nirvāna and samsāra vary as do day and night. The only connection between them is the progress of the aspirant who in the process of his training during many rebirths slowly transcends the realm of darkness, and by way of the realm of dawn finally enters that of the full light of day. Transmigration and liberation are here in opposition, as are darkness and light for the Manichaeans and for the dualist Christian sects—the whole range from the Paulicians, Thondraciens and Carthusians to the French Hinschists.

Mahāyāna seeks to dispel this dualism. The manifold world with its inherent suffering dissolves into a dream, but in it is nevertheless seen a hidden reflection of eternal truth, overcast by the cloud of delusion. Even the humblest being has the Buddha-nature, and so carries a potential, future ray of perfection. With this conception Buddhism has considerably changed its attitude to the world, not least by plumbing ever deeper levels in its attempt to explain the cosmos. These levels now give it a metaphysical background. Within certain limits a parallel is thus established with all those religions that originally saw an unbridgeable gulf between actual, earthly being and its expected, eschatological glorification. But as in course of time their faith had to accommodate itself to the circumstances of life, the realization of the Kingdom of Heaven seemed to become possible even in the present, and was finally considered as the thing to strive for.

Detailed research into the change and development of Buddhist doctrines under the further influence of Far Eastern thought would be immensely rewarding, as would an examination into what is still truly Buddhist in these new developments. Various scholars have just started to work along these lines. [7]

CONCLUSIONS

For thousands of years man has found himself in a world the origin of which is as impenetrable as the happenings in it. In ever new forms he seeks to grasp it, to explain its mysteries, and to find a way through the tangle of the insoluble problems it presents. Man is not an intellectual being only who searches for an explanation of all manifestation in the light of cold reason alone. He is also governed by his feelings, desires, hopes, fears, intuitions, imaginations, and fantasies so that the rational and irrational or emotional elements in him are mixed in one inextricable whole.

Besides being engaged in the search for a theoretical solution of the secrets of being, man also tries to find practical rules by which he may meaningfully regulate his behaviour both in his individual life and within the framework of society. Thus he produces systems designed to accord with his conceptions of the world as well as with what he believes he has perceived behind and beyond it.

Hence his attempts to fashion into one more or less complete whole all speculative insights, emotional experiences, decisions of will, and actions which he considers to be correct and necessary. All religions and philosophical systems derive from precisely these attempts.

Men differ from each other individually. They are born in different countries and climates, live at different periods of time, grow up in differing environments and traditions. Likewise the philosophical systems evolved in the course of millennia differ accordingly. The enormous variety of these systems is not easily perceived, for many of them seem to have much in common—either because they originated from a common tradition (as have the manifold forms of Jewish-Christian-Islamic theism), or because they owe their existence to similar psychological factors (Hindu and Chinese theism).

Within the historical development of one religion, particular divergences may be veiled—partly because their creeds, dogmas, rites, etc., became rigid in the course of centuries, or because their original content was more or less modified in later times. Classification into a number of types of religion and traditional forms is therefore possible.

The view that in his history of six hundred thousand years man once possessed a religion that was common to all, or will at one time in the future have one common to and acknowledged by all, is as unlikely as is the contention that all men at one time either have had or will have the same food, clothing, language, art, music, and moral code. Fundamentally common to all religions is only the metaphysical element, imperceptible to mortal man, which forms his mysterious ground of being. Also common to all is the pious awe man experiences when confronted by this mystery, his urge to unveil it, and his continuously renewed attempts to explain it conceptually or emotionally; also his striving to render it concretely effective for his everyday life by means of magic, cult, or ethics.

A comparison of the various religions conclusively proves that the same objective facts, plus similar intellectual demands, emotional moods and psychological needs within the same historical period and in the same mental climate may produce totally different dogmatic expressions.[1] Most illustrative in this context is a comparison between Christian and Buddhist teaching. Both are highly developed religions, and both seek to bring man to salvation—liberation. They have much in common with regards to morality, cult, and forms of organization.[2]

They also differ radically precisely in their metaphysical foundations, especially along the lines treated in this book. The central dogma of Western religions is the belief in a personal, transcendent creator and ruler beside whom no other divine being is conceived as active in nature. Buddhism kept the nature gods of the Indian religions, and also admitted those of other countries it entered, but it sees all *devas* as bound in *saṃsāra*. This difference is of secondary importance only, for in the actual teaching of liberation the Buddhist *devas* have no special place. It is also relatively unimportant for *practical* religiosity whether the undoubted need of many people to apply for help and protection to a multitude of supernatural beings is satisfied by the cult of numerous lower deities, or by the belief in angels, saints, *pīrs*, or other intermediaries.

123

The problem of the origin of the world is decisive in many religions, and is mostly approached by assuming an original creator of all that is. This, however, is inconceivable for many Asians, who consider it but idle speculation on the grounds that it seems dubious whether the causal law is applicable to the world; and further that if God created the world, then the obvious question arises as to what is the cause of God. Buddhism regards this question of a first cause as futile and refuses to speculate about it. For practical purposes the statement suffices that the present world has come into being by reason of the karmic consequences of a previous world—just as a tree grows from a seed, but the seed came from a previously existing tree.

For the Buddhist the question of the just rule of the world is solved by the doctrine of karmic law which is immanent in the world, acts automatically and mechanically, and requires no god to keep it going.

The further belief in a moral world order as manifested by karmic consequences frees Buddhism from the supposition of an instigator of the moral laws, and of a strict judge who guards his moral commandments and accordingly rewards or punishes in a hereafter. Since Buddhism does not believe in a historical process leading to the future perfection of the world, it also needs no belief in providential guidance.

In accordance with its non-theistic attitude Buddhism declines to believe in a divine revelation, in saints inspired by God or in divine incarnations who have proclaimed the liberating truth. In the doctrine of the Buddha's rediscovering the ancient way to liberation and presenting it once more to erring mankind, and by the dogma that the sermons existing in voluminous canonical scriptures are an authoritative account of metaphysical truths by omniscient Buddhas, Buddhism has found a perfectly justified alternative to the beliefs in revelation which are typical of 'book' religions.

A decisive factor in all religions is that the faithful in need or danger may expect help from supernatural powers if they are appealed to with gifts and prayers. Hīnayāna expresses this by assuming the popular gods as the dispensers of worldly blessings. These are supplemented in Mahāyāna by the conception of helpful Bodhisattvas and Buddhas.

The orthodox Hīnayānist sees in the Buddha simply a guide

to liberation. The Buddhist does not believe in a god who can grant his devotee liberation from the bonds of impermanence. In Mahāyāna, however, the faith in Amitābha Buddha and other compassionate ones has resulted in the belief that a saviour by his mercy may extricate a devout believer from the vortex of rebirths.

The veneration of higher beings is, however, not exclusively activated by the egotistical hope of being thus saved from misfortune, but is often actuated by a deeply rooted need of the human being, which is to look up to a personified ideal. Goethe expresses this well when he says that 'man inclines towards veneration'. In theistic religions this veneration is projected on to God for 'none is good but the one God' (Mark 10,18), or is projected on his incarnation in this world. In Buddhism, Buddha is the ideal of perfection. In him, the believer beholds all that is good, true, and beautiful, and he offers his veneration to him.

In Nathan Söderblom's words, 'the holy is the great concept in the religious realm. . . . Genuine religion may do without concrete formulation of the divine, but every genuine religion differentiates between the holy and the profane. Attaching exaggerated importance to the divine frequently resulted in excluding from the realm of religion primitive forms which, though profoundly religious, were labelled as magic. Equally excluded were Buddhism and other higher systems of liberation and piety because they did not contain a belief in God. However, the only certain mark (of religiosity) is the holy.'[3]

Buddhism shares with all other religions the idea of the holiness of certain concepts, rites, places, and persons. Taking this as the decisive factor, Buddhism shows itself as a genuine religion, and not only as a particular metaphysical explanation of the world, or way of life.

In Hinayāna thought, Nirvāna is the 'holy' which as the 'totally other' is above or beyond impermanence, in Mahāyāna it is shūnyatā or vijñaptimātratā. The latter's similarity with one aspect of the god concept has been discussed above.

In conclusion it may be said that Buddhism in spite of all doctrinal differences is nevertheless based on the same assumptions, feelings and hopes as the theistic religions. The fundamental difference is that the latter combine in the god idea a great number of mutually exclusive concepts (the omniscient and omnipotent creator of an evil world; the severe judge and compassionate saviour, etc.), whereas in Buddhism the different elements of a religious world concept appear attributed to various factors.

The multiplicity and variety of the beliefs of mankind may all be explained as attempts to express the ineffable. Their manifold forms may be variously regarded and classified, just as the same stars were variously interpreted by ancient cultures, and were grouped into different heavenly constellations.

NOTE ON THE BUDDHIST SCRIPTURES

By M. O'C. WALSHE

Siddhattha Gautama, the historical founder of the religion known today as Buddhism, lived in northern India from about 560–480 BC. In a sense Buddhism grew out of the soil of Hinduism in much the same way as Christianity did out of Judaism. Buddhism is so called because its founder Gautama became the *Buddha*, the Awakened or Enlightened One. It teaches that such awakening or enlightenment is possible for all men to achieve. It is through ignorance and craving that we are impelled through the weary series of rebirths instead of attaining the unutterable peace of Nirvāna (*nibbāna* in Pāli).* Buddhism is sometimes called pessimistic because it sees life in the world as fraught with suffering and frustration, but it also shows a way of release from this situation.

The Buddha taught the Four Noble Truths: that life is painful and frustrating (*dukkha*); that the reason for this is in our minds, in the craving which leads us to grasp at that which can never bring satisfaction; that this craving, and hence the frustration born of it, can be overcome; and that there is a path to the end of craving, the end of suffering, to Enlightenment and Nirvāna. This is the Noble Eightfold Path of right understanding, right aims; right speech, action and livelihood; right effort, right mindfulness and right concentration (*samādhi*). The first two steps are aspects of wisdom, the next three deal with ethics, and the last three with the practice of meditation.

* *Pāli*: The religious language of Theravāda Buddhism. The word means 'text', hence the language of the sacred texts. Its precise origin is disputed, and few Western scholars accept the claim that it is the original language of the Buddha himself (*Māgadhi?*), though the difference may only be comparatively slight. It is the oldest and most conservative of the Middle Indic dialects (*Prākrits*) and stands to Classical Sanskrit in a relation somewhat similar to that of Italian to Latin. The Pāli scriptures (*Tipitaka*) were long preserved orally, being committed to writing about 80 BC under King Vattagāmini of Ceylon.

Without some wisdom, we will never start to tread the path; without some degree of moral purity we shall fail to progress; by meditation (training the mind) we can attain the goal.

The essence of Buddhist meditation, whether it be that of Zen in Japan or the *Vipassanā* (insight) method of the Theravāda school, is the gaining of clear awareness of things as they truly are. This involves an understanding of *karma*, whereby our volitional acts, good or bad, will have their inevitable consequences pleasant or painful for us, in this or some future existence, and the wisdom which, by withdrawal from the allurements of things sensual, transcends *karma* and, with it, all forms of conditioned existence.

Right understanding also involves profound insight into the Three Marks of Existence: that all things are impermanent, frustrating and impersonal (without 'self-nature'). This book deals with the concept of deity in Buddhism, and makes it clear that there is no idea of a personal divine (or 'supreme self') in the ultimate sense. The deathless element itself is not a personal god, it is *anattā* (without self'), in Sanskrit frequently also called the void (*shūnyatā*). 'Personality' of any sort is purely relative, and though there are 'gods' and other beings, they are only relatively real. The man, too, who gains enlightenment must first have become fully aware of the spurious nature of his own 'self'. Strictly speaking, there is no 'entering into Nirvāna', since there is no self to enter, but Nirvāna can nevertheless be attained.

The law of dependent origination shows how all things in the relative world (*samsāra*, which includes the highest, temporary, 'heavens' as well as the lowest, equally temporary, 'hells') are interdependent. Through ignorance and craving we are born, and the same ignorant craving ensures that we shall be born again and again, in this realm or that according to our deeds, unless and until we gain liberation through insight.

This teaching is common to all schools of Buddhism. In Southern Buddhism, the Theravāda ('teaching of the elders') found today in Ceylon, Burma, Thailand and Cambodia, it may be assumed that something very like the original teaching of the Buddha has been preserved. The scriptures of the Theravāda school are in Pāli, and have nearly all been translated into English by the Pāli Text Society, founded in 1881 by Prof. Rhys Davids. These voluminous scriptures fall into three divisions or 'baskets': *Vinaya* or the *Book of Discipline* (for monks), the *Suttas* or *Discourses of the Buddha* and his chief disciples, and *Abhidhamma* or *Further Teaching*.

It has been shown that Pāli cannot have been the Buddha's original language, and the Theravāda school of today is the only survivor of some eighteen early schools. How far it may differ from 'primitive Buddhism' is not known, but though some of its doctrinal formulations may be later, there is little reason to doubt that it substantially represents the spirit of the Buddha's own doctrine and, most important, the path of practice he prescribed. It is at any rate easy to derive all admittedly or seemingly later developments convincingly from something very like the system enshrined in the Pāli Canon.

The aim of the Theravāda Buddhist is to become an *arahat*, i.e. to become enlightened by one's own efforts. At some stage this goal came to be regarded as selfish (though in fact it involves the overcoming of the very notion of 'self'), and the ideal of the *Bodhisattva*, pledged to postpone his own 'entry into Nirvāna' for the sake of all beings, arose instead. The schools in which this ideal was taught came to be known as the 'Mahāyāna' or 'Great Vehicle (or Career)', and the Mahāyānists coined the term 'Hīnayāna' ('Lesser Vehicle') for the older schools. The Mahāyāna schools (which differ widely among themselves) collectively form Northern Buddhism, being spread over China, Tibet, Korea, Japan and Mongolia. In the Mahāyāna schools, elaborate doctrinal and speculative systems were set up. In some, a bewildering multiplicity of Buddhas and Bodhisattvas appeared, but the reader of this book will appreciate that any appearance of polytheism is deceptive.

But while it is easy to point to the differences between the various Buddhist schools, it is important to remember the underlying unity. The great teachers of the Mahāyāna never lost their grip on the basic principles, however much these may have been elaborated or seemingly modified out of recognition. Thus the Bodhisattva who would 'save all beings' must at the same time be clearly aware that—since all is void—there are in reality no 'beings' to save! The doctrine of the Pure Land school seems at first sight to have departed a long way from the original teaching. According to this school, the teaching of which

I   129 finds its most extreme expression in the Shin sect of Japan, the non-historical Amitābha Buddha, realizing the difficulty for ordinary people of attaining Enlightenment by their own efforts, has vowed to establish a western paradise in which all will be reborn who have sincere faith in him. There they will be enabled to gain enlightenment without the difficulties that beset them on earth. The idea of 'self-help' is here completely replaced by reliance on the help of Amitābha Buddha. Yet the faith required for rebirth in the Pure Land is that of 'pure egolessness', and Amitābha Buddha himself symbolizes or represents the *Dharmakāya* or absolute truth. The superficial contrast with the directness of Zen, which with its insistence on one's own efforts comes near to the Theravāda ideal, is striking, and yet in the metaphysical dialectic of self and not-self the two ways are less different than they seem. They illustrate the fact that *all* methods of gaining enlightenment propounded by the Buddhas and great teachers are in the last resort but 'skilled devices', rafts for crossing the stream. When the stream is crossed, one throws away the raft.

SOME IMPORTANT SCHOOLS OF BUDDHISM

The Buddha, North India, *c.* 560–480 BC

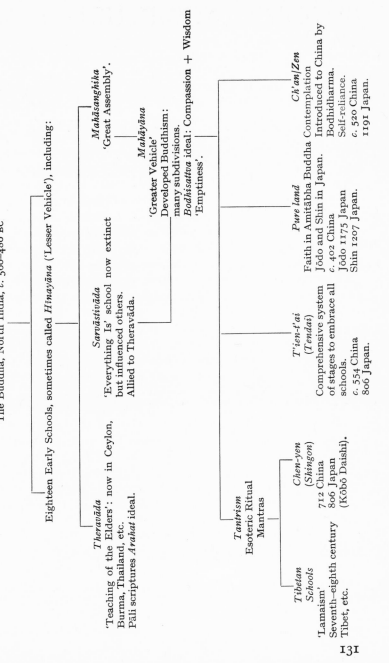

Eighteen Early Schools, sometimes called *Hīnayāna* ('Lesser Vehicle'), including:

Theravāda
'Teaching of the Elders': now in Ceylon, Burma, Thailand, etc.
Pāli scriptures *Arahat* ideal.

Sarvāstivāda
'Everything Is' school now extinct but influenced others.
Allied to Theravāda.

Mahāsanghika
'Great Assembly'.

Mahāyāna
'Greater Vehicle'
Developed Buddhism: many subdivisions.
Bodhisattva ideal: Compassion + Wisdom
'Emptiness'.

Tantrism
Esoteric Ritual
Mantras

Tibetan Schools
'Lamaism'
Seventh–eighth century
Tibet, etc.

Chen-yen (Shingon)
712 China
806 Japan
(Kōbō Daishi).

T'ien-t'ai (Tendai)
Comprehensive system of stages to embrace all schools.
c. 554 China
806 Japan.

Pure land
Faith in Amitābha Buddha
Jōdo and Shin in Japan.
c. 402 China
Jōdo 1175 Japan
Shin 1207 Japan.

Ch'an/Zen
Contemplation
Introduced to China by Bodhidharma.
Self-reliance.
c. 520 China
1191 Japan.

BUDDHIST SCRIPTURES

The scriptures of the various Buddhist schools are vast and in various languages.

The Theravāda scriptures are in Pāli (the Pāli Canon or *Tipitaka, Three Baskets*).

Vinaya Pitaka. Book of Discipline.

Sutta Pitaka. Discourses, divided into:

Dīgha Nikāya	*Longer Discourses* (translated as *Dialogues of the Buddha*)
Majjhima Nikāya	*Middle Length Sayings*
Samyutta Nikāya	*Kindred Sayings*
Anguttara Nikāya	*Gradual Sayings*
Khuddhaka Nikāya	*Minor Anthologies* (includes the well-known *Dhammapada* or *Verses of the Law*)

Abhidhamma Pitaka. Further Teaching (compendious treatment of doctrine).

The scriptures of the other schools were originally mainly in a form of Sanskrit. They include material (the *Āgamas*) corresponding closely to the Pāli *Nikāyas*, and also, less closely, to the *Abhidhamma*. Many texts are known only in Chinese or Tibetan translations.

Special Mahāyāna scriptures include the vast collection of *Prajñāpāramitā, (Perfection of Wisdom)* texts, including the Diamond Sūtra (*Vajracchedikā*), and the short Heart Sūtra in which the doctrine of 'voidness' is expounded in brief. Other important works are the Lotus Sūtra (*Saddharma-pundarīka*) and Aśvaghosa's *Awakening of Faith*. A work of importance for Zen is the Platform Sūtra of the Sixth Patriarch Hui-nêng (*d.* 713), of which several translations exist.

SELECTIONS FROM THE BUDDHIST SCRIPTURES

The following scriptural extracts are (with one exception [20])
referred to in the main text of this book.
The English translation of the Pāli Canon has been freely
used. Wherever English and German versions differ, the latter
has been followed. This choice does not express a preference.
It was made in order to render the author's views as accurately
as possible.
E = English translation, G = German. PTS = Pāli Text Society

Anguttara Nikāya
  E: *The Book of Gradual Sayings*, 5 vols, PTS 1933–36
  G: trans. Nyanatiloka, 5 vols, Munich, 1922–23

Dīgha Nikāya
  E: *Dialogues of the Buddha*, 3 vols, Sacred Books of the
       Buddhists, 1899–1921
  G: trans. R. Otto Franke, *Quellen der Religionsgeschichte* 4,
       Göttingen, 1913

Jātaka and *Jātaka Commentary*
  E: *Jātaka Stories*, trans. E. B. Cowell *et al.*, 6 vols, Cam-
       bridge, 1895–1913
  G: trans. Paul Dutoit, 7 vols, Leipzig, 1908–21

Majjhima Nikāya
  E: *Middle Length Sayings*, 3 vols, PTS 1954–59
  G: trans. Kurt Schmidt (Rowohlts Klassiker), Reinbek,
       1961
       trans. K. E. Neumann, 3 vols, Leipzig, 1896–1902

Milinda-pañha
  E: *Milinda's Questions*, trans. I. B. Horner, 2 vols, Sacred
       Books of the Buddhists, 1963
  G: trans. Nyanaponika, 2 vols, Leipzig, 1919

Samyutta Nikāya
  E: *The Book of Kindred Sayings*, 5 vols, PTS 1917–30
  G: trans. W. Geiger, 2 vols, Munich, 1925.
Visuddhimagga
  E: *The Path of Purification*, trans. Ñānamoli, Colombo, 1956
  G: trans. Nyanatiloka, Constance, 1952
Bodhicaryāvatāra
  E: *The Path of Light*, trans. L. D. Barnett, 2nd ed., London,
       1947
  G: trans. R. Schmidt, *Dokumente der Religion* 2, Paderborn,
       1923
Saddharma-puṇḍarīka
  E: *The Lotus of the Wonderful Law*, trans. W. E. Soothill,
       Oxford, 1930
  G: trans. H. von Glasenapp, Heidelberg, 1952

Other Works
  Frauwallner, *Philosophie*
     Erich Frauwallner, *Die Philosophie des Buddhismus*, Philo-
        soph. *Studientexte* 2, 2nd ed., Berlin, 1958
  Glasenapp, *Pfad zur Erleuchtung*
     Helmuth von Glasenapp, *Der Pfad zur Erleuchtung, Grund-
        texte der buddh. Heilslehre*, Düsseldorf, 1956
  Glassenapp, *Weisheit*
     Helmuth von Glasenapp, *Die Weisheit des Buddha*, Baden-
        Baden, 1946
  Nyanatiloka, *Weg*
     Nyanatiloka, *Der Weg zur Erlösung*, Constance, 1956
     E: *The Path to Deliverance*, 2nd ed., Colombo, 1959
  Seidenstücker, *Pāli-Buddhismus*
     Karl Seidenstücker, *Pāli-Buddhismus in Übersetzungen*,
        2nd ed., Munich, 1923

ANGUTTARA NIKĀYA

I

Impossibility and Possibility

(1) It is impossible, monks, it cannot come to pass, that one who is possessed of right view should regard anything (a conditioned factor of being, *samkhāra*) as permanent. It is impossible. Yet, monks, it is possible that a worldling may do so.

(2) It is impossible, monks, it cannot come to pass, that one who is possessed of right view should regard anything (see above) as happiness. It is impossible. Yet, monks, it is possible that a worldling may do so.

(3) It is impossible, monks, it cannot come to pass, that one who is possessed of right view should regard anything (a factor of being, *dhamma*) as a self. It is impossible. Yet, monks, it is possible that a worldling may do so.

(4) It is impossible, monks, it cannot come to pass, that one who is possessed of right view should slay his mother . . .

(5) . . . should slay his father . . .

(6) . . . should slay an *arahat* . . .

(7) . . . should with evil intent draw the blood of a *tathāgata* . . .

(8) . . . should cause schism in the Order . . .

(9) . . . should proclaim some other teacher. It is impossible. Yet, monks, it is possible that a worldling may do so.

(10) It is impossible, monks, it cannot come to pass, that in one world system at one and the same time there should arise two *arahats*, two fully enlightened ones (*sammāsambuddha*). It is impossible. Yet, monks, it is possible for one *arahat*, one fully enlightened one, to arise in one world system.

(11) It is impossible, monks, it cannot come to pass, that in one world system at one and the same time there should arise two universal monarchs. Yet, monks, it is possible for one to arise in one world system.

(12) It is impossible, monks, it cannot come to pass that a woman should be an *arahat*, a fully enlightened one (*sammāsambuddha*). It is impossible. Yet, monks, it is possible for a man to be one.

(13) It is impossible, monks, it cannot come to pass, that a woman should be a universal monarch. It is impossible. Yet, monks, it is possible for a man to be one.

(17–19) It is impossible, monks, it cannot come to pass, that the fruit of a deed ill done by body, word, or thought, should be pleasant, dear, delightful. That is impossible. Yet, monks, it is possible that the fruit of a deed ill done by body, word, or thought, should be unpleasant, hateful, and miserable.

(20–22) It is impossible, monks, it cannot come to pass, that the fruit of a deed well done by body, word, or thought, should be unpleasant, hateful, and miserable. That is impossible. Yet, monks, it is possible that the fruit of a deed well done by body, word, or thought, should be pleasant, dear, and delightful.

(23–25) It is impossible, monks, it cannot come to pass, that one who did evil with body, word, or thought, should as a result of that when his body disintegrates after death, be reborn in a happy place, in a heavenly realm. But the opposite may well be.

(26–28) It is impossible, monks, it cannot come to pass, that one who did good with body, word, or thought, should as a result of that when his body disintegrates after death, be reborn in an unhappy place, a place of woe, in the misery of hellish tortures. But the opposite may well be.

(Vol. 1, Ch. 15)

2

Monks, there are certain recluses and Brahmins who teach thus, who hold this view:—Whatsoever weal or woe or neutral feeling is experienced, all that is due to the creation of a supreme god. I approach them and say: 'Is it true, as they say, that the venerable sirs hold the view and teach that whatsoever weal or woe or neutral feeling is experienced, all this is due to the creation of a supreme god?' Thus, questioned by me they reply: 'Yes, we do.' Then I say to them: 'So then, owing to the creation of a supreme god, men will become murderers, thieves, unchaste, liars, slanderers, covetous, malicious, and heretical. Those who rely on the creation of a supreme god, those lack the desire, and the energy, to do what is to be done and to refrain

from doing what is not to be done. So then, the necessity for action or inaction not being found to exist in them, the term "recluse" cannot reasonably be applied to yourselves since you live in a state of bewilderment without heed or restraint.' Such, monks, is my second reasonable rebuke to those recluses and Brahmins who thus teach, who hold such views.
(Vols I–III, Ch. 61, 3)

3

By right action, Visākhā, the impure mind is purified. And how, Visākhā, is the impure mind purified by right action? Herein the virtuous disciple calls to mind the gods: there are the gods of the four great kings, the gods of the thirty-three, the gods of Yama's (Underworld) Realm, the happy gods, those that delight in creation, and those that control the creations of others, the gods of the Brahmā world, and still more. Such faith exists in me as the faith, blessed with which those gods deceased from this world were reborn in that world. Such virtue as theirs exists in me, such religious knowledge as theirs exists in me. Such is my generosity, and my insight. As the disciple thus calls to mind the faith, virtue, religious knowledge, generosity, and wisdom of himself and the gods, his mind is calmed, joy arises, and what impurities of mind there are, they vanish just as impure silver is refined by right processing.

And how, Visākhā, is impure silver refined by right processing? By means of a furnace, of salt-earth, red chalk, bellows, tongs, and by the adequate effort of a person. And how, Visākhā, does the impure mind become purified by right processing? Herein the virtuous disciple calls to mind the gods: There are the gods of the four great kings, the gods of the thirty-three, the gods of Yama's realm, the happy gods, those that delight in creation, and those that control the creations of others, the gods of the Brahmā world, and still more. Such faith exists in me as the faith, blessed with which those gods deceased from this world, were reborn in that world. Such virtue as theirs exists in me, such religious knowledge as theirs exists in me. Such is my generosity, and my insight. As the disciple calls to mind the faith, virtue, religious knowledge, generosity, and insight of

himself and the gods, his mind is calmed, joy arises, and what impurities of mind there are, they vanish.
(Vols I–III, Ch. 7, 70)

4

(2) Just then the Exalted One stepped aside from the road and sat himself down under a tree, sitting cross-legged, holding his body upright, mindful and self-possessed. Dona the Brahmin who had followed the footsteps of the Exalted One thus beheld him sitting at the foot of a tree. Seeing him comely, faith-inspiring, with senses calmed, tranquil of mind, in full self-possession and repose, tamed and protected, the hero with guarded senses, he drew near and addressed him:
'Might the lord be a god?'
'Not am I, Brahmin, destined to be a god.'
'Or might the lord perhaps be a spirit?'
'Not am I, Brahmin, destined to be a spirit.'
'Then might the lord perhaps be a ghost?'
'Not am I, Brahmin, destined to be a ghost.'
'Then the lord is after all a human being?'
'Not am I, Brahmin, destined to be a human being.'
'Asked "Might the lord be a god, . . . a spirit . . . a ghost . . . a human being?" you reply "Not am I, Brahmin, destined to be god, . . . a spirit . . . a ghost . . . a human being." What, pray, might the lord be?'
(3) That delusion, Brahmin, that would make me a god, just that delusion is extinguished in me, is torn from the root as a palm-tree is uprooted, is destroyed and will not enter existence again. That delusion, Brahmin, that would make me a spirit, or a ghost, or a human being, just that delusion is extinguished in me, is torn from the root as a palm-tree is uprooted, is destroyed and will not enter existence again.
Just as, Brahmin, the blue, red and white lotus, though born in the water, grown up in the water, when it reaches the surface stands unsullied by the water, just so, Brahmin, though born in the world, grown up in the world, I have overcome the world and now abide unsullied by the world. Wherefore you, Brahmin, may take me as the Enlightened One.
(Vols II–IV, Ch. 4, 36)

5

'Have you, Ānanda, heard that the Vajjians honour, respect, revere and venerate the cult places within and outside (the towns), and that they do not deny them the customary oblations?'

'Thus have I heard, Venerable One.'

'Therefore, Ānanda, as long as the Vajjians honour, respect, revere and venerate the cult places within and outside (the towns), and do not deny them the customary oblations, they may expect blessings only, and no decrease.'

(Vols IV, VII, Ch. 3, 20)

6

In former days, monks, there lived a teacher named Sunetta, a founder of religion, who had wholly overcome all sense pleasures. He had many hundreds of disciples, to whom he taught the way leading to rebirth among the gods of the Brahmā world. All those who grasped the words taught by Sunetta in their fulness, on distintegration of the body after death reached a Brahmā world. But those who partially grasped his instructions reappeared, some among the gods who have control of the creations of others (*para-nimmita-vasarattī devā*), some among the gods who delight in creating (*nimmāna-ratī devā*), others among the happy gods (*tusitā devā*), and others again among the gods of the underworld (*yāmā devā*); some among wealthy nobles, or among wealthy Brahmins, or wealthy householders. Now Sunetta the teacher thought thus: 'It is not seemly that after death I should have the same mode of existence as my disciples. What if I aimed for something still higher?' And Sunetta the teacher cultivated the thought of loving-kindness for seven years, and then for seven world-cycles returned not to this world. He arose in the sphere of the radiant gods (*ābhassarā devā*) ... in the empty Brahmā palace ... as Mahā-Brahmā, the invincible, omnipotent, who sees everything. Thirty-six times he was Sakka, some hundred times lord of the world, master of virtues, owner of the four quarters, victorious, secure of his domain, endowed with the seven jewels. He had more than a thousand sons, heroes who could destroy all enemies had

139

there been any. Thus he lived on this earth he had conquered as far as the sea, by his virtue only, without a stroke of the sword. Yet, monks, although Sunetta lived so long, and lasted such a time, he was not freed from birth, old age, and death, from weeping and lamentation, from grief, pain and desperation. He was not free from ill, I say. And what is the reason? It was by not seeing into, by not penetrating four conditions. What four? Noble conduct, noble concentration, noble wisdom, and noble liberation. However, monks, when noble conduct, noble concentration, noble wisdom, and noble liberation are seen into and penetrated, the thirst for existence is cut off, the stream of existence runs dry, and there is no more coming-to-be. (Vols IV, VII, Ch. 7, 62)

7

Knowledge and Vision

Once the Exalted One was staying on the summit of Mount Gayā at Gayā and there he addressed the monks, saying: 'Monks.' 'Venerable One', they replied. And the Exalted One said: 'Before my awakening, monks, when I was not yet fully awakened but only a Bodhisattva, I perceived radiance, but I saw no forms. To me there, monks, came the thought: "If I both were to perceive radiance and to see forms, knowledge and vision in me would thus be better purified." Later on, living zealous, earnest, resolute, I both perceived the radiance and saw the forms, but I did not stand with, talk to, or engage in conversation with any of those gods.

'To me there, monks, came the thought: "If I were to perceive the radiance, see the forms, stand with, talk to, or engage those gods in conversation, knowledge and vision in me would thus be better purified." Later on, living zealous, earnest, resolute, I did these things . . ., but of those gods I knew not whether they were from this or that heavenly realm.

'To me there, monks, came the thought: "If I were to perceive the radiance, see the forms, and stand with, talk to or engage those gods in conversation, and also knew from which heavenly realm they were, knowledge and vision in me would thus be better purified." Later on, living zealous, earnest, resolute, I did these things . . ., and also knew where they were from, but did not know by result of which deeds they had passed away from here and arisen there, what their food was, what weal and woe they experienced, how long they lived, how long their life-span was, and whether I had lived with them before or not.

'To me there, monks, came the thought: "If I were to perceive the radiance; see the forms; stand with, talk to and engage them in conversation; know they are of such a realm; know their faring on was thus because of their deeds; their food, experience, weal and woe such; their lives and life-span so long; know whether I had dwelt with them or not, knowledge and vision in me would thus be better purified." Later on, living zealous, earnest, resolute, I did . . . and knew all these things. . . .

'So long, monks, as this eightfold series of knowledge and vision of the gods was not fully purified in me, I was uncertain whether I had attained to unsurpassed, highest enlightenment in the world of gods, Māra, Brahmā, or in the world of men with its recluses and priests, gods and men. But when the eightfold series of knowledge and vision was fully purified, I was certain that in the world of gods, Māra, and Brahmā, and among re-cluses and priests, gods and men, my enlightenment was unsurpassed and complete. Then knowledge and vision arose in me, and I knew: "Firm and irrevocable is my heart's release. This is my last birth; there is no more becoming for me." '

(Vol. 4, VIII, VII, Ch. 64)

8

Thus have I heard: Once the venerable Sāriputra dwelt near Rājagaha at the squirrels' feeding-ground in the bamboo grove. There he addressed the monks saying: 'Nirvāna, my brothers, is happiness. Nirvāna, my brothers, is happiness.'

Now when he had thus spoken, the venerable Udāyi said to him:

'But how, my brother, can there be happiness when feelings no longer exist?'

'When feelings no longer exist, O brother, verily just that is happiness.'

(Vol. 4, IX, IV, Ch. 34)

9

DHAMMAPADA

(Verse 276)

> You yourself must make the effort;
> Buddhas do but point the way.
> Living mindful, meditating,
> You escape from Māra's sway.

IO

DĪGHA-NIKĀYA

(30) There are, monks, some ascetics and Brahmins who are eternalists, and who on four grounds proclaim that both the self and the world are eternal. And what are those four grounds? (31) In the first place, monks, some ascetics and Brahmins by means of ardour, of exertion, of devotion, of mindful earnestness, of right mental effort reach such concentration of heart that they recall various former existences (of their transmigrations)—in one birth, or in two, or three, or four, or five, . . . ten, twenty . . . fifty, a hundred, a thousand . . . or in several thousand or hundred thousand existences—to the effect that he knows: 'There I had such and such a name, was of such and such a family and caste, lived on such and such food, experienced such and such happiness and pain, and lived to such and such an age. And when I deceased from that existence, I was reborn in such and such other . . .' Thus he recalls his various previous existences in full detail. And so he says to himself: 'Eternal is my self; and the world, bringing forth nothing new, is steadfast as a mountain, unwavering as a pillar firmly fixed. Though living beings move hither and thither, decease and reappear, transmigrating in *samsāra*, it is after all eternally the same. It is for this reason that I can recall, by means of ardour, of exertion . . . various former existences. . . . And therefore I know that my self and the world are eternal, bringing forth nothing new, steadfast as a mountain, unwavering as a pillar firmly fixed. And that, though living beings move hither and thither, decease and reappear, transmigrating in *samsāra*, it remains after all eternally the same.'

(32) What is the second case of the eternalists? Some ascetic or Brahmin by means of ardour, of exertion, of devotion, of mindful earnestness, of right mental effort reaches such concentration of heart that he recalls various former existences (of his transmigration)—one world cycle, two, three, four, five, ten world cycles: 'There I had such and such a name, was of such and such family and caste . . .'.
And therefore he proclaims: 'Eternal is my self, and the world . . .'.
(33) What is the third case of the eternalists? Ten, twenty, thirty, forty world cycles. . . .
(34) What is the fourth case of the eternalists? In this case an ascetic or Brahmin is addicted to logic and reasoning. He proclaims the following conclusion derived from his argumentative logical sophistry: 'Eternal is the self, and the world bringing forth nothing new, is steadfast as a mountain, unwavering as a pillar firmly fixed. Though living beings move hither and thither, decease and reappear, transmigrating in *samsāra*, it is after all eternally the same.'
(35) These, monks, are those ascetics and Brahmins who are eternalists, and who on four grounds proclaim that both the self and the world are eternal. All without exception do so in these four ways, or in the one or other of the same. There are no other than these four.
(36) Now, monks, the *tathāgata* knows that these speculations, thus arrived at and diligently fostered, will have such and such result, and such and such effect on future rebirths. That the *tathāgata* knows, and also what is beyond this knowledge. But he does not value such knowledge, for in his heart is another knowledge, the knowledge of liberation. And since he in truth has understood and realized the arising and disappearing of feelings, their pleasure and pain, and how to become free of them he is liberated, is the *tathāgata*.
(37) These, monks, are those other things, profound, difficult to realize, hard to understand, peaceful and sublime, not to be grasped by mere logic, subtle, comprehensible to the wise only. Those the *tathāgata* has realized, has seen face to face, and is proclaiming them. And it is concerning these that the *tathāgata* is rightly praised.
(Vol. 2, 1, 1, 30)

II

Then the one who was first reborn, thinks thus to himself: 'I am Brahmā, the Great Brahmā, the Supreme One, the Mighty, the All-seeing, the Ruler, the Lord of all, the Maker, the Creator, the Chief of all, appointing to each his place, the Ancient of days, the Father of all that is and will be. These beings are of my creation. And why is that so? A while ago I thought: "Would that other beings, too, might come to this existence! This was my heart's desire, and here are the beings now, come into existence." And those beings themselves think thus: "This is the revered Brahmā, the Great Brahmā, the Supreme One. . . . The revered Brahmā created us all. For as we see, he was here first, and we came after him." '
(Vol. 2, 1, 2, 5)

I2

(19) There are, monks, ascetics and Brahmins who hold the doctrine of Nirvāna existing already in the visible world, and who in five ways maintain true Nirvāna, in this visible world, of an existing self.

(20) Hereon, monks, some ascetic or Brahmin may have the following opinion, the following view: 'Whensoever this self, in full enjoyment and possession of the five sense pleasures, indulges in them, the self has attained true Nirvāna in this visible world.' Thus do some maintain true Nirvāna, in this visible world, of an existing self.

(21) To him another says: 'There is, Venerable One, this self you describe. I do not deny it. But the self does not attain true Nirvāna in the way you describe. And why not? The sense pleasures are transitory, they involve pain, their very nature is to fluctuate. And grief, lamentation, pain, sorrow and woe arise out of their inconsistency and change. But whensoever the self, putting away sense pleasures and evil dispositions, enters into and abides in the first Jhāna, the state of joy and happiness, born of detachment, accompanied by purposeful reflection and investigation, then has the self attained true Nirvāna in this visible world.'

(22) To him another says: 'There is, Venerable One, this self you describe. I do not deny it. But the self does not attain true Nirvāna in the way you describe. And why not? Because inasmuch as that state involves reasoning and investigation it is stamped as gross. But whensoever the self, abandoning both reason and investigation, enters into and abides in the second Jhāna, the state of joy and happiness, without reflection or investigation, born of serenity, a state of inner calm productive of elevation and unification of the heart, then the self has attained true Nirvāna in this visible world.'

(23) To him another says: 'There is, Venerable One, this self you describe. I do not deny it. But the self does not attain true Nirvāna in the way you describe. And why not? Because inasmuch as that state involves the sense of joy, and exhilaration of heart, it is stamped as gross. But whensoever the self transcends joy and remains detached, mindful and self-possessed, experiences happiness physically and so enters into and abides in the third Jhāna which the *arahats* call "detached, concentrated, and happy", then has the self attained true Nirvāna in this visible world.'

(24) To him another says: 'There is, Venerable One, this self you describe. I do not deny it. But the self does not attain true Nirvāna in the way you describe. And why not? Because inasmuch as that state involves constant awareness of happiness it is stamped as gross. But whensoever the self, by putting away happiness, by putting away pain, by the previous dying away of both joy and grief, has entered into and abides in the fourth Jhāna—a state made pure by self-possession and equanimity, without pain, and without happiness—then the self has attained true Nirvāna in this visible world.'

(25) Monks, these are the ascetics and Brahmins who hold the doctrine of Nirvāna existing already in the visible world, and who in five ways maintain true Nirvāna of an existing self in this visible world. All maintain it in those five ways, and there is no other except these five.

(26) Now, monks, the *tathāgata* knows . . . (identical with extract 10, 36, above).

These, monks, are those other things, profound . . . (identical with 10, 37, above).

Vol. 2, 3, 19–26.

13

(81) And it was not long, Kevaddha, before the Great Brahmā appeared. The monk drew close and asked: 'Where, friend, do the four great elements—earth, water, fire, and air—cease, leaving no trace behind?' The Great Brahmā replied: 'I, monk, am Brahmā, the great Brahmā, the Supreme, the Mighty, the All-seeing, the Ruler, the Lord of all, the Controller, the Creator, the Chief of all, appointing to each his place, the Ancient of days, the Father of all that is and will be.'

(82) Again the monk asked Brahmā: 'I did not query, friend, whether you are indeed Brahmā, the Great Brahmā, the Mighty . . ., but rather as to where the four elements earth, water, fire, and air, cease, leaving no trace behind.' Again Brahmā answered: 'I am Brahmā, the Great Brahmā . . .'.

(83) And a third time the monk addressed Brahmā: 'I did not query, friend, whether you are indeed Brahmā, the Great Brahmā . . . but rather as to where the four elements of earth, water, fire, and air cease, leaving no trace behind.' Then the Great Brahmā took that monk by the arm and led him aside, and said: 'These gods of the Brahmā world here, monk, hold that there is nothing I cannot see, nothing I do not know, and nothing that is not manifest to me. Therefore I did not answer you in their presence. I do not know, monk, where the four elements of earth, water, fire, and air cease without leaving a trace. You have acted wrong, you have done ill by ignoring the Exalted One and going elsewhere to find an answer to your question. Go now to the Exalted One, ask him your question, and accept his answer.'

(Vol. 2, 11, 81–83)

14

(14) 'Then you say, Vāsettha, that none of the Brahmins, or of their teachers, or of their teachers' teachers even up to the seventh generation, has ever seen Brahmā face to face. And that even the Rishis of old, such as Atthaka, Vāmaka, Vāmadeva, Vessāmitta, Yamataggi, Angirasa, Bhāradvāja, Vāsettha, Kassapa, Bhagu, the authors and utterers of the verses, of the ancient forms of words which the Brahmins of today so carefully

intone and recite precisely as they have been handed down—even they did not maintain to know or have seen where or whence or whither Brahmā is. Thus the present-day Brahmins, versed in the *Three Vedas*, proclaim: "What we know not, what we have not seen, to a state of union with that we can show the way, and can say 'This is the straight path, this is the direct way which makes for liberation, and leads him who follows it to union with Brahmā'". What do you think, Vāsettha? Does it not follow that the talk of the Brahmins, versed though they be in the *Three Vedas*, turns out to be foolish talk?'

'So it is, Venerable Gautama.'

(15) 'Verily, Vāsettha, that Brahmins versed in the *Three Vedas* should be able to show the way to a state of union with that which they do not know, neither have seen—such a condition of things can in no wise be. It is as when a string of blind men clings one to another, the foremost cannot see, neither can the middle one see, nor can the hindmost see—just so is the talk of the Brahmins versed in the *Three Vedas* but blind talk: the first sees not, the middle one sees not, nor can the last see. The talk then of these Brahmins versed in the *Three Vedas* turns out to be ridiculous, mere words, a vain and empty thing.'

(16) 'Now what do you think, Vāsettha? Can the Brahmins versed in the *Three Vedas* like other, ordinary people, see sun and moon, and do they pray to and worship them, and do they with folded hands turn towards the places whence they rise and where they set?'

'Yes, Venerable Gautama.'

(17) 'Now what do you think, Vāsettha? The Brahmins versed in the *Three Vedas* who like other, ordinary people see the sun and the moon, and pray to and worship them, and with folded hands turn towards the places whence they rise and where they set—can those Brahmins point out the way to a state of union with this sun and moon, saying: "This is the straight path, this is the direct way which makes for liberation, and leads him who follows it to a state of union with sun or moon?" '

'No, Venerable Gautama.'

(18) 'Then you say, Vāsettha, that the Brahmins are not able to point out the way to union with that which in common with other ordinary people they really see, sun and moon and the places whence they arise and where they set. . . . And you ad-

mitted that none of the Brahmins, or of their teachers, or of
their teachers' teachers even up to the seventh generation,
has ever seen Brahmā face to face. And that even the Rishis of
old, such as Atthaka . . . did not maintain to know or have
seen where or whence or whither Brahmā is. And so, in fact,
these Brahmins versed in the *Three Vedas* proclaim: What we
know not, what we have not seen, to a state of union with that
we can show the way, and can say: "This is the straight path,
this is the direct way which makes for liberation, and leads him
who follows it to union with Brahmā." What do you think,
Vāsettha? Does it not follow that the talk of the Brahmins,
versed though they be in the *Three Vedas*, turns out to be
foolish talk?'

'So it is, Venerable Gautama.'

'Very good, Vāsettha. That the Brahmins versed in the *Three
Vedas* should be able to show the way to a state of union with
that which they do not know, neither have seen—such a condition of things can in no wise be.'

(19) 'Just, Vāsettha, as if a man should say: "I love the most
beautiful woman in the land, and wish to make her my own."
And people should ask him, "This most beautiful woman in the
land, whom you so love and wish to make your own, do you
know whether that beautiful woman is a noble lady, or a Brahmin woman, or of the trader caste, or a Sūdra?" But when so
asked, he should answer "No". And when asked: "Friend. This
most beautiful woman in the land, whom you so love and wish
to make your own, do you know what the name of that most
beautiful woman is, or what is her family, whether she be tall
or short or of medium height, whether her skin is black, dark,
or fair, or in what village or town or city she lives?" And when
so asked, he should again answer "No". Being finally asked:
"So then, friend, whom you know not, neither have seen, her
do you love and wish to make her your own?", he should
answer "Yes". What do you think, Vāsettha? Would it not
follow that the talk of that man was foolish talk?'

'So it is, Lord.'

(20) 'And just so, Vāsettha, as you admit, none has ever seen
Brahmā face to face, not one of the Brahmins though versed
they be in the *Three Vedas*, nor . . .' (as in (18) above).

(Vol. 2, 13, 14–20)

148

15

(22) And the Exalted One seated himself on the seat prepared for him; and when he was seated, he addressed the venerable Ānanda, and said: 'Please, Ānanda, fetch me some water, for I am thirsty and would like a drink.' The venerable Ānanda replied: 'But just now, lord, about five hundred carts have crossed over. The water in the shallow brook here is stirred up by the wheels, and is foul and turbid. But over there, lord, not far away, is the Kakutthā river with clear, pleasant, cool, and fresh water, easy to get to, and delightful. There the Exalted One may both drink and bathe.'

(23) And a second time the Exalted One addressed the venerable Ānanda and said: 'Please, Ānanda, fetch me some water, for I am thirsty and would like a drink.' Again the venerable Ānanda replied: 'But just now, lord, about five hundred . . .'

(24) And a third time the Exalted One addressed the venerable Ānanda and said: 'Please, Ānanda, fetch me some water, for I am thirsty and would like a drink.' 'Yes, lord,' now obediently replied Ānanda, took the bowl and went down to the brook. And behold, the little brook which had been stirred up by the wheels and become foul and turbid, was now flowing clear and bright, and free from all turbidity.

(25) Ānanda thought: 'How wonderful, how marvellous is the miraculous might and power of the *tathāgata*! This brook, stirred up . . . now as I come up to it, runs clear and bright, and free from all turbidity.' And taking water in the bowl, he returned to the Exalted One, and said: 'How wonderful, how marvellous is the miraculous might and power of the *tathāgata*! Let the Exalted One drink the water! Let him who trod the path to the very end, drink the water!' And the Exalted One drank the water.

(Vol. 3, 16, 4, 22–25)

16

Now the Exalted One addressed the venerable Ānanda and said: 'It may be, Ānanda, that in some of you the thought may arise: "The word of the master is ended, we no longer have

a teacher." But it is not thus, Ānanda, that you should regard it. The teaching, and the rules of the order which I have set forth and laid down for you all, let them be your teacher after I am gone.'
(Vol. 3, 16, 6, 1)

17

At that period, monks, there will arise in the world an Exalted One named Metteyya, *arahat*, fully awakened, full of wisdom and a perfect guide, himself having trodden the path to the very end; with knowledge of the worlds, unsurpassed as an educator, teacher of gods and men, an Exalted Buddha, just as in the present period I am now. From his own understanding and penetration of it, he will proclaim (the nature of) this universe with its gods, Māras, and gods of the Brahmā worlds, and (the nature of) living beings including ascetics, Brahmins, gods and men, just as I proclaim them from my own understanding and penetration of it. And he will proclaim the teaching that is lovely in its origin, lovely in its progress, and lovely in its consummation; he will proclaim it both in the essence of its meaning and in its outward form; the higher life will he make known in all its fullness and in all its purity, even as I do now. He will be the head of an order of many thousand monks, just as in the present period I am the head of an order of many hundreds.
(Vol. 4, 26, 25)

JĀTAKA STORIES

18

The God of Rain

At that instant Sakka's stone throne covered with yellow drapings grew hot beneath him, and he sought to discover the cause. Realizing what was the matter, he summoned the king of the gods of the storm clouds and said: 'Friend, the Master is standing on the steps of the Jetavana lotus pond and wishes to bathe. Make haste and pour down rain in a single torrent over all the

kingdom of Kosala.' Obediently the king clad himself in one cloud as an undergarment, and another cloud as an outer garment, and chanting the rain-song, he darted eastward. He appeared in the east as a cloud as large as a threshing-floor which grew and grew till it was as big as a hundred, as a thousand threshing-floors; and he thundered and lightened, and then let it rain, let it pour down as if a water-pot had been turned over. The deluge was all over Kosala. Unbroken was the downpour, quickly filling the lotus pond of Jetavana, and stopping only when the water was level with the topmost step.
(*Jāt.* 75, introd.)

19

Once upon a time when Brahmadatta was reigning in Benares, the Bodhisattva was born a Brahmin in the north country, and on the day of his birth his parents lit a birth-fire. In his sixteenth year, they addressed him thus: 'Son, on the day of your birth we lit a birth-fire for you. Now choose. If you wish to lead the family life, learn the *Three Vedas*; but if you wish to attain to the Brahmā realm, take your fire with you into the forest and there tend it, so as to win Mahā Brahmā's favour and hereafter to enter into the Brahmā realm.' Telling his parents that the family life had no charms for him, he went into the forest and dwelt in a hermitage tending his fire.

One day an ox was given him in the nearby village, and when he had driven it home to his hermitage, the thought came to him to sacrifice it to Agni, Lord of Fire. But finding that he had no salt, and feeling that the Lord of Fire could not eat his meat-offering without it, he resolved to go back and bring a supply from the village. While he was gone, a band of hunters came up and, seeing the ox, killed him and roasted themselves a dinner. And what they did not eat they carried off, leaving only the tail and hide, and the shanks.

Finding only these sorry remains on his return, the Brahmin exclaimed: 'As this Exalted Agni cannot so much as look after his own, how shall he look after me? It is a waste of time to serve him, bringing neither good nor profit.' Having lost all desire to tend Fire, he said: 'My Lord of Fire, if you cannot manage to protect yourself, how shall you protect me? The

meat being gone, you must make shift with what remains.'
So saying, he threw on the fire the tail and the rest of the
robbers' leavings and uttered this stanza:

'You unwise knower of beings,* here's the tail for you;
And think yourself in luck to get so much.
The prime meat's gone; put up with tail today.'

So saying, the Great Being put the fire out with water, and
renounced the world after the way of the wise ones. And thus
he won perfection and knowledge, and attained the Brahmā
world.
(*Jāt.* 144)

20

If there exists some Lord all powerful to fulfil
In every creature bliss or woe, and action good or ill,
That Lord is stained with sin. Man does but work his will.
(From *Jāt.* 528)

21

Talk Against the Brahmins' Sacrificial Cults

He [the Bodhisattva] gathered all the Nāga multitude together,
and scolded Arittha thus: 'Arittha, you have spoken falsely
when you described the Vedas, the sacrifices, and the Brahmins;
for the sacrifice of victims by Brahmins according to Vedic rules
is not held to be desirable, and it does not lead to a heavenly
realm. See what unreality there is in your words.' And he
repeated the *gāthās* describing the various kinds of sacrifice:

These Veda studies are the wise man's toils,
The lure which tempts the victims whom he spoils;

A mirage formed to catch the careless eye,
But which the prudent passes safely by.

The Vedas have no hidden power to save
The traitor, or the coward or the knave;

* Another name for Agni.

The fire, though tended well for long years past,
Leaves his base master without hope at last.

Though all earth's trees in one vast heap were piled
To satisfy the fire's insatiate child,

Still would it crave for more, insatiate still—
How could a Nāga hope that maw to fill?

Milk ever changes—thus where milk has been
Butter and curds in natural course are seen;

And the same thirst for change pervades the fire,
Once stirred to life it mounts still higher and higher.

Fire bursts not forth in wood that's dry or new,
Fire needs an effort ere it leaps to view;

If dry, fresh timber of itself could burn,
Spontaneous would each forest blaze in turn.

If he wins merit who to feed the flame
Piles wood and straw, the merit is the same

When cooks light fires or blacksmiths at their trade
Or those who burn the corpses of the dead.

But none, however zealously he prays
Or heaps the fuel round to feed the blaze,

Gains any merit by his mummeries—
The fire for all its crest of smoke soon dies.

Were fire the honoured being that you think,
Would it thus dwell with refuse and with stink,

Feeding on carrion with a foul delight,
Where men in horror hasten from the sight?

Some worship as a god the crested flame,
Barbarians give to water that high name;

But both alike have wandered from their road:
Neither is worthy to be called a god.

To worship fire, the common drudge of all,
Senseless and blind and deaf to every call,

And then one's self to live a life of sin—
How could one dream that this a heaven could win?

These Brahmins all a livelihood require,
And so they tell us Brahmā worships fire;

Why should the increate who all things planned
Worship himself the creature of his hand?

Doctrines and rules of their own, absurd and vain,
Our sires imagined wealth and power to gain;

'Brahmins he made for study; for command
He made the Khattiyas; Vessas plough the land;

Suddas he servants made to obey the rest;
Thus from the first went forth his high behest.'

We see these rules enforced before our eyes,
None but the Brahmins offer sacrifice,

None but the Khattiya exercises sway,
The Vessas plough, the Suddas must obey.

These greedy liars propagate deceit,
And fools believe the fictions they repeat;

He who has eyes can see the sickening sight;
Why does not Brahmā set his creatures right?

If his wide power no limit can restrain,
Why is his hand so rarely spread to bless?

Why are his creatures all condemned to pain?
Why does he not to all give happiness?

Why do fraud, lies, and ignorance prevail?
Why triumphs falsehood—truth and justice fail?

I count your Brahmā one th' injust among,
Who made a world in which to shelter wrong.

Those men are counted pure who only kill
Frogs, worms, bees, snakes or insects as they will—

These are your savage customs which I hate—
Such as Kamboja* hordes might emulate.

* A north-western tribe, considered barbarians.

Then he continued to show up their falsehood:

If he who kills is counted innocent
And if the victim safe to heaven is sent,

Let Brahmins Brahmins kill—so all were well—
And those who listen to the words they tell.

We see no cattle asking to be slain
That they a new and better life may gain—

Rather they go unwilling to their death
And in vain struggles yield their latest breath.

To veil the post, the victim and the blow
The Brahmins let their choicest rhetoric flow;

'The post shall as a cow of plenty be
Securing all thy heart's desires to thee;'

But if the wood thus round their victim spread
Had been as full of treasure as they said,

As full of silver, gold and gems for us,
With heaven's unknown delights as overplus,

They would have offered for themselves alone
And kept the rich reversion as their own.

These cruel cheats, as ignorant as vile,
Weave their long frauds the simple to beguile,

'Offer thy wealth, cut nails and beard and hair,
And thou shalt have thy bosom's fondest prayer.'

The offerer, simple to the heart's content,
Comes with his purse, they gather round him fast,

Like crows around an owl, on mischief bent,
And leave him bankrupt and stripped bare at last,

The solid coin which he erewhile possessed,
Exchanged for promises which none can test.

Like grasping strangers sent by those who reign
The cultivators' earnings to distrain,

These rob wherever they prowl with evil eye—
No law condemns them, yet they ought to die.

The priest a shoot of Butea* must hold
As part o' the rite sacred from days of old;

Indra's right arm 'tis called; but were it so
Would Indra triumph o'er his demon foe?

Indra's own arm can give him better aid,
'Twas no vain sham which made hell's hosts afraid.

'Each mountain range which now some kingdom guards
Was once a heap in ancient altar-yards,

And pious worshippers with patient hands
Piled up the mound at some great lord's commands.'

So Brahmins say—fie on the idle boast,
Mountains are heaped aloft at other cost;

And the brick mound, search as you may, contains
No veins of iron for the miner's pains.

A holy seer well known in ancient days,
On the seashore was praying, legend says;

There was he drowned, and since this fate befell
The ocean's waves have been undrinkable.

Rivers have drowned their learned men at will
By hundreds and have kept their waters still;

Their streams flow on and never taste the worse,
Why should the sea alone incur the curse?

And the salt streams which run upon the land
Spring from no curse but own the digger's hand.

At first there were no women and no men;
'Twas mind first brought mankind to light—and then,

Though they all started equal in the race,
Their various failures made them soon change place;

* A tree, *Butea frondosa*.

It was no lack of merit in the past,
But present faults which made them first or last.

A clever low-caste lad would use his wit,
And read the hymns nor find his head-piece split;

The Brahmins made the Vedas to their cost
When others gained the knowledge which they lost.

Thus sentences are made and learned by rote
In metric forms not easily forgot—

The obscurity but tempts the foolish mind,
They swallow all they're told with impulse blind.

Brahmins are not like violent beasts of prey,
No tigers, lions of the woods are they;

They are to cows and oxen near akin,
Differing outside they are as dull within.

If the victorious king would cease to fight
And live in peace with his friends and follow right,

Conquering those passions which his bosom rend,
What happy lives would all his subjects spend!

The Brahmin's Veda, Khattiya's policy,
Both arbitrary and delusive be,

They blindly grope their way along a road
By some huge inundation overflowed.

In Brahmin's Veda, Khattiya's policy,
One secret meaning we alike can see;

For after all, loss, gain and glory, and shame
Touch the four castes alike, to all the same.

As householders to gain a livelihood
Count all pursuits legitimate and good,

So Brahmins now in our degenerate day
Will gain a livelihood in any way.

The householder is led by love of gain,
Blindly he follows, dragged in pleasure's train,

Trying all trades, deceitful and a fool,
Fallen, alas, how far from wisdom's rule.

The Great Being, having thus confuted their arguments, established his own doctrine; and when they heard his exposition the assembly of Nāgas was filled with joy. The Great Being delivered the hunter-Brahmin from the Nāga world, and did not utter one contemptuous word.

(From *Jāt.* 543)

MAJJHĪMA NIKĀYA

22

You would cling to what is eternal, permanent, not subject to change. You would embrace a teaching of Self which frees the believer from grief and pain. Do you know such a thing, or such a teaching? I know of none. And as there is no such self, nor anything pertaining to it, how could it, in fact, be attained? This being so, it follows that a teaching proclaiming: 'The world and the self are the same; to that I shall attain after death—imperishable, permanent, eternal', is but a foolish teaching.

23

Thus have I heard. Once while the venerable Mahāmoggallāna was staying in the Bhagga country at Sumsumāragira in Bhesakalā wood in the deer park, he was pacing to and fro in the open when Māra, the Evil One, entered his belly and got into his stomach. Wondering why his belly should feel as heavy as a sack of beans, Mahāmoggallāna, his walk over, went to his cell and sat down to think it out by himself. Detecting Māra's presence in his inside, he exclaimed:
'Begone, Evil Māra, begone! Do not annoy a truth-finder, or a truth-finder's disciple, lest you lay up for yourself enduring hurt and harm.'
Thought Māra to himself: 'This recluse says all this without knowing or discerning that it is I. Why, even his master would take time to know it was I; and how should this disciple know?'
Hereon Mahāmoggallāna said to Māra, the Evil One:

'Yes, I know you, Evil One. Imagine not that I do not. You are Māra, the Evil One; and you are thinking that it was without knowing or discerning that it was you, that I bade you begone and not annoy a truth-finder, or a truth-finder's disciple, lest you should lay up for yourself enduring hurt and harm; but you imagine that even my master would take time to know it was you; and how should a disciple know?'

'So this recluse really does know and discern that it is I', thought Māra; and he issued from Mahāmoggallāna's mouth and perched on the crutch to hold the door bar. And the venerable Mahāmoggallāna saw Māra, the Evil One, there and addressed him:

'Thus I see you here, Evil One! Let go the hope "He does not see me", for there, Evil One, you crouch on the door bar.'

(From 50)

24

Ānanda: 'Have you ever heard of the thirty-three gods?'

Vidūdabha: 'Oh, yes. And so has king Pasenadi.'

'Tell me, can king Pasenadi expel or banish the thirty-three gods from their abodes?'

'Why, he cannot even see them, much less expel or banish them.'

'Just in the same way, the malign gods cannot even see the benign gods, much less expel or banish them from their abodes.'

Now the king asked the Exalted One the name of this monk.

'He is called Ānanda.' 'Ānanda, the joyous', said the king, 'and joyous he looks! What the venerable Ānanda said seems to be well reasoned. Further, lord, does Brahmā exist?'

'Sire, why do you ask whether Brahmā exists?'

'I ask whether Brahmā will appear in this world, or not?'

'A malign Brahmā will, a benign Brahmā does not.'

(From 90)

25

Now the Exalted One looked at Kāpathika, and Kāpathika said:

'The verses and hymns transmitted from the Brahmins of old along the line of unbroken oral transmission, those only the Brahmins admit as truth; everything else is vain. What does the Lord Gautama say?'

The Exalted one said: 'Tell me, is there among all the Brahmins a single one who claims that he personally sees and knows that this alone is truth, and everything else is vain?'

'No, Lord Gautama.'

'Or is there a single teacher of Brahmins, or a teacher of teachers, back to the seventh generation, who can claim that he personally sees and knows that this alone is truth, and everything else is vain?'

'No, Lord Gautama.'

'Or the Rishis of old, who composed the verses and hymns, such as Atthaka, Vāmaka, Vāmadeva, Vessāmitta, Yamataggi, Angirasa, Bhāradvāja, Vāsettha, Kassapa, Bhagu—did they claim personally to see and know that this alone is truth, and everything else is vain?'

'No, Lord Gautama.'

'It is like a string of blind men, each holding on to his neighbour, the first cannot see, nor can the one in the middle, nor can the hindmost. Such a string of blind men, methinks, is the Brahmin tradition, wherein the first never saw, nor did the one in the middle see, nor does the last. This being so, does it not follow that the Brahmins' belief is groundless?'

Kāpathika replied: 'It is not faith alone which inspires Brahmins, but also the tradition they have inherited.' 'At the outset you based yourself on faith,' said the Exalted One, 'and now you are shifting to authority. There are five activities which are ambiguous in this world, to wit: to believe, to like, to reiterate, to consider carefully, and to examine patiently. One may firmly believe something, and yet this may prove to be in itself empty, vain and false; or a thing may fail to inspire belief but yet in itself prove real, veritable and sure. One likes something, and yet in itself it may prove to be empty, vain and false; or a thing may fail to please but yet in itself prove real, veritable and sure. One reiterates something well, one considers it carefully, one examines it patiently, and yet in itself it may prove to be empty, vain and false; or if one does not reiterate something well, does not consider it carefully, not examine it patiently it may prove real, veritable and sure. Maintenance of truth does not entitle an intelligent man to aver that here alone resides all truth and that everything else is vain.'

Then Kāpathika said: 'Please tell me, Lord Gautama, how then can one secure maintenance of truth?'

The Exalted One replied: 'If a man has faith, then in his profession of faith he maintains the truth he has but does not claim absolutely that this is all the truth and that everything else is vain. Or if a man likes something and then says "I like this", or if he reiterates something and says "I reiterate this", or if he considers and says "I have considered this", or if he patiently examines something and says "I have examined this", he maintains the truth he has, but does not claim absolutely that this is all the truth and that everything else is vain. By this means I teach how to maintain the truth, but this is not even approaching truth.'

(From 95)

26

Sangārava: 'Fruitful indeed and noble was your striving, Lord Gautama, worthy of an all-enlightened *arahat*. But tell me, Lord Gautama, are there gods?

The Exalted One: 'It is clearly observable whether there are gods.'

'Why do you give that answer to my question, Gautama? You reply "It is clearly observable whether there are gods". Then, is it false and untrue?'

'Anyone who, when asked if gods there be, answers that there are gods, and that this is clearly observable—why an intelligent man will arrive at the same conclusion as to whether there are gods.'

'Why did you not make this clear at the outset, Lord Gautama?'

'The world is loud in agreement that there are gods.'

(From 107)

27

At this point Ganaka-Moggallāna asked the Exalted One whether, with his guidance and instruction by him, all his disciples or only some of them attained to Nirvāna. The

Exalted One said: 'Some attain to Nirvāna, and some do not.'
Ganaka-Moggallāna asked further: 'What is the cause and condition why, though Nirvāna exists and the road to it exists
and you show the way, it is only some and not all disciples
who, with this guidance and instruction, succeed in attaining
Nirvāna?'
'That leads me to ask you a counter-question. Please answer
it as you deem fit. Do you know the way to Rājagaha?'
'Yes, I do.'
'Suppose there came to you a man who wanted to go to Rājagaha, and asked you to tell him the way thither; and suppose
you told him: "This way leads to Rājagaha, continue on it for
a while, and you will first see a certain village, then a certain
township a little further on, and again a little further on you
will see Rājagaha with its lovely park, pleasant wood, the fine
lawns, and the lotus pond." Suppose further that with this
guidance and instruction from you, that man took a wrong
turning at a cross-road and went in the opposite direction.
Suppose now a second man came to you who wanted to go to
Rājagaha and you told him the route exactly as you had told
the first man; and suppose that with this guidance and instruction from you, he got safely to Rājagaha. So then, what is the
cause and condition why, while Rājagaha exists, and the road
to it exists, and you tell them the way, that one man reaches
Rājagaha and the other not?'
'What more can I do, Lord Gautama? I only indicate the way.'
'Just in the same way, Brahmin, while Nirvāna exists and the
road to it exists and I tell them the way, some of my disciples
do, and others do not, succeed with this guidance to attain
Nirvāna. What more can I do? I only indicate the way.'
(From 107)

MILINDA-PANHA

28

Nāgasena's Study of the Vedas
Then the Brahmin Sonuttara gave a teacher's fee of a thousand
coins to a Brahmin teacher, and when he had had a sleeping
place prepared in a well-separated room inside the house, he

spoke thus to the Brahmin teacher: 'You, Brahmin, must make this boy study the hymns and chants.'

And the Brahmin teacher chanted them and ordered the boy to learn them by heart, and young Nāgasena did so. After no more than a single repetition the *Three Vedas* were learned by heart, properly intoned in voice, properly remembered in sequence, properly pondered. And by himself he gained insight into the *Three Vedas* with their vocabularies and rituals, with the phonology and exegesis, and the oral traditions as the fifth. And he became familiar with the words and the grammar, and well acquainted with the science of nature, and with the marks of a great man.

Then the boy Nāgasena said thus to his father: 'Father, is there anything else to be learned in this Brahmin caste, or is this all there is?'

'Dear Nāgasena, there is nothing further.'

Then the boy Nāgasena, having passed his teacher's examination, left the house and due to an inborn inclination, driven by an inner urge, went into the forest to live the homeless life. There, dwelling in solitude, he meditated on his learning and his knowledge. Pondering the Vedas and finding them empty as to their origination, content, and consummation, he became sad and unhappy. 'Empty indeed are these Vedas, void indeed are these Vedas, without pith and gist.'

(Vol. I, p. 14)

29

As Nirvāna is not born of a cause, how can there be a way to the realization of it?

'In the world, venerable Nāgasena, things are produced by karmic action, or by cause, or by temperature. Tell me, what in the world is not produced by karmic action, by cause, or by temperature?'

'In the world there are these two, sire, which are neither produced by karmic action, nor by cause, nor by temperature: space and Nirvāna.'

'Do not, venerable Nāgasena, misuse the words of the Victorious One. Do not explain the problem without understanding it.'

'But what have I said, sire, that you thus speak to me?'

'Is it correct, venerable Nāgasena, to assert that Nirvāna and space are not produced by either karmic action, nor cause, nor by temperature? The Exalted One repeatedly pointed out the way to the realization of Nirvāna to his disciples. And yet you maintain that Nirvāna is not born from cause?'

'It is true, sire, the Exalted One repeatedly pointed out the way to the realization of Nirvāna to his disciples. But he did not point out a cause for the arising of Nirvāna.'

'Here, venerable Nāgasena, we are entering from darkness into greater darkness . . . if you maintain that though there be a means to the realization of Nirvāna, yet there is no cause for the arising of it (more accurately: of this *dharma* or factor of being: *dhamma*). If there is . . . a means to the realization of Nirvāna, then a cause for Nirvāna is required too. Inasmuch as there is the father of a child, for that reason one would require also a father of the father . . . inasmuch, sire, if there be a cause for the realization of Nirvāna, for that reason one would require a cause also for the arising of Nirvāna. . . .'

'Nirvāna, sire, does not arise; therefore, a cause for the arising of Nirvāna has not been pointed out.'

'Please, venerable Nāgasena, present some proof, convince me by plausible reason so that I may know: There is a cause for the realization of Nirvāna; there is no cause for the arising of Nirvāna.'

'Well then, sire, lend an attentive ear, listen closely and I will tell you the reason for this. Would a man, sire, with his natural strength, be able to go up from here to a Himalaya, a monarch of mountains?'

'Yes, venerable sir.'

'But would that man, sire, with his natural strength be able to bring a Himalaya, a monarch of mountains, here?'

'O no, venerable sir.'

'Would it be possible for a man who with his natural strength has crossed the great sea in a ship to reach the farther shore?'

'Yes, venerable sir.'

'But would it be possible, sire, for that man with his natural strength to bring the farther shore of the great sea here?'

'O no, venerable sir.'

'Even so, sire, it is possible to point out the way for the realization of Nirvāna, but impossible to show a cause for the arising of

Nirvāna. For what reason? Because of the uncreatedness of the Law (more accurately: *dharma* or factor of being).'

'Is then, venerable Nāgasena, Nirvāna uncreated?'

'Yes, sire, Nirvāna is uncreated; it has not been created. One cannot say of Nirvāna, sire, that it has arisen or that it has not arisen, or that it can arise, or that it is past, present or future, or that it is cognizable by the eye or the ear or the nose or the tongue or the body.'

'In that case, venerable Nāgasena, you explain Nirvāna as something non-existent and indicate that Nirvāna is not.'

'Nirvāna is, sire. Nirvāna is realized by mind (*manoviññeyyam*). A noble disciple, practising rightly, with a mind that has become purified, lofty, straight, freed, transcending, sees Nirvāna.'

'But, venerable sir, what is this Nirvāna like? Please convince me by reason, inasmuch as its existence can be illustrated by analogies.'

'Is there, sire, what is called wind?'

'Yes, venerable sir.'

'Please, sire, show me the wind, and explain its colour and form, and tell me whether it is thin or thick, long or short.'

'It is not possible, venerable Nāgasena, for the wind to be shown. For the wind does not lend itself to being grasped by the hands or to being touched. But yet that "wind" is.'

'If it is not possible, sire, for the wind to be shown, well then, the wind is not.'

'I know, venerable Nāgasena, that there is wind; I am convinced of it in my heart, but I am not able to point out the wind.'

'Even so, sire, Nirvāna is, though it is not possible to point out Nirvāna, nor to explain it by colour and form.'

'Excellent, venerable Nāgasena. Well pointed out is the simile, well expressed the argument. Thus it is, therefore do I accept it: there is Nirvāna.'

(Vol. 2—seventh division, 5)

30

Are there Ghosts (Yakshas)?

'Venerable Nāgasena, are there ghosts in the world?'

'Yes, sire, there are ghosts in the world.'

'But do these ghosts, venerable Nāgasena, decease from their (ghost) realm?'

'Yes, sire, they do.'

'Then why, venerable Nāgasena, does one not see the corpses of those dead ghosts, and why is no odour emitted from the corpses?

'One does see the physical frame of dead ghosts, sire, and an odour is emitted from their corpses. One sees them in the form of insects, ants, moths, snakes, scorpions, centipedes, birds, and wild beasts.'

'Who else, venerable Nāgasena, that had been asked this question could have answered it except one as discerning as you?' (Vol. 2, seventh division, 7)

31

SAMYUTTA NIKĀYA

Suriya, the Sun god

(1) Now at that time, Suriya, son of the gods, was seized by Rāhu, lord of demons (*asuras*). Then Suriya calling the Exalted One to mind, invoked him by verse:

(2)   O Buddha! Hero! Glory to thee!
          Thou that art wholly set at liberty!
          Lo! I am fallen into sore distress.
          Be thou my refuge and my hiding-place!

(3) Then the Exalted One addressed a verse to Rāhu, lord of demons, on behalf of Suriya, son of the gods:

          To the *tathāgata*, the *arahat*
          Hath Suriya for help and refuge gone.
          O Rāhu, set the sun* at liberty!
          The Buddhas take compassion on the world.
          Nay, Rāhu, thou that walkest in the sky,
          Him that thou chokest, darkening the world,
          Swallow him not, the craftsman of the light,

          * Suriya, the sun god.

The shining being of the disc, the fiery heat,
My kith and kin—Rāhu, free set the sun*.

(4) Then Rāhu, lord of demons, let go Suriya, son of the gods,
and hurried into the presence of Vepacitti, lord of demons,
where he stood at one side, trembling and with stiffened hair.
And Vepacitti addressed him, standing there, in these lines:

(5)   Now why as one o'erta'en by sudden fright,
         Didst thou, O Rāhu, let the sun go free?
         Here comest thou in agitated plight—
         Why standst thou there so terrified to see?

(6) Rāhu:
         'Thy head will into seven pieces rive,
         Nor shalt thou e'er be happy whilst thou live,
         If thou doest not Suriya let go free.'
         Thus spake the Buddha, and thus frightened me.

(Vol. 1, 2, 1, 10)

32

(1) Thus have I heard. In the land of Kosala a monk was once
staying in a forest.
(2) Now at that time, while engaged in his daily practice, the
monk indulged in wrong and evil thoughts connected with
worldly matters.
(3) Then a god who lived in that forest, moved by compassion
for that monk and desiring to urge him on,
(4) drew near and addressed him with the verses:

         Into the wood fain for detachment come,
         Lo! How thy vagrant heart wanders without.
         As man, for company give up all longings,
         Then shalt thou happy be and free of lusts.
         Let go dissatisfaction! Heedful be!
         And heedfulness shalt bear in mind.
         Hard is it to brush off the dust of hell.

         * Suriya, the sun god.

Be not swept down with dust of sense-desires.
Just as a bird dust-flecked, shaking itself,
Throws off the dust [adhering to its plumes],
So the good monk, heedful and strenuous,
Shaking himself, throws off the adhering dust.

(5) Then the monk, urged by the god, returned to the right way.
(Vol. I, 9, I)

33

Uncontrolled Senses

(1) In the land of Kosala, many monks dwelt in a forest. And
they were arrogant, puffed-up, unsteady, noisy, loose of speech,
forgetful, heedless, without concentration, feeble of mind, with
uncontrolled sense-desires.
(2) Then a god, who lived in that forest, moved by compassion
for those monks and desiring to urge them on,
(3) drew near and addressed them with the verses:

Modestly lived the monks of yore,
Who true disciples were of Gautama.
Unhankering they sought their frugal alms,
Unhankering, their lodging and their couch.
The impermanence of things they understood,
And hence of misery they made an end.
Now, having turned insatiable
Like headmen of the village [taking toll],
They idly covet but their neighbours' goods,
And eat and eat until they sink to rest.
The order used to greet I with my folded hands,
But now I do so only to the few.
The others, cast-out and forlorn,
Resemble ghosts a-loitering about.
My message is for those who heedless live.
To earnest, striving monks I pay respect.

(4) Then the monks, urged by the god, returned to the right
way.
(Vol. I, 9, 13)

34

The Patience of Sakka, King of the Gods

(1–3) The Exalted One was staying at Sāvatthī, in the jeta grove of Anāthapindika, and there he said: Monks, a long time ago gods and demons (*asuras*) were to meet in battle.

(4) And Vepacitti, lord of demons, addressed the demons, saying: 'If, dear sirs, in the impending battle between gods and demons, the demons are victorious and the gods defeated, you shall fetter Sakka, king of the gods, both hands and both feet, and with a fifth (chain) round the neck, and thus bring him before me in the city of the *asuras*.'

(5) And, monks, Sakka, the king of the gods, also addressed the thirty-three Gods saying: 'If, dear sirs, in the impending battle between gods and demons, the gods are victorious and the demons defeated, you shall fetter Vepacitti, lord of demons, both hands and both feet, and with a fifth (chain) round the neck, and thus bring him before me in the assembly hall Sudhammā.'

(6) Now in the battle, monks, the gods were victorious, the demons were defeated.

(7) And the thirty-three gods fettered Vepacitti, lord of demons, both hands and both feet, and with a fifth (chain) round the neck, and brought him before Sakka, king of the gods, in the assembly hall Sudhammā.

(8) And the lord of demons, Vesappatti, thus fettered railed at and reviled Sakka, king of the gods, as he entered and when he left the hall, with coarse and scurrilous words.

(9) Then, monks, Mātali, the charioteer, addressed Sakka, king of the gods, with the verse:

> Now is it, Sakka, that thou art afraid,
> Or because thou art weak that thou forbear'st,
> When thou dost hear these speeches scurrilous
> By Vepacitti cast into thy teeth?

(10) Sakka:

> Nay, not from fear or weakness do I bear
> With Vepacitti. How should any man

Who lacks not understanding, such as I,
Engage himself to bandy with a fool?

(11) Mātali:

But fools may wax ever more wroth
If there be none to put a stop to them.
Wherefore by heavy chastisement and sharp
Let the strong-minded man retain the fool.

(12) Sakka:

But in my judgement this alone avails
To stop [the railing] of a foolish man:—
When he who has a mind alert and sees
Another filled with rage, grows calm and still.

(13) Mātali:

In this, that thou dost patiently forbear,
A grievous error, Vāsava,* I see.
For when the fool does fancy: ''Tis from fear
He bears with me,' the dolt will press you hard,
Like bull [that charges] more when you do flee.

(14) Sakka:

O let him fancy as he will—or won't—
That I do bear with him because of fear.
'Mong highest matters of our spirit's growth
Nought ranks above forbearing patiently.
Yea, surely he that has the upper hand
And beareth patiently with him that's down—
Ever to tolerate the weaker side—
This the supreme forbearance has been called.
Whoso does think the strength of fools is strength,
Will say of the strong man: A weakling he!

* A name of Sakka or Indra.

For the strong man whom righteousness does guard,
To bandy words comes not into his thought.
Worse of the two is he who, when reviled,
Reviles again. Who does not, when reviled
Revile again, a twofold victory wins.

Both of the other and himself he seeks
The good; for he the other's angry mood
Doth understand and groweth calm and still.
He who of both is a physician, since
Himself he healeth and the other too,
Folk deem him fool, they knowing not the norm.

(15—16) Verily, monks, this Sakka, king of the gods, harvesting
the fruits of his own merits, and ruling over and governing the
thirty-three gods, will be of those who commend forbearance
and gentleness. Now in this order, monks, you will enhance your
virtue when you who have gone forth under the *dharma* and the
discipline so well proclaimed, become forbearing and gentle.
(Vol. I, II, I, 4)

35

The Gods and the Vow

(1) Another discourse at Sāvatthī.
(2) (The Exalted One thus addressed the monks): 'In the days,
monks, when Sakka, king of the gods, was a man, he made and
kept seven vows whereby he attained his celestial sovereignty.'
(3) 'What were the seven vows?'
(4) 'As long as I live, may I maintain my parents. As long as
I live, may I revere the head of the family. As long as I live,
may I use gentle language. As long as I live, may I utter no
slander. As long as I live, with a mind free from stain and selfishness, may I conduct myself in the home with generosity,
with clean hands, happy to give, amenable to petitions, delight-
ing in sharing gifts. As long as I live, may I speak the truth.
As long as I live, may I not give way to anger; if anger arises,
may I swiftly repress it.'

(5) By undertaking and carrying out these vows when he was a human being, Sakka attained his celestial position.

(6)   Whoso his mother and his father keeps,
         The senior in his family reveres,
         Converseth gently and with soft-toned speech,
         And all that makes for slander puts aside,

         Who sets himself all meanness to suppress,
         A man of truth, his temper 'neath control:
         On such an one the three and thirty gods
         Do verily confer the name: good man.

(Vol. i, ii, 2, i)

36

(19) Just as if, monks, a man faring through the forest, through the great wood, should see an ancient path, and an ancient road traversed by men of former days. And he were to go along it, and going along it he should see an ancient city, an ancient prince's domain, wherein dwelt men of former days, having gardens, groves, pools, foundations of walls, a goodly spot.
(20) And that man, monks, should bring word to the prince, or the prince's minister: 'Pardon, lord, know this. I have seen as I fared through the forest, through the great wood, an ancient path, an ancient road traversed by men of former days. I have been along it, and going along it I have seen an ancient city, an ancient prince's domain, wherein dwelt men of former days, having gardens, groves, pools, foundations of walls, a goodly spot. Lord, restore that city.'
(21) And, monks, the prince or his minister should restore that city. That city should thereafter become prosperous and flourishing, populous, teeming with folk, should grow and thrive. Even so have I, monks, seen an ancient path, an ancient road traversed by the rightly enlightened ones of former times.
(22) And what, monks, is that ancient path, that ancient road traversed by the rightly enlightened ones of former times? Just this noble eightfold path, to wit, right views, right aims, right speech, right action, right livelihood, right effort, right mindfulness, right concentration. This, monks, is that ancient

path, that ancient road traversed by the rightly enlightened ones of former times.

(Vol. 2, 12, 65, 19–22)

37

UDĀNA

Thus have I heard: Once the Exalted One was staying at Sāvatthi, in the jeta grove of Anāthapindika. At that time he addressed the monks, taught, admonished and encouraged them, and gave them the joy of his exposition of Nirvāna. And the monks listened attentively and followed his words with full concentration.

Now the Exalted One, realizing the import of this, uttered the famous words:

There is, monks, that which is neither earth nor water, neither fire nor air; nor infinite space, nor infinite field of consciousness, nor no-thing-ness; neither perception nor non-perception; not this world, nor any other, neither sun nor moon. That, monks, I call neither coming nor going, nor standing still; neither coming-to-be, nor ceasing-to-be. It is without support, without beginning, without foundation; just that is the end of suffering. 'Difficult to see is that not-I, and difficult to grasp is the truth; for him who knows, the thirst is slaked; for him who sees, there is no-thing.

'There is, monks, an unborn, unoriginated, uncreated, unformed. If, monks, there were no unborn, unoriginated, uncreated, unformed, there would likewise be no escape from the born, originated, created, formed. But as, monks, there is this unborn, unoriginated, uncreated, unformed, therefore escape from the born, originated, created, formed, is possible.

'What is dependent, that also moves; what is independent does not move. Where there is no movement, there is rest; where rest is, there is no desire; where there is no desire, there is neither coming nor going, no ceasing-to-be, no further coming-to-be. Where there is no ceasing-to-be nor further coming-to-be, there is neither this shore nor the other shore, nor anything between them. Even this is the end of suffering.'

(8, 1–4)

38

VINAYA

When Upaka the mendicant (*Ājīvika*) saw the Exalted One, he said to him: 'You look joyful, and your complexion is clear and bright. Why did you renounce the world, who is your teacher, and which doctrine do you profess?'
The Exalted One answered in these verses:

> All-vanquishing, all-knowing, lo! am I,
> from all wrong thinking wholly purged and free.
> All things discarded, cravings rooted out,
> —whom should I follow?—I have found out all.
> No teacher's mine, no equal. Counterpart
> to me there's none throughout the whole wide world.
> The *arahat* am I, teacher supreme,
> utter Enlightenment is mine alone;
> unfever'd calm is mine, Nirvāna's peace.
> I seek the Kāsis' city, there to start
> my doctrine's wheel, a world purblind to save,
> sounding the tocsin's call to deathlessness.

'So, friend, you claim to be the *arahat*, the perfect conqueror?'

> 'Like me, those conquer who the passions quell;
> —by conquering bad *dharmas* I am conqueror.'

When he had thus answered, Upaka said: 'Perhaps, friend,' and, shaking his head, went away on a different road.
(*Mahāvagga* I, 6, 7–9; identical with *Majjhima-Nikāya* 26).

VISUDDHIMAGGA OF BUDDHAGHOSA

39

Local Etymologies of the word 'Arahat'.

The meditator with unshakeable trust who as the first of the ten meditations wants to develop the recollection of the Enlightened

One, should go into solitary retreat in a favourable abode and recollect the special qualities of the Enlightened One, the Exalted One, as follows: 'This Exalted One is indeed the *arahat*, the All-Enlightened One, the Perfect One in insight and conduct, the Accomplished One, the knower of worlds, the incomparable leader of men to be tamed, the master of gods and men, the Enlightened One, the Exalted One.' And this is the way of recollection: 'This Exalted One is indeed the *arahat*, the All-Enlightened One . . . the Exalted One.' Thus he should recollect. And for the following reasons he should thus recollect:

Because he is 'remote', has 'conquered the enemies', has 'broken the spokes of the wheel', is 'worthy' of the needful things, and 'hides from doing wrong'—for these reasons the Exalted One is the '*arahat*' (the Accomplished One).

Because he is 'remote' (*āraka*) from all defiling passions, has destroyed them together with the adhering imprints, and far, far from them treads the path, because he is thus remote, he is the '*arahā*' (the Remote One).

> A man remote indeed we call
> From something he has not at all;
> The Noble One who has no stain
> May well the name *arahā* gain.

And because, treading the path, he has 'conquered' (*hata*) the 'enemies' (*ari, arayo*), the defiling passions, because he has conquered the enemies, he is the '*arahat*' (conqueror of enemies).

> The enemies that were deployed,
> Greed and the rest, have been destroyed
> By his, the Noble's, wisdom's sword,
> So he is *arahat*, all accord.

He is also acclaimed *arahat* because he has 'broken' (*hata*) the 'spokes of the wheel'. This is the wheel of the round of being, with its hub made of ignorance and of craving for becoming, with its spokes consisting of formations of merit and the rest, with its rim of old age and death, and which is pierced by the axle caused by the arising of the defiling passions. This wheel is joined to the chariot of triple becoming, and has been turning ceaselessly since time without beginning. All these wheel's spokes were destroyed by him on the throne of Bodhi, as he stood firm with the feet of energy on the ground of virtue, wielding with the hands of faith the *karma*-destroying axe of insight.

Or alternatively the wheel of the round of being (*samsāra-cakka*) is also the beginningless round of becoming. The hub is ignorance (*avijjā*) for it gives rise to everything else; the rim is old age and death, for they terminate it; the spokes are the voluptuous ten links of the round of being (*Pattica-samuppāda*, the dependent origination of everything) the root of which is ignorance, and old age and death their termination.

(*Visuddhimagga*, 7th chapter, 198)

ABHĪDHARMAKOSHA OF VASUBANDHU

40

Suppression by Insight (pratisankhyā-nirodha)

Suppression by insight is severance (*visam-yoga*). It is the severance from soiled (*sāsrava*) conditions. By insight is meant insight into the four noble truths, i.e. of suffering, etc., and thus one kind of wisdom (*prajñā*). And the suppression achieved by it is suppression by insight. . . . *Question*: Is suppression by insight one and the same for all soiled conditions? *Answer:* No. *Question:* How is it then? *Answer:* It is different in each individual case.

There are as many separating things as there are connecting ones. Otherwise the dissolution of some defiling passions by insight into suffering would result in the effective suppression of all defiling passions. In that case practice with the other opposites (*pratipaksha*) would be superfluous. *Question:* But it is said that the suppression is incomparable (*asabhāga*). What does this mean? *Answer:* This means that suppression has no identical cause (*sabhāgahetu*), and that by itself it cannot be the identical cause for something else; it does not (mean), however, that there is nothing identical with it. With this, suppression by insight has been explained.

(1, 6 ab)

BODHICARYAVATĀRĀ OF SHĀNTIDEVA

4I

(119) 'God is the cause of the world.' Tell me, who is God? The elements? Then why all the trouble about a mere word?

(120) Besides (the elements) are manifold, impermanent, without (intelligence) and activity; without anything divine or venerable; impure. Also (the elements) earth, etc. are not God.

(121) Neither is space God; space lacks activity, and so is not *ātman*—that we have already excluded (*ibid.*, ch. 8). (Would you say that God is too great to conceive?) An unthinkable creator is likewise unthinkable, so that nothing further can be said.

(122) ('But if God is inconceivable as to his essence, yet his works are conceivable.') What has he created and desired? Might it be *ātman*? No, for *ātman* is eternal. Might it be the elements? (They, too, are eternal.) Should God desire to create himself? He is eternal. Insight is (also not created by God), as insight (at all times) precedes the object and has no beginning.

(123) Likewise do pain and pleasure precede action? Tell me, then: What has God created? If cause (is ever active and) has no beginning (i.e. does not just become active at a given point in time), how then can the result have a beginning? (After each chaos, the universe of itself begins anew: it is not caused by an eternal and permanent God.)

(124) Why does God not accomplish in one (the creation, continuance, and destruction of the universe)? He is responsible to nobody except himself. He has created all else. Then why does he hesitate to act?

(125) Does he have to take into account the nexus (of conditions, as the potter needs clay, etc., to make a pot)? Then God is not the cause (you talk about). He is not free to act if the nexus of conditions exists; nor is he free to act should this nexus prove to be faulty.

(126) If God acts without wishing to do so, he obviously is subject to somebody else; (if he acts) desiring to do so, he is subject to desire. And thus his action is not free.

(9, 119–126)

MADHYAMAKAKĀRIKA OF NĀGĀRJUNA

42

'Stolen things are of no value',
So did the Buddha teach us.
The *dharmas* are without a self,
And are by nature empty.

(13, 1)

43

(31)   Just as the master does produce
A magic man by magic means,
And then again by magic means
This magic man produce another,
(32)   Thus is a magic man each single doer,
And magic is what he did do,
Which he, the unreal magic being,
By magic only did produce.

(17, 13)

44

The passions, actions (*karma*), bodies, actors and fruits (of *karma* which the actors reap) are as a mirage, a reflection in the air, a dream.

(17, 33)

45

Emptiness, if misconceived
Brings misery to the fool,
As does a snake when wrongly grasped,
Like magic wrongly used.

(24, 11)

46

(19) Birth-and-death (*samsāra*) are not different from Nirvāna, and Nirvāna is not different from birth-and-death.

(20) The boundary line of Nirvāna is also the boundary line of birth-and-death. There is nothing that separates those two from each other.

(25, 19–20)

SADDHARMAPUNDARĪKA

47

It is like unto a great cloud
Rising above the world,
Covering all things everywhere,
A gracious cloud full of moisture;
Lightning-flames flash and dazzle,
Voice of thunder vibrates afar,
Bringing joy and ease to all.
The sun's rays are veiled,
And the earth is cooled;
The cloud lowers and spreads
As if it might be caught and gathered;
Its rain everywhere equally
Descends on all sides,
Streaming and pouring unstinted,
Permeating the land.
On mountains, by rivers, in valleys,
In hidden recesses there grow
The plants, trees and herbs;
Trees, both great and small,
The shoots of the ripening grain,
Grape vine and sugar cane.
Fertilized are these by the rain,
And abundantly enriched;
The dry ground is soaked,
Herbs and trees flourish together.
From the one water which
Issued from that cloud,

Plants, trees, thickets, forests,
According to need receive moisture.
All the various trees,
Lofty, medium, low,
Each according to its size,
Grows and develops
Roots, stalks, branches, leaves,
Blossoms and fruit in their brilliant colours;
Wherever the one rain reaches,
All become fresh and glossy.
According as their bodies, forms
And nature are great or small,
So the enriching (rain),
Though it is one and the same,
Yet makes each of them flourish.
I appear in the world
Like unto this great cloud,
To pour enrichment on all
Parched living beings,
To free them from their misery
To attain the joy of peace,
Joy of the present world,
And joy of Nirvāna.
Ever to all beings
I preach the Law equally;
Pour it copiously on the world
Like the all-enriching rain.
On honoured and humble,
High and low,
Quick-witted and dull-witted,
Equally I rain the Law rain
Unwearyingly.

(5, 5) (Soothill, 125–128 abridged)

48

He who can explain this *sūtra*
When I myself have long since gone,
With my supernatural powers
I'll send him helpers all along.

Be he scolded, be he beaten,
Be he laid upon with stones,
Those illusory forms I gathered
All around him guard him well.

Should he dwell alone in woodlands,
Meditating on truth alone,
Trying hard to grasp its meaning
Yet not clear on every point,

I shall approach the meditator
In my Bodhisattva-form,
Shall myself explain it to him,
So that he, too, sees the light.

If he solitary in mountains
Seeks the end of all his strife,
I will send him gods and spirits
who shall keep him company.

(10, 27)

REFERENCE NOTES

The following abbreviations have been used in the notes:

Abhk.	*Abhidharmakosha* de Vasubandhu, traduit et annoté par Louis de La Vallée Poussin, 6 vols, Paris et Louvain 1923–1931.
Ang.	*Anguttara-Nikāya,* Pāli Text Society.
Bareau	André Bareau, *L'Absolu en Philosophie Bouddhique,* Paris, Centre de Documentation Universitaire, 1951.
Bodhicary.	*Bodhicaryāvatāra,* ed. de La Valleé Poussin, Bibl. Indica, Calcutta 1901–1914.
Dīgh.	*Dīgha-Nikāya,* Pāli Text Society.
ERE	*Encyclopaedia of Religion and Ethics,* 13 vols, Edinburgh 1908–1926.
Hōbōgirin	*Hōbōgirin, Dictionnaire encyclopédique du Bouddhisme d'après les sources chinoises et japonaises,* 2 fascicules, Tokyo 1929, 1930.
Jat.	*Jātaka,* ed. Fausböll, London 1877–1897.
Majjh.	*Majjhima-Nikāya,* Pāli Text Society.
Mil.	*Milinda-pañha,* London 1928
Mk.	*Madhyamaka-kārikās,* Bibliotheca Buddhica.
Mppsh.	*Mahāprajñāpāramitāshāstra, Le Traité de la grande vertu de sagesse,* traduit par Étienne Lamotte, 2 vols to date, 1944, 1949; Louvain.
Samy.	*Samyutta-Nikāya,* Pāli Text Society.
Sphutārthā	Yashomitra's *Abhidharmakoshavyākhyā,* ed. Unrai Wogihara, 7 vols, Tokyo 1932–1936.

The reference notes to literature quoted are listed under chapter headings.

[1], etc., refer to the selections from Buddhist scriptures.

INTRODUCTION

1 H. von Glasenapp, *Kant und die Religionen des Ostens,* Kitzingen 1964, p. 60.

2 *Kants Werke,* ed. Preussische Akademie der Wissenschaften, vol. 9, p. 385.

3 Transl. K. Weidinger, *Zeitschrift für Missionskunde und Religionswissenschaft* 47, 1932, p. 129 ff.

4 *Essentials of Buddhist Philosophy*, 2nd ed., Honolulu, 1949, p. 45.
5 A. Schopenhauer, *Parerga und Paralipomena I*, definitive ed., p. 111; Hübscher, p. 123.
6 A. Schopenhauer, *Satz vom Grunde*, paragraph 34, definitive ed., p. 121; Hübscher, p. 128. Also comp. H. von Glasenapp, *Das Gottesproblem bei Schopenhauer und in den metaphysischen Systemen der Inder*, 28. *Jarhbuch der Schopenhauer-Gesellschaft*, 1941, p. 153 ff.
7 In W. Bauer, *Griechisch-Deutsches Wörterbuch zu den Schriften des Neuen Testaments und der übrigen urchristlichen Literatur*, 4th ed., Berlin 1949, under *Atheos*, vol. 1, col. 36. Also comp. F. Max Müller, *Gifford Lectures on Natural Religion*, p. 228.
8 Wilhelm Schmidt, *Ursprung und Werden der Religion*, Münster, 1930, p. 4.
9 Kobbert, 'Religio' in Pauly-Wissowa, *Real-Encyclopädie der klassischen Altertumswissenschaft*, revised edn., 2nd series, vol. 1, Stuttgart, 1920, p. 565; also comp. Kobbert, *De verborum 'religio' atque 'religiosus' usu apud Romanos*, Königsberg, 1910.
10 The theme of this book has been developed from a short essay of the same title published in the periodical *Scientia*, Milano, 1941, pp. 77–83.

CHAPTER I

1 *Ang.*, 6, 9 f., III, 284–288.
2 Comp. *Ang.*, 3, 70, 8, I, p. 210 f.; xx 11, 12, 8, V, p. 331 f.
3 *Les inscriptions d'Asoka*, text edn with French transl. by Jules Bloch, Paris, 1950, p. 98.
4 *Ibid.*, p. 146. For the meaning of these words, comp. Pierre Meile, '*Misā devehi*' in *Journal Asiatique*, 1949, p. 193 ff.
5 In *Culla-Niddesa*, p. 307, and *Khuddakapātha* commentary, p. 123.
6 *Jat.*, I, 425.
7 *Dhammapada*, Commentary III, 246.
8 *Dīgh.*, 32, 10, III, p. 205.
9 G. P. Malalasekera, *Dictionary of Pāli Proper Names*, London, 1937–1938, I, p. 854; II, p. 273. *Ibid.* I, p. 1118; Rhys Davids-Stede, *Pāli Dictionary*, entry '*deva*'; *Nāgārjuna Mppsh.* I, pp. 331 and 440.
10 *Dīgh.*, 16, 1, 31, II, p. 88.
11 *Ang.*, 5, 58, 5, III, p. 77.
12 Malalasekera, note 9, II, p. 854.
13 *Ibid.*, II, p. 1255.

14 *Samy.*, 32, III, p. 254 f.
15 So *Samy.*, 12, 23, 27, II, p. 32.
16 Commentary to the *Theragāthā*, 325 ff.
17 *Mahāvamsa* I, 33 f.
18 *Jāt.*, 442, IV, p. 17; 539, VI, p. 35.
19 *Dīgh.*, 16, 1, 26 f., II, p. 87.
20 von Glasenapp, *Die Philosophie der Inder*, Stuttgart, 1949, p. 213.
21 *Milinda-pañha*, p. 259 f.
22 *Ang.*, 8, 46, 4, IV, p. 265.
23 *Mppsh.*, I, p. 482, comp. *Avadānashataka* I, p. 292.
24 Malalasekera, note 9, I, p. 1119.
25 Legendary derivation of their name in W. Geiger's translation of *Samyutta-Nikāya*, I, p. 27.
26 *Dīgh.*, 20, 7 ff., II, pp. 265 ff.; *Majjh.* 120, III, p. 99 ff.
27 Comp. the tables in K. Seidenstücker, *Pāli-Buddhismus in Übersetzungen*, 2nd edn, München 1923, p. 112; J. Masson, *Religion populaire dans le canon pāli*, Louvain, 1942, p. 146; and *Abhidharmakosha*, Book III.
28 In my *Die Religionen Indiens*, Stuttgart 1943, 2nd edn Stuttgart 1956, p. 240 f., I have compiled the important details with ref. to the *Abhidharmakosha*.
29 Wodilla, *Niedere Gottheiten des Buddhismus*, Erlangen, 1928.
30 A. Getty, *Ganesha*, Oxford, 1936, and the Tübingen dissertation by J. Rassat, 1955. Details on the specific gods in Malalasekera, note 9, and Masson, note 27.
31 *Mppsh.*, I, p. 605.
32 *Samy.*, 11, 2, 2, I, p. 229.
33 Māra, comp. E. Windisch, *Māra und Buddha*, Leipzig, 1895; H. Oldenberg, *Buddha*, 10th edn, Stuttgart, 1923, pp. 62, 100 ff., 135 f., 353 ff. and *Aus Indien und Iran*; L. de La Valleé Poussin, *ERE* 8, p. 406; J. Masson, note 27, p. 99 ff.
34 A number of them in *Samy.* 4, I, p. 103 ff.
35 For example *Dīgh.* 13, 40, I, p. 250.
36 Oldenberg, note 33, p. 62; Masson, note 27, p. 52; *Hōbōgirin*, entry '*Bon*', p. 113 f.
37 *Samy.*, 48, 57, V, p. 233.
38 *Hōbōgirin*, p. 115 b.
39 The brahmanic legend about Vishnu sleeping in the world ocean, and Brahmā sitting on a lotus that has grown out from his own navel, is told in Nāgārjuna, *Mppsh.* I, p. 466.
40 Comp. *Dharmasangraha*, para. 4 ff.
41 Comp. *Abhk.* 3, 2b, II, p. 2.

42 *Abhk.*, 8, 3c, V, p. 135.
43 *Abhk.*, 1, 22, b–d4, I, p. 43.
44 *Abhk.*, 2, 15–16b, I, p. 133.
45 *Abhk.*, 2, 14, I, p. 132, and 3, 3a, II, p. 4.
46 *Majjh.*, 1, I, p. 2, and *Majjh.* 49, I, p. 329.
47 *Mppsh.*, I, p. 141.

Chapter I

[2], Parallels from Comparative Religion.
1 K. Florenz in Chantepie de la Saussaye, *Lehrbuch der Religions-geschichte*, 4th edn, Tübingen, 1925, I, pp. 280 and 291.

CHAPTER II

1 The *Ishvara-kartritva-nirākriti* attributed to Nāgārjuna, ed. by Stcherbatsky in Zapiski, 1906, p. 58, and Kalyānarakshita's *Tshvara-bhanga*, mentioned in de La Vallée Poussin, *Vijñapti-mātratā-siddhi*, Paris, 1928, p. 30, were not available to me.
2 *Abhk.*, 5, 8, IV, p. 19; *Sphutārthā*, pp. 445, 26.
3 *Ang.*, 10, 29, 2, V, p. 59.
4 Besides the quotation in the appendix 'Selections from the Buddhist Scriptures, [14], see *Dīgh.* 9, 35.
5 *Abhk.*, 9, V, p. 287.
6 *Abhk.*, 5, 62-d2, I, p. 312; *Sphutārthā*, p. 238.
7 *Mppsh.*, I, p. 562; the quotation there seems to have been taken from the *Bhagavadgītā*, 10, 20 and 41, or some similar work which mentions the '*vibhūtis*' of Vishnu.
8 *Abhk.*, 2, 64d, I, pp. 311–13.
9 *Sphutārthā* p. 237.
10 *Ibid.*, pp. 237, 23.
11 Essay 'Buddhism and the Enlightenment of Man', *The Listener*, London, Jan. 7, 1954.
12 Ashvaghosha, *Buddhacarita* 9, 53.
13 *Majjh.*, 101, II, pp. 222, 227, also refers to the teaching that everything can be reduced to the will of God.
14 *Abhk.*, 4, 68d, III, p. 148.
15 Comp. Ashvagosha, *Vajrasūcī*, para. 20, on the teaching of *Purushasūkta*, *Rigveda* 10, 90, according to which the four castes are said to have emerged from a divine original being. A. Weber, *Abh. Berliner Akademie* 1859, p. 227 ff.; *Indische Striefen I*, Berlin, 1868, p. 186 ff.
16. *Dīghanikāya*, Selections of, trans. by R. O. Franke, Göttingen-Leipzig 1913, p. 25 f.; comp. *Sphutārthā*, p. 448 f.
17 H. Beckh, *Buddhismus*, Berlin, 1916, I, p. 121 f; II, p. 126 f.

18 Comp. in *Orientalische Literaturzeitung*, 1953, 11/12 (special ref. to col. 509 f.). My review of *Christus und die Religionen der Erde*, ed. by Franz König, Freiburg, 1952, and my essay '*Der Buddhismus in der Vorstellungswelt der Hindus*, in *Festschrift für Friedrich Weller*, Leipzig, 1954, p. 174.

Chapter II

[2] Parallels from Comparative Religion.

1 A detailed refutation of the existence of a supreme god is given in Mallishena's commentary to Hemacandra's *Syādvāda-manjarī*; German trans. by H. Jacobi, *Die Entwicklung der Gottesidee bei den Indern*, Bonn, 1923, pp. 102–12. In my *Der Jainismus*, Berlin, 1925, pp. 214–22, I have examined these and other arguments, and have cited further literature on p. 470 thereof.

2 Kumārila, *Mīmāmsāshlokavārtika* to *Sūtra V*, Section 16 *Sambandhākshepaparihāra*, *Kārikā*, 43–85.

3 'Vācaspatimishra', commentary to Ishvarakrishna's *Kārikā*, verse 57.

4 H. H. Wilson, *Religious Sects of the Hindus*, London, 1862, p. 359 ff.; comp. ERE 2, p. 186.

5 H. von Glasenapp, *Religiöse Reformbewegungen im heutigen Indien*, Leipzig, 1928, pp. 36–47; the bibliography in Hindi and English on p. 69 is now to be extended by: *Dev-shāstra*, now 4 vols, Lahore, 1935; *Ātma Kathā, arthāt Dev Samāj sthāpak kī jubalī aidres*, 1935; *Satya aur mithyā dharmm matom ke vishvāsiyom kī pachān*, 1925; further, *The Dev Shastra*, Eng. trans., 2 vols, Lahore n.d.; P. V. Kanal, *Altruism, High Road to Higher Life*, 6 vols, Moga, 1940–1951; P. V. Kanal, *Man's Life After Death*, Lahore, 1946; and especially his *Bhagwan Dev Atma*, Lahore, 1942, which praises the Master and his teaching in 700 pages.

6 David Hume, *Philosophical Works*, Boston, 1854, IV, pp. 429–93; the quotations from pp. 434 and 454.

7 Heinrich Hackmann, *Chinesische Philosophie*, München, 1927, p. 26.

8 Otto Franke, *Die Chinesen*, in Chantepie de la Saussaye's text-book, I/2–1, p. 244 f.

CHAPTER III

1 Alberuni's *India*, Eng. by E. Sachau, London, 1910, I, p. 50.

2 *Overseas Hindustan Times*, March 21, 1953.

3 *Ang.*, 3, 134, I, p. 286.

4 *Samy.*, 12, 20, 3, II, p. 25.

5 *Samy.*, 12, 10, II, p. 10.
6 S. Kuroda, *Mahāyāna*, Leipzig, 1904, p. 24.
7 *Dīgh.*, 33, 1, 9, 12, III, p. 212; *Abhk.* 7, 28c, V, p. 69.
8 On the spiritual insufficiency of women, *Mppsh.* I, p. 232.
9 *Jāt.*, 425, III, p. 477 f. = *Suvarnaprabhāsa*, ed. by Nobel, p. 214.
10 *Samy.*, 1, 2, 10, I, p. 9.
11 Shāntideva, *Shikshā-samuccaya*, p. 322 of the edn *Bibliotheca Buddhica.*
12 *Dīgh.*, 27, 8, III, p. 84.
13 When it is said of the Buddha (above, *Dīgh.* 27, 8, III, p. 84):
   '*Dhamma-kāyo iti pi, Brahmā-kāyo iti pi, Brahmā-bhūto iti pi*',
   I do not believe that this refers to the Brahmā of the Vedanta
   but rather to the god Brahmā whose virtues are usually praised
   in Pāli Buddhism (*Dīgh.* 13, 31, I, p. 247), and who is portrayed
   as a true Bhikkhu (*ibid.* 80). Analogous to *Ang.* 10, 115, 4, V, p.
   226, where it is said of the Buddha: '*cakkhu-bhūto, ñāna-bhūto,
   brahmā-bhūto*, this is to be translated as: 'He is an embodied
   Brahmā, or a Brahmā in human form, or he has fully become
   a divine being of moral purity.'

Chapter III
(2) Parallels from Comparative Religion.
1 S. Eitrem in Pauly-Wissowa (Introduction/9), 15th vol., col.
   2453, Stuttgart, 1932.
2 Pauly-Wissowa (Introduction/9), 7th vol., col. 2622.
3 Exhaustive information in the relevant articles in Pauly-
   Wissowa. Also comp. W. Engel, *Die Schicksalsidee im Altertum*
   (Erlangen 1926); A. Meyer, *Vorsehungsglaube und Schicksalsidee
   in ihrem Verhältnis bei Philo von Alexandrien*, Dr.-Diss.,
   Tübingen, 1939.
4 Hermann Schneider, *Die Götter der Germanen*, Tübingen, 1938,
   p. 155.
5 *Sūre* 45, 23.
6 Werner Caskel, '*Das Schicksal in der altarabischen Poesie,*'
   Morgenländische Texte und Forschungen, ed. by A. Fischer, I,
   5, Leipzig, 1926, pp. 21 and 54. Comp. *ibid.* Nöldeke, *Vorstel-
   lungen der Araber vom Schicksal, Zeitschrift für Völkerpsychologie
   und Sprachwissenschaft* III, 1865, pp. 130–35, and Schrameyer,
   Über den Fatalismus der vorislamischen Araber, Diss., Bonn, 1881.
7 O. Franke, *Die Chinesen*, in de la Saussaye's textbook (I/2–1),
   I, 203.
8 Léon Wieger, *Histoire des croyances religieuses et des opinions
   philosophiques en Chine*, 3rd edn, Hien-hien, 1927, p. 669.
9 Re different interpretations, comp. Olaf Graf, *Dschu-Hsi-Djin*

Si Lu, Die jungkonfuzianische, Summa mit dem Kommentar des Yä Tsai, translated, with comments, Tokyo, Sophia University Press, 1953, I, p. 240.

10 E. V. Zenker, *Geschichte der chinesischen Philosophie*, Reichen berg, 1927/27, II, p. 262.

11 Grassmann, *Wörterbuch zum Rigveda*, Leipzig, 1873, p. 282.

12 *Rigveda* I, 92, 3.

13 H. Oldenberg, *Die Religion des Veda*, 1894, 3rd edn 1923, pp. 194–96.

14 Heinrich Lüders, *Varuna*, Göttingen, 1951, I, p. 14.

15 *Rigveda* 3, 54, 3: *Yuvor ritam rodasī satyam astu;* 10, 190, 1: *ritam ca satyam cābhīddhāt tapaso 'dhy ajāyata;* German text in Geldner's translation.

16 *Rigveda* 10, 92, 4.

17 *Rigveda* 4, 21, 3.

18 *Rigveda* 5, 62, 1.

19 *Katharmoi*, Str. 135; W. Kranz, *Vorsokratische Denker*, Berlin, 1939, p. 100.

20 H. von. Glasenapp, *Die Philosophie der Inder*, Stuttgart, 1949, p. 445.

21 H. von Glasenapp, '*Unsterblichkeit und Erlösung in den indischen Religionen*', Schriften der Königsberger Gelehrten Gesellschaft, 14. *Jahr, Geisteswissenschaftl. Klasse, Heft* 1, Halle 1938.

22 A. R. Wadia in his contribution to *Contemporary Indian Philosophy*, ed. by S. Radhakrishnan and J. H. Muirhead, 2nd edn, London, 1952, p. 623; also comp. p. 627 f.

23 A critical essay of such theories: W. E. Mühlmann, *Das Problem des Urmonotheismus, Theolog. Literaturzeitung*, 78. Jahrgang, Dec. 1953, cols. 705–18.

CHAPTER IV

1 *Jāt.*, I, p. 129.

2 Recent research on the life of the Buddha especially in A. Foucher *La vie du Bouddha d'après les textes et les monuments de l'Inde*, Paris, 1949; also comp. Lamotte's discussion in *Muséon*, vol. 62, Louvain, 1949, pp. 251–60.

3 André Bareau, *La Date du Nirvāna, Journal Asiatique*, 1953, pp. 27–62.

4 According to *Abhk.* 3, 13a, II, p. 44 the fancy of the mother only.

5 [15] in the 'Selections', and also *Dīgh.* 16, 1, 3, II, p. 89.

6 Introd. to *Jāt.*, 78, I, pp. 345–49.

7 Introd. to *Jāt.*, 483, IV, pp. 263–65.

8 *Dīpavamsa* 1–2.
9 Foucher (IV, note 2), p. 27.
10 *Apadāna* I, pp. 299–301.
11 *Mppsh.*, I, p. 507 ff.
12 Supporting material in *Mppsh.* I, p. 115.
13 The voluminous literature on it in *Mppsh.* I, p. 271.
14 Foucher (IV, note 2), p. 58 ff.
15 *Mil.*, p. 75.
16 *Mppsh.*, I, pp. 437–452, esp. p. 446 ff.
17 Shāntideva, *Shikshā-samuccaya*, p. 334 ff.
18 *Mppsh.*, I, p. 272.
19 *Mahāvastu* I, p. 158.
20 E. Waldschmidt, *Wunderkräfte des Buddha*, selected from the *Mahāparinirvāna-Sūtra*, Nachr. der Akademie Göttingen, 1948, also comp. *Dashabala-Sūtra* in *Bruchstücke aus dem zentralasiatischem Sanskritkanon*, edn by Waldschmidt, Berlin, 1932, p. 207 ff.
21 *Majjh.*, 12, I, pp. 69–71; *Ang.* 10, 21, V, p. 32, etc.
22 *Abhk.*, 7, 28, V, p. 66 ff.
23 *Mppsh.*, I, pp. 13, 148. f
24 *Abhk.*, V, p. 254, note 4.
25 *Mil.*, pp. 102, 107.
26 *Mil.*, p. 134.
27 *Buddhavamsa* I, 64: *Atthasālinī*, para. 374.
28 *Abhk.*, 7, 34, V, p. 82.
29 *Mil.*, p. 236.
30 *Mil.*, p. 75.
31 Comp. *Mppsh.*, I, p. 467, note 1.
32 *Mil.*, p. 273.
33 *Mil.*, p. 107.
34 *Mil.*, p. 111.
35 *Abhk.* 4, 12c, III, p. 41.
36 *Mil.*, p. 186.
37 *Abhk.*, 7, 33, V, p. 77 f.
38 *Mil.*, p. 164.
39 *Mil.*, p. 172.
40 *Mil.*, p. 70.
41 *Kathā-vatthu* 21, 4.
42 *Mppsh.*, I, p. 157.
43 *Mil.*, p. 218.
44 *Mil.*, p. 164.
45 *Samy.*, 2, 3, 10, I, p. 67.
46 *Mil.*, p. 96 f.

47 *Mil.*, p. 96.
48 *Mil.*, p. 309.
49 *Mil.*, p. 177.
50 *Vibhāshā*, 173, 9.
51 *Abhk.*, 1, 31d, note 4, I, p. 59.
52 Cf. note 51.
53 *Kathā-vatthu*, 18, 4.
54 *Kathā-vatthu*, 2, 10.
55 *Mahāvastu*, I, p. 168 ff.
56 Comp. my essay *Der Buddha des Lotus des Guten Gesetzes*, in *Jahrbuch des Museums für Länder- und Völkerkunde*, Linden-Museum in Stuttgart, 1951, Heidelberg, 1952, where some parts are translated.
57 *ERE*, 8, p. 145.
58 *Abhk.*, 7, 30a, V, p. 71.
59 See [1]; also comp. *Abhk.*, 3, 95–6, II, p. 198.
60 *Mil.*, p. 237.
61 *Abhk.*, 3, 95–96, II, p. 201.
62 *Abhk.*, 3, 94a-b, II, p. 192 f.
63 *Dīgh.*, 14, 4, II, p. 2 f; *Samy.*, 12, 2, 4, II, pp. 5–9.
64 *Abhk.*, 4, 110, III, p. 227.
65 *Mahāvastu*, I, p. 57.
66 *Abhk.*, 3, 95–96, II, p. 200; *Mppsh.*, I, p. 540.
67 See *Hōbōgirin*, I, p. 26, on previous lives of Amitābha.
68 *Mil.*, p. 80.
69 Takakusu. *Essentials of Buddhist Philosophy*, 2nd edn, Honolulu, 1949, p. 166.
70 *Mppsh.*, I, pp. 594, 602.
71 *Abhk.*, 7, 34, V, p. 79 f.
72 Theories on different types of *Nirvānas* in *Mppsh.*, I, p. 381 f.
73 *Abhk.*, 7, 34, V, p. 81.
74 *Abhk.*, 4, 56, III, p. 123.
75 *Abhk.*, 2, 36, I, p. 183.
76 *Abhk.*, 7, 34, V, p. 79.
77 *Samy.*, 22, 87, 13, III, p. 120; comp. *Itivuttaka*, p. 91.
78 Comp. *Hōbōgirin*, p. 176b.
79 *Mppsh.*, I, p. 546.
80 *Mahāyānasangraha-bhāshya*, 19 in Bareau, p. 227.
81 *Mahāyānasangraha-shāstra*, 34, Bareau, p. 213.
82 Candrakírti in his commentary to Nāgārjuna's *Kārikā*, 25, 24.
83 *Hōbōgirin*, I, p. 27 f; Takakusu (note 69 above), p. 172; Ryōtai Hatani, *Realization of Buddhist Nirvāna*, ed. Educational Department of West Hongwanji, Kyōto, 1926.

84 *Hōbōgirin*, I, p. 184b middle.
85 H. von Glasenapp, *Buddhistische Mysterien*, Stuttgart, 1940; R. Tajima, *Étude sur le Mahāvairocana-Sūtra*, Paris, 1936.
86 Tajima (see note 85 above), p. 40.
87 *Ibid.*, p. 42.
88 *Ibid.*, p. 55.
89 *Ibid.*, p. 139.
90 *Ibid.*, p. 89.
91 Shashi Bhusan Dasgupta, *An Introduction to Tantric Buddhism*, University of Calcutta, 1950; Herbert V. Guenther, *Yuganaddha, The Tantric View of Life*, Chowkhamba Sanskrit Series, *Studies*, Vol. III, Benares, 1952.
92 *Jñāna-siddhi*, Ch. 15.
93 MS. of *Vyakta-bhāvānugata-tattva-siddhi* in Dasgupta (note 91 above), pp. 89, 93.
94 *Mahāvastu*, I, p. 266.
95 *Mppsh.*, I, p. 602. On 'Confusion of the Buddha and the Bodhisattva', comp. de La Vallée Poussin, *ERE* 1, p. 97a.
96 See *Hōbōgirin*, I, p. 4, for corresponding parrallels in Shingon.
97 Asanga, *Sūtrālankāra*, 9, 77.
98 *Gaekwad's Oriental Series*, vol. 90, Baroda, 1941.
99 *Ibid.*, p. 8.
100 M. Winternitz, *Geschichte der indischen Literatur*, Leipzig, 1920, II, p. 238.
101 *Sang-hyang Kamāhāyanikan*, ed. by J. Kats, The Hague, 1910; comp. J. S. Speyer in *Zeitschrift der Deutschen Morgenländischen Gesellschaft*, 67, 1913, pp. 374–62; Sir Charles Eliot, *Hinduism and Buddhism*, London, 1921, III, p. 173; Kern, art. *Java*, *ERE*, 7, p. 495 ff.
102 B. H. Hodgson, *Essays on the Languages, Literature and Religion of Nepal and Tibet*, London, 1874, and de La Vallée Poussin, art. *Ādi-Buddha*, *ERE*, 1, pp. 93–100.

Chapter IV

(2) Parallels from Comparative Religion.

1 *Majjh.*, 71, I, p. 483.
2 *Jāt*, I, p. 2.
3 *Ibid.*, p. 16.
4 Comp. H. von Glasenapp, *Der Jainismus*, Berlin, 1925, pp. 293 f, 296.
5 *Die Religion in Geschichte und Gegenwart*, 2nd edn, Tübingen, 1927–1932, III, 569.

6 *Majjh.*, 38, I, p. 265.
7 *Abhk.*, 3, 13a-b, II, p. 44.
8 *Abhk.*, 4, 108, III, p. 221 f.
9 P. Toldo (note 30 below), I, p. 321.
10 *Ibid.*, p. 322.
11 *Ibid.*, p. 324.
12 Tor Andrae, *Die Person Mohammeds in Lehre und Glaube seiner Gemeinde*, Stockholm, 1918, p. 30.
13 Günter (note 30, below), p. 89.
14 Andrea (note 12), p. 32.
15 Günter (note 30), p. 89.
16 *Ibid.*, p. 112.
17 *Ibid.*, p. 67.
18 *Majjh.*, 26, I, p. 186 f.
19 *ERE*, 7, p. 355b ff.
20 *Dīgh.*, 11; *Vinaya, Cullavagga*, V, 8, II, p. 110 f: the story of Pindola.
21 *Udāna*, 8, 8.
22 *Samy.*, 22, 87, III, p. 119 f.
23 Günter (note 30), p. 78.
24 *Ibid.*, p. 65 f.
25 *Ibid.*, p. 77.
26 Andrea (note 12), p. 46.
27 *Dīgh.*, 87, I, p. 77 f.
28 Andrea (note 12), p. 55.
29 *Jāt.*, IV, p. 265.
30 Peter Toldo, *Leben und Wunder der Heiligen im Mittelalter*, in *Studien zur vergleichenden Religionsgeschichte*, I, 1901, p. 320 ff., and the following vols; J. E. Stadler, *Heiligenlexikon*, 5 vols, 1858–1862; Heinrich Günter, *Christliche Legende des Abendlandes*, Heidelberg, 1910, also *Buddha in der abendländischen Legende?*, Leipzig, 1922.
31 Andrea (note 12), pp. 362, 364.
32 A. Hilgenfeld, *Ketzergeschichten des Urchristentums*, Leipzig, 1884, p. 297; Andrea (note 12), p. 364, and for the following A. Fortescue, *Docetism, ERE*, 4, p. 833b.
33 *Korān*, 4, 161 ff; 6, 83 ff, and various verses in *Sūre* 19.
34 *ERE*, 6, p. 507.
35 *Ang.*, 4, 160, II, p. 147; 7, 56, IV, p. 84.
36 I. Goldziher, *Vorlesungen über den Islam*, 2nd edn by F. Babinger Heidelberg, 1925, p. 208.
37 See C. G. Jung's essay *The Psychology of Eastern Meditation*, Coll. Works, Vol. XI, pp. 560–63, on *Amitāyur-dhyāna-sūtra*,

trans. J. Takakusu in *Buddhist Mahāyāna Sūtras*, Part II, pp. 159–201.

38 *Cherubinischer Wandersmann*, I, 61; III, 248.

39 Jalāl-ad-din Rumi, *Masnavi*, Whinfield, p. 53; Goldziher (note 36), p. 172.

40 Otto von Glasenapp, *Indische Gedichte aus vier Jahrtausenden*, Berlin, 1925, p. 101.

CHAPTER V

1 *Abhk.*, 2, 46, I, p. 237.
2 *Abhk.*, 2, 45, I, p. 224.
3 *Abhk.*, 2, 55d, I, p. 276.
4 *Abhk.*, 5, 62, IV, p. 107.
5 *Abhk.*, 1, 22a-b, I, p. 41.
6 See Bareau's excellent exposition to which I owe a lot.
7 *Abhk.*, 1, 6c-d, I, p. 10.
8 *Abhk.*, 2, 55d, I, p. 279.
9 *Abhk.*, 6, 21a, IV, p. 171; *Sphutārthā*, 538.
10 *Abhk.*, 1, 5d, I, p. 8.
11 *Abhk.*, I, p. 201, note.
12 *Abhk.*, 4, 81d, III, p. 180 f.
13 Bareau, p. 215.
14 *Ibid.*, p. 235.
15 *Ibid.*, p. 260.
16 *Samy.*, 43, 1, 2, IV, p. 359.
17 *Samy.*, 44, 1, 30 ff, IV, p. 378 f.
18 Comp. *Vinaya, Parivāra*, III, 1, V, p. 86.
19 C. G. Jung, *Psychology and Alchemy*, German edn, Zürich, 1944, p. 23, note.
20 Commentary to *Dīgh.* (III), p. 899 f; Malalasekera, Ch. 1, note 9, II, p. 303.
21 *Ang.*, 7, 53, IV, p. 77.
22 *Abhk.*, 2, 55d, I, p. 284.
23 *Ang.*, 7, 16, 3, IV, p. 13.
24 *Puggalapaññatti*, I, 19, p. 13.
25 De La Vallée Poussin, note II/1, *Vijñapti-mātratā-siddhi*, Paris, 1928, p. 670, bibliography.
26 *Chāndogya-Upanishad*, 7, 25, 2 and 8, 2, 1 ff.
27 Bareau, p. 106.
28 *Abhk.*, 4, 2, III, p. 4.
29 *Samy.*, 12, 61, II, p. 95.
30 *Mk.*, 10.
31 *Mk.*, 15.

N

32 *Mppsh.* I, p. 357.
33 F. Edgerton, *Buddhist Hybrid Sanskrit Dictionary*, New Haven, 1953, p. 380.
34 Candrakīrti to *Mk.* I, p. 57, m.
35 *Mppsh.* II, 1094.
36 *Mppsh.* II, 1094; comp. *Abhk.* 8, 25, V, p. 187.
37 *Mppsh.* 39, note.
38 Madhva, *Brahmā-sūtra-anuvyākhyāna*, p. 31a; H. von Glasenapp, *Madhvas Philosophie des Vishnuglaubens*, Bonn and Leipzig, 1923, p. 21.
39 Takakusu, *Essentials of Buddhist Philosophy*, 2nd edn. Honolulu, 1949, p. 74.
40 Th. Stcherbatsky, *Madhyānta-vibhanga. Discourse on Discrimination between Middle and Extremes*, trans. from the Sanskrit, *Bibliotheca Buddhica XXX*, Leningrad and Moscow, 1936, Introduction, p. VI.
41 Various useful references in Sōgen Yamakami, *Systems of Buddhist Thought*, Calcutta, 1912, and in Takakusu (note 39 above).
42 Shashi Bhusan Dasgupta, *An Introduction to Tantric Buddhism*, University of Calcutta, 1950, p. 92, notes.
43 *Hōbōgirin*, under '*Busshin*', p. 178a.

Chapter V

[2] Parallels from Comparative Religion.

1 *Sputārthā*, p. 15 (to *Abhk.* I, 5).
2 H. von Glasenap, *Die Philosophie der Inder*, Stuttgart, 1949, p. 371.
3 H. von Glasenapp, *Entwicklungsstufen des indischen Denkens*, Halle, 1940, p. 67 f.
4 *Lankāvatāra-Sūtra*, ed. Bunyiu Nanjio, Kyoto, 1923, pp. 182–86; Eng. trans. by D. T. Suzuki, London, 1932, pp. 157–61; Bareau, p. 284.
5 H. von Glasenapp, *Vedānta und Buddhismus*, Abh. Mainzer Akademie, 1950, p. 15.
6 G. Mensching, in *Theolog. Lit. Ztg.* 1951, No. 12, col. 725.
7 On China, comp. Walter Liebenthal: *The Book of Chao, Monumenta Serica 13*, Peking, 1948; *Shih Hui-yüan's Buddhism as Set Forth in his Writings*, in *Journal of the American Oriental Society* 70 (1950), pp. 243–59; *The Immortality of the Soul in Chinese Thought, Monumenta Nipponica*, vol. 8, Tokyo, 1952, pp. 372–96; *Was ist chinesischer Buddhismus?* in *Asiat. Studien*. Schweiz, 6. Jahrg. 1954, p. 116 f.

CONCLUSIONS

1 H. von Glasenapp, *Die Religionen der Menschheit. Ihre Gegensätze und ihre Übereinstimmungen*, Wien, 1954.
2 H. von Glasenapp, *Die fünf Grossen Religionen*, Düsseldorf, 1951, p. 476 ff. New edn 1963, new title: *Die fünf Weltreligionen*.
3 Nathan Söderblom, article 'Holiness' in *ERE* 6, p. 731 ff.

*For Further Reading**

Buddhist Texts Through the Ages, ed. by Edward Conze, American Edition by Philosophical Library, New York.
Conze, Edward, *Buddhism*, Philosophical Library, New York.
Murti, *The Central Philosophy of Buddhism*, Allen & Unwin.
Takakusu, *The Essentials of Buddhist Philosophy*, Honolulu, 1947 (there is a later edition, too).

* Chosen by the translator.

GLOSSARY

Where necessary, the grammatical gender has been indicated: m—masculine, f—feminine, n—neuter; pl—plural. Skr—Sanskrit, P—Pāli. Editions or translations published by the Pāli Text Society are indicated by PTS.

Abhidhamma-Pitaka (n): 'Basket of dogmatic/scholastic metaphysics', a part of the Pāli Canon.
Abhidharmakosha: 'Treasury of dogmatics', by Vasubandhu.
Ahura Mazda: Parsee god of light.
Ālaya-vijñāna (n): 'Store-consciousness'.
Amida: Japan. for Amitābha.
Amitābha: 'Having immeasurable splendour', mythical Buddha.
Anātman (Skr), *Anattā* (P, m): without self, without continuous existence.
Andhakas (pl.): Hīnayāna school.
Anguttara-Nikāya (m): 'Collection of discourses compiled according to the number of subjects treated in each Sutta', section of the *Sutta-Pitaka* (*Gradual Sayings* PTS).
Apadāna (n): Book of legends in the *Khuddaka-Nikāya*.
Apollonius of Tyana: Greek worker of miracles, first century.
Asanga: Brother of the Mahāyāna teacher Vasubandhu, fourth–fifth century; Mahāyāna doctrinalist, author of *Mahāyāna-sangraha-shāstra* and of *Sūtrālankāra*.
Asankhyeya (n): World age.
Ashoka: Indian king, third century BC.
Ashvaghosha: Famous Buddhist poet, author of a biography of the Buddha in Sanskrit, first century.
Āsrava (m): 'Influence', tendency to passion, a factor of being.
Ātman (Skr), *Attā* (P, m): 'Self' as an imperishable, spiritual entity.
Avadānashataka (n): Legends of the Buddha and of holy men, in Sanskrit.
Avatāra (m): Incarnation.
Bhagavadgītā (f): 'Song of the Exalted One', sixth book of the *Mahābhārata*.
Bhakti (f): Devotion to God.
Bhikkhu: Monk.
Bodhi (f): Enlightenment.

196

Bodhicaryāvatāra (m): 'Revealing the path to enlightenment', by Shāntideva.

Bodhisattva (m): 'Enlightened being', Buddha before he attained perfect enlightenment.

Brahmā (m): Name of a god.

Brahman (Skr, n): The Absolute, the cosmic ground of being, upon which all moral order depends.

Brahmā-Samāj (m): Modern religious reform movement.

Brahmins, Brahmans (pl.) Hindu caste of priests.

Buddha (historical, about 500 BC).

Buddha (mythical aspect).

Buddhaghosa: Pāli author, fifth century; *Visuddhimagga*.

Buddhavamsa (m): Relating the history of the Buddha and his predecessors, section of the *Khuddaka-Nikāya*.

Caitanya: Brahmin theologist, about A D 1500.

Candrakīrti: Mahāyāna theologian, seventh century.

Cathari (pl.): Medieval religious sect.

Chuang-tse: Chinese Taoist philosopher, fourth century.

Chu-hsi: Chinese philosopher, reformer of Confucianism, twelfth century.

Condition(al)ism: A teaching that holds everything as conditional.

Confucius: Latin for Kung-tse, Chinese philosopher, fifth century BC.

Creatio ex nihilo: Creation from nothing.

Culla-Niddesa (m): Old commentary to a part of the *Suttanipāta*, itself a section of the *Khuddaka-Nikāya*.

Deus otiosus: 'idle' god, a god who does not interfere in the course of the world.

Dev-Samāj (m): Modern religious reform movement.

Dhamma (P, m): *Dharma* (Skr).

Dhammapada (n): 'Words of the doctrine', *Khuddhaka-Nikāya*.

Dharma (m): World order, or world norm; factor of being; law, teaching.

Dharmakāya (m): *Dharma* body, the absolute body of Buddhahood, without any attributes.

Dharma-sangīti-sūtra (n): Brahminic guide-book of the law.

Dhyāna (Skt) *Jhāna* (P): meditative absorption.

Dhyānibuddhas (pl)): Meditation Buddhas.

Diamond vehicle: Vajrayāna.

Dīgha-Nikāya (m): 'Collection of the long discourses', part of the *Sutta-Pitaka* ('Dialogues of the Buddha' PTS).

Docetism, docetic: Originally holding the heresy that Christ's body was not human but phantasmal, or of celestial substance. By inference, denial of corporeal reality.

Ens-realissimum (n): the most real, highest being.

Gaudapāda: Brahmin philosopher, eighth century.

Gilgamesh legend: Babylonian legend.

Gnosis (f): Christian theological speculation of the first centuries, judged heretical by the church.

Gosāla: Contemporary of the Buddha, founder of the Ajīvikas.

Great Vehicle: *Mahāyāna*.

Guru: Teacher.

Hallāj: Islamic mystic, tenth century.

Harivarman: Founder of the Satyasiddhi school, third–fourth century.

Hīnayāna: 'Small Vehicle', older stream of Buddhism.

Iamblichus, Greek Neo-Platonist, about AD 300.

Īshvara: God, lord of the world.

Īshvarakrishna: Sānkhya philosopher, fourth century.

Itivuttaka (n): 'Thus have I heard', part of the *Khuddaka-Pitaka*.

Jains (pl.): Members of the Jain sect, a religious movement that arose in India contemporary with Buddhism.

Jalāl-ed-din Rumi: Persian mystic poet, thirteenth century.

Jambudvīpa (m): India; according to the old Indian conception, a continent in the centre of the surface of the world.

Jātaka (n): Stories about the previous existences of the Buddha, belonging to the *Khuddaka-Nikāya*.

Jhāna: see *Dhyāna*.

Jīvanmukti (f): Liberation realized within this life.

Jīvita (n): Force or strength of life.

Jōdo School: 'School of the Pure Land', Japan. Mahāyāna school.

Kabīr: Indian poet, fifteenth century.

Kālacakra system: late form of Indian Vajrayāna, much influenced by Hinduism.

Kalpa (m): World age.

Kārandavyūha (m): Mahāyāna scripture.

Kārikā (f): Teaching verse.

Karma or *Karman* (n): 'Act' or action; also name of the causal nexus, the moral law of cause and result.

Khuddaka-Nikāya (m): 'Collection of the short discourses, part of the *Sutta-Pitaka*.

Kōbō Daishi: Founder of Japanese Shingon school, ninth century.

Kumārila: Brahmin philosopher, eighth century.

Lalita-vistara (m): 'The complicated presentation of the play', Sanskrit work, on the legends of the Buddha.

Lankāvatāra (n): 'The proclamation of the teaching in Lanka' (Ceylon), Mahāyāna scripture.

Lao-tse: Chinese philosopher, founder of Taoism, dates unknown.
Logos speculation: Speculation on 'the word has become flesh'.
Lokottaravādins (pl): Transcendentalist Hinayāna school.
Lotus book: *Sad-dharma-pundarīka*.
Madhva: Brahmin theologist, thirteenth century.
Mādhyamakas (pl): Nāgārjuna's school.
Mādhyamaka-kārikās (pl): 'Teaching verses of the doctrine of the mean', by Nāgārjuna.
Mahābhārata (n): Brahminic epic.
Mahāparinibbāna-Sutta (n): Name of a text in the *Sutta-Pitaka*, not to be confused with *Mahaparinirvāna Sūtra* a quite different Mahā-yāna work.
Mahāprājñāparāmitā-shāstra (n): 'The book of the great teaching of complete enlightenment', attributed to Nāgārjuna.
Mahāsānghikas (pl): 'Members of the Great Community', Hīnayāna school.
Mahāvagga (m): Part of the *Vinaya-Pitaka*.
Mahāvamsa (m): 'Great Chronicle', Pāli historical work.
Mahāvastu (n): 'Book of the great events', Hinayāna work in hybrid Sanskrit.
Mahāvīra: Teaching name of the founder of Jainism, fifth century BC.
Mahāyāna: 'Great Vehicle', younger stream of Buddhism.
Mahishāsakas (pl): Hinayāna school.
Maitreya (Skr), Metteya (P): Future Buddha.
Majjhima-Nikāya: 'Collection of the middle-length discourses', Part of the *Sutta-Pitaka*. ('Middle Length Sayings' PTS.)
Manas (n): The organ of thinking.
Mandala (n): Mystic circle, diagram.
Manichaeism: The teaching of the Persian Mani, third century.
Māyā (f): Illusion.
Mazdaism (from Ahura Mazda): Parsee religion.
Metteya: Maitreya.
Milinda-pañha (m): 'The questions of Milinda', text of Pāli literature.
Mīmāmsā (f): Brahminic guide-book of rituals; believers in: Mīmām-sakas.
Nāgārjunga: Mahāyāna patriarch, second century; author of *Mādhyamaka-kārikās*.
Nibbāna (P, n): *Nirvāna* (Skr).
Nidānakathā (f): Biography of the Buddha in Pāli, attributed to Buddaghosa, fifth century.
Nirmānakāya: Transformation body.
Nirodha: Extinction.

Nirodha-samāpatti: Extinction of all concious processes.

Nirvāna (Skr): *Nibbāna* (P).

Nyāya (m): the fundamental teaching of logical argumentation, philosophical system of the Brahmins.

Pāli: Medieval Indian literary language, canonical language of Hinayāna Buddhism.

Pāli Canon: *Tipitaka* ('three baskets'), collection of Hīnayāna scriptures transmitted in Ceylon, Burma, Thailand, etc. (Southern Buddhist countries), consisting of *Sutta-Pitaka, Vinaya-Pitaka*, and *Abhidhamma-Pitaka*.

Pan-en-theism: Teaching that everything is contained in God.

Parsism, Mazdaism: Old-Persian religion founded by Zoroaster.

Paticcasamuppāda (P), *Pratītyasamutpāda* (Skr): Causal nexus of dependent origination.

Paulicians: Gnostic-Manichaean sect in the Orient, since seventh century.

Prajñāpāramitā: 'Perfection of Insight' (often translated 'perfection of wisdom'); also the name of a group of Mahāyāna texts, and of the philosophical teaching of Nāgārjuna.

Pratītyasamutpāda (Skr): see *Paticcasamuppāda*.

Prithagjana (Skr), *Puthujjana* (P): worldling.

Pseudo-Matthew: Apocryphal gospel.

Pubbaseliyas (pl): Hinayāna school.

Puggalapaññatti: 'Characterization of the individuality', belonging to the *Abhidhamma-Pitaka*.

Purushasūkta: Purusha song in the *Rigveda;* Purusha: divine original being.

Quidditas: Suchness; a something; essence; *Tatathā*.

Rāmakrishna: Philosopher of the Vedanta, 1836–1886.

Rāmānuja: Brahminic theologian, eleventh century.

Rigveda: Oldest part of the Vedic literature.

Sad-dharma-pundarīka: 'Lotus of the Good Law', Mahāyāna scripture, second century.

Samana: Ascetic.

Sambhāra: The achievement of merit and knowledge during previous lives.

Samjñā: Conscious volition; perception.

Sammītiyas (pl): Hīnayāna school.

Samsāra: The cycle of becoming.

Samskāra: Volition, stirring of.

Samskāra (Skr), *Sankhāra* (P): conditioned factor of being, drive.

Samyutta-Nikāya: 'Collection of Discourses of related content', part of the *Sutta-Pitaka* ('Kindred Sayings' PTS).

Samskrita-dharma: Conditioned factor of being.

Sangha: Community of monks.

Sankhāra (P): *Samskāra*. (Skr).

Sānkhya: A non-theistic Brahmin teaching.

Sānkhya-kārikā: Main *Sānkhya* scripture, by Īshvarakrishna.

Sarvāstivādins (pl), also: Vaibhāshikas, Hīnayāna school.

Sanskrit: *samskrita* ('fashioned'), old-Indian literary language.

Satornil: an early Gnostic.

Satya-siddhi School: Hīnayāna school, founded by Harivarman.

Sautrāntikas (pl): Hīnayāna school, developed from the Sarvāstivādins.

Shaiva: Devotee of Shiva, one of the two main streams of Hinduism.

Shaktism: (*shakti* = power): a religious movement which conceives the power that moves the world as feminine.

Shankara: Founder of a Vedanta school, about AD 800.

Shāntideva: Mahāyāna writer, end seventh century, author of *Shikshā-samuccaya*.

Shāstra(s): Book of teaching(s).

Shikshā-samuccaya: Treatise on the teachings of Mahāyāna Buddhism, by Shāntideva.

Shingon school: 'School of the true word', Japan. Vajrayāna school founded by Kōbō Daishi.

Shin school: Japan. Mahāyāna school.

Shūna (Skr): empty.

Shūnyatā (f): Emptiness; what is without a self, without permanent substance; unlimited.

Shūnyavāda: The teaching of emptiness, one of the main streams of Mahāyāna.

Solipsism: A teaching according to which the 'I' with its conscious contents is the only reality.

Sphutārthā: 'Commentary of clear explanations', commentary on the *Abhidharmakosha*, by Yashomitra.

Sthiramati: Mahāyāna theologian.

Sukhāvati-vyūha: 'Detailed description of the Pure Land', the paradise of Amitabha, a Mahāyāna work.

Sūtra (Skr.), *Sutta* (P): Teaching text.

Sutta-Pitaka: 'Basket of Discourses', part of the Pāli Canon, containing the five collections of *Dīgha-*, *Majjhima-*, *Samyutta-*, *Anguttara-*, and *Khuddaka-Nikāya*.

Tantra: 'Woven', system of rites and doctrines.

Tantrism: The magical stream in Indian religions since the sixth century.

Taoism: Chinese world concept, founded by Lao-tsu.

Tathāgata: The 'thus gone': Buddha.

Thaumaturge: Worker of miracles.

Theopantism: Teaching of divine immanence.

Theragāthā (pl): 'Songs of the monks', *Therīgāthā:* 'Songs of the nuns', parts of the *Khuddaka-Nikāya.*

Theravādins (pl); 'The older, reverend monks', Hīnayāna school of Ceylon, Burma, Thailand, etc.

Theurgy: production of effects by supernatural or magical agency.

Thondracians (pl): Medieval Armenian sect.

Tīrthankara: A Jain teacher.

Triratna: 'Three jewels', the three essential things, i.e. Buddha, Dharma, Sangha.

Tulku (Tibetan): Incarnation.

Udāna: 'Inspired words' of the Buddha, part of the *Khuddaka-Nikāya.* ('Verses of Uplift' PTS.)

Upādāna-skandhas (Skr.) (*-khandhas* P): The (five) 'aggregates of attachment', which make up a personality: i.e. body, feelings, perceptions, impulses, consciousness.

Upanishads (pl): 'Secret teachings', philosophical tractates, considered part of the Vedic literature.

Upāya: Skilful means.

Uttarapāthakas (pl): Hīnayāna school.

Vācaspatimishra: Brahmin philosopher, ninth century.

Vāda: Teaching.

Vaibhāshikas (pl): Sarvāstivādins.

Vairocana: 'the one like the sun', mythical Buddha.

Vaisheshika: atomistic natural philosophy of the Brahmins.

Vaishnavas (pl): Vishnuites.

Vajrasattva: mythical Buddha of the Tantric schools.

Vajrasūcī: 'Diamond needle', a Buddhist treatise arguing against the caste system, attributed to Ashvaghosa.

Vajrayāna: 'Diamond Vehicle', youngest stream of Buddhism.

Valentinus: A Gnostic, second century. His adherents: Valentinians.

Vallabha: Brahmin theologian about AD 1500.

Varāhamihira: Indian astronomer and astrologer, sixth century.

Varnāshramadharma: The duties of caste.

Vasubandhu: traditionally thought to be the brother of Asanga, fourth–fifth centuries, Hīnayāna teacher of the Sarvāstivādin school, author of the *Abhidharmakosha;* in the light of recent research, not identical with the Mahāyāna author Vasubandhu.

Vātsīputrīyas (pl): Hīnayāna school.

Veda (m): 'Knowledge', holy scriptures of Hinduism. In a more limited meaning they consist of sacrificial hymns.

Vedānta: 'End of Veda', the *Upanishads* at the end of the Veda; also name of the systems based upon them, especially that of Shankara.

Vibbhāshā: A commentary of the Sarvāstivādin school.

Vijñāna: Consciousness.

Vijñānavāda: The teaching of 'consciousness only', also called *Yogācāra*; main representative: Asanga.

Vijñapti-mātratā: Pure consciousness.

Vimāna-vatthu: Part of the *Khuddhaka-Nikāya*.

Vinaya: Discipline of the monks.

Vinaya-Pitaka: 'Basket of the discipline for monks', part of the Pāli Canon. ('Book of Discipline' PTS.)

Vishnuites, Vaishnavas (pl): Devotees of Vishnu, one of the two main streams of Hinduism.

Visuddhimagga: *The Path of Purification*, work of Buddhaghosa.

Yājñavalkya: A thinker in the *Upanishads*.

Yashomitra: Author of the *Sphutārthā*.

Yoga: 'Yoking' of thinking, spiritual training.

Yogācāra: 'Change by Yoga', see *Vijñānavāda*.

Yogavāsishtha: Brahmin philosophical treatise, ninth century.

Zarathustra (Greek: *Zoroaster*): Persian religious founder, seventh century B C.

INDEX